"My father didn't die—he escaped."

He was a movie star, the king of nightclubs, the definitive recording artist of his time. He stamped his sense of style on the postwar generation. His death at eighty-two was mourned the world over by people who heard his music as the soundtrack of their lives, and who saw him as one of their own.

Frank Sinatra seemed to have it all: genius, wealth, the love of beautiful women, glamorous friends from Las Vegas to the White House. Why then would Tina Sinatra, his youngest daughter, refer to his death as an "escape"? What *happened* to make his life so difficult?

In this startling and remarkably outspoken memoir, Tina Sinatra reveals to us an acutely restless, lonely, and conflicted man. Through his marriages and front-page romances and the melancholy gaps in between, Frank Sinatra searched for a contentment that eluded him.

My Father's Daughter, with its unflinching account of Sinatra's flaws and foibles, will shock many of his fans. At the same time, it is a deeply affectionate portrait written with love and warmth, a celebration of a daughter's fond esteem for her father and respect for his great legacy.

The world remembers Frank Sinatra as one of the giants of show business. In this book from someone *inside* the legend, Tina Sinatra remembers him as something more: a father and a man.

My Father's Daughter
A MEMOIR

Includes photographs from the family collection

My Father's Daughter

A MEMOIR

Tina Sinatra

WITH JEFF COPLON

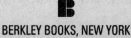

BERKLEY BOOKS, NEW YORK

MY FATHER'S DAUGHTER

A Berkley Book / published by arrangement with
Simon & Schuster, Inc.

PRINTING HISTORY
Simon & Schuster hardcover edition / October 2000
Berkley paperback edition / October 2001

Visit our website at
www.penguinputnam.com

ISBN: 0-425-18198-7

BERKLEY®
Berkley Books are published by The Berkley Publishing Group,
a division of Penguin Putnam Inc., 375 Hudson Street,
New York, New York 10014.
BERKLEY and the "B" design
are trademarks belonging to Penguin Putnam Inc.

PRINTED IN THE UNITED STATES OF AMERICA

10 9 8 7 6 5 4 3 2 1

Acknowledgments

The author would like to acknowledge her family, for their patience and love; Lisa Tan for her undaunting dedication; and David Rosenthal and Michael Korda, for their tenacity and objectivity.

She is also grateful to Chuck Adams, Leslie Ellen, Natalie Goldstein, Rebecca Head, Amy Hill, Liz McNamara, Emily Remes, Katy Riegel, Jackie Seow, and Cheryl Weinstein, whose efforts at Simon & Schuster were truly indispensable.

for Turkey

My
Father's
Daughter

Part One

A RESTLESS SPIRIT

1

Two Loves

M Y FATHER WAS an only child, and a lonely child. He was born in 1915, in Hoboken, New Jersey, the son of immigrants who'd arrived in this country with the will to make their way and not a whole hell of a lot else. They ran a restaurant and saloon, where Dad sang propped up on the player piano, and they outlasted Prohibition and the hard times that followed.

Dolly Sinatra was the social animal, the politically connected one, who spent her spare time buying votes for the local Democratic machine. (A woman with advanced ideas, she would chain herself to City Hall at a protest for women's suffrage in 1919.) As Dolly's ambitions broadened, she finagled a fireman's post for her husband, Marty, a job that stole him away from home for days at a time. They were doting parents, and their skinny, blue-eyed son was the center of their universe. But they were also working overtime to make sure he'd have a better life. They weren't always seeing Dad off to school, or asking how his day had gone when he got home.

No one talked about "nurturing" when my father was young. Which was just as well, because he didn't get too much of it.

My father was seventeen and my mother only fifteen when they met at the Jersey shore and fell in love at first sight. The country was still waist-deep in the Depression, and Dad was dreaming his dream—of becoming the biggest singer in the world—long before it seemed plausible. His parents slapped down his grand ideas; everyone mocked him, except for Nancy Barbato. From that first moment she shared Dad's dream and became a part of it. In a time of widespread discouragement, these two young people were earnest and optimistic. They were sure they would make it, together.

I think this was the reason my father would hold Mom so close for the rest of his life—because she'd been there, without a negative word, from the start. Dad married his best friend. Later he'd say it was the smartest thing he'd ever done with his life, if only he'd been able to stick with it.

❋

My parents were wed on February 4, 1939, but their joy was tempered by false rumors that it was a shotgun marriage. They'd already been shaken by Dad's arrest on an archaic morals charge, pressed two months earlier by a *married* woman in Bergen County after a romp in a rumble seat. While the charge was dropped, it made their small-town newspaper. It would mark the beginning of a prolonged smear campaign, spearheaded by what Dad referred to as the "garter-belt Mafia": J. Edgar Hoover and the Hearst columnists Westbrook Pegler and Lee Mortimer.

My parents spent their honeymoon working on their three-room Jersey City apartment. Dad loved taking pictures, so they converted a second bathroom into a darkroom. Funds were limited, even after my father hooked up with Harry James, but my mother recalls those first years together as their happiest. As Mom said, "The little things mattered." When Dad was out on a winter tour, she sent him a pair of gloves with a dollar bill rolled up inside each finger, her way of making sure he'd eat enough.

To cut their expenses, they shared their apartment with a drummer and his wife. When Mom was pregnant with my sister, Nancy, she got a craving for a ham and cheese sandwich. "We didn't have any money," she recalled, "but we had a lot of empty Coke bottles. Frank gathered them up, cashed them in to buy me my sandwich and a slice of apple pie. When he came back, he said, 'Nobody touch that. That's for Nancy.'

"That was a good time. It wasn't about being rich and famous—it was about real feelings."

After little Nancy was born, in June of 1940, Mom stayed steadfast at the home front, answering her husband's fan mail, crafting his signature floppy bow ties. As the bobby-soxers went wild at the Paramount and my father bathed in adulation on a daily basis, she sensed him changing. *It went to his head*, she'd say. She knew that Dad had a roving eye and that he was being tempted. She was too much of a realist to imagine he could resist.

My father was a very Italian male from the first half of the twentieth century. Home was the place where you respected your mother, and then your wife. As long as you provided for your family and always came back to them, what you did outside, discreetly, was your own business. Dolly Sinatra was tough and demanding, but she'd also spoiled and pampered her son into believing he could do no wrong.

From early on, Dad's life fed his art. Without the rueful voice of experience, he couldn't possibly have become the consummate singer of love songs. His rakish persona was a big part of his mystique and appeal.

They'd moved to a more sophisticated world, but my parents were still kids in their twenties, not long removed from small-town New Jersey. My father had come so far, so fast, that he forgot he was a saloonkeeper's son who'd married his childhood sweetheart. He was truly confused—and also, as Mom would note, childlike and self-centered. I think my dad desperately wanted to do the best he could for the people he loved, but ultimately he would do what he needed to do for *himself*. (In that he was his mother's son.) When those two forces collided, the result would be life-altering. Somebody had to get hurt.

In our case, everybody got hurt.

For years Mom thought she could ride out her husband's indiscretions. She didn't like or accept them, but neither did she take them too seriously. As far as she knew, it was a common weakness; her father had done the same thing to her mother. She would compromise herself to a point, and repress her bruised feelings, because the family came first. Having little Nancy's father home—even if only in between road trips—meant everything. The alternative was inconceivable.

My mother was a proud woman who recognized her own importance. She knew that my father couldn't have held himself together without her faith and support. Dad was young and attractive and ridiculously famous; he was seduced by his own celebrity, no question. But even as he was becoming the most important entertainer on the planet, he needed an anchor. He ached for someone to come home to from those whirlwind weeks on the road. He never stopped missing his family—and never stopped to think that his infidelities might jeopardize it. Dad believed that his marriage was inviolate.

As he wrote to Mom from San Francisco, while on tour in 1941, "I have never stopped loving you. You are my life and there is nothing or no one that can ever change it." My father acknowledged that his words might be suspect "because of past happenings," but added that he was "going to do my damnedest" to change.

"You were right from the first, I guess," Dad continued. "He is a great man who can resist temptation. I guess I am not that great." But I think that my mother believed him when he closed, "I'll love you and cherish you till my last day on earth—and then some. Honest."

Honest he was. He *would* cherish her to the end. But there was always something else, someone else, on his horizon.

In 1944, with Dad becoming more prominent in Hollywood musicals (and did anyone look cuter in a sailor suit?), he moved his family from New Jersey to Toluca Lake, an upper-middle-class neighborhood in the San Fernando Valley. He bought a big pink house once owned by Mary Astor, near W. C. Fields and Bob Hope.

With my brother, Frankie, a babe in arms, my mother welcomed the change. The Valley still smelled of orange groves, not smog—it was heaven. Mom's parents and six siblings soon followed her out west so she wouldn't lack for company. And she figured, reasonably enough, that the move would shore up their marriage; her husband would be able to stay home while he made his movies.

My sister tells me that Toluca Lake was as close as she ever got to a normal family life. Dad was a hands-on parent, just as he'd been in New Jersey, where he once woke his baby daughter in the middle of the night for her first sight of snow. In California he gave Nancy painting lessons and taught her how to swim in the pool. They'd go rowing on the lake, or float on a flat wooden raft out of *Huckleberry Finn*. They had their daily routines, and even ate breakfast together now and then.

Unfortunately, Mom had traded one fishbowl for a bigger one, with *much* bigger fish. When my father was a band performer, he had his share of one-night stands—that was the way of the road. But once he moved his home and work to California, the nameless faces became women with above-the-title credits. Show business was a fishbowl then, much as it is today. There were no secrets.

Dad's philandering eventually set him on a collision course with Metro-Goldwyn-Mayer and its absurd morals clause. He was married, after all, and Louis B. Mayer expected him to behave that way, at least in public. Of course, Dad was the last person to be told what he could or could not do. Like Dolly, he resented authority in any guise—especially when he knew he was wrong. The more you yanked him by the neck, the less he liked it, and the more he'd dig in his heels. (Speaking for myself, the fruit wouldn't fall far from the tree.)

Here was insult added to Mom's injury, the public humiliation she'd hoped to avoid. It came to a head late in 1945, when Mom found a diamond bracelet in her new convertible's glove box and left it there, assuming it was to be a surprise gift from Dad. A few days later, at my parents' New Year's Eve party, she found the actress Marilyn Maxwell wearing the damn thing! My mother had gumption. She told the woman off and ordered her out of her home. But she knew there were regiments of Marilyns out there, and that the line formed uncomfortably close to home.

It was a pivotal point in the erosion of their marriage. "When you have a successful man," Mom would tell me more than half a century later, "certain women will try to snare him. And if you have a man with an inclination for that sort of thing, it's no surprise when he gives in to them."

His fans and flirtations fed off my father's public persona—the brash, reckless Frank who needed a home-cooked meal. What he displayed to them was real enough. It's the other part of him that they didn't see or understand. The loving, tender, vulnerable part. The part he brought home to the pink house on Toluca Lake, to the woman who'd known him way back when.

☼

Shortly after their New Year's Eve blowup, Mom became pregnant for the third time. Dad sincerely wanted to change his ways, but Mom was skeptical. When you fear that someone will let you down, you don't expect too much. My mother loved my father. After seven years, she remained committed to their marriage. But she had serious reservations about their future. They'd barely settled into their new life in California when a film called *It Happened in Brooklyn* lured Dad back to New York—and to a brief affair with Lana Turner that made headlines in sixty-point type. Mom saw the pattern worsening. She already had two young children.

She had no intention of having another.

But my father had a different point of view. He'd fallen in love with Mom's family, in all of its teeming commotion. My father had been accustomed to eating alone, one reason he was so skinny. But mealtime was a raucous event at the Barbato household, with the mother cooking and the father beaming and the Victrola playing Verdi in the background, and half a dozen kids around the table. "I used to love the racket," Dad would recall. "Where I grew up, it was so quiet all the time." My father was starving for company, for *family*, and he ate at the Barbatos' table every chance he could. Dinnertime gatherings would remain a central ritual throughout his life.

Once he was married, Dad thought a large family would fill up his life. He'd say to Mom, "I want to have as many kids as we possibly can." And so when Mom floated the idea of ending her third pregnancy, he was aghast.

An abortion was a haunting thing for my father, a flashback to dark times in Hoboken, where Dolly had served as the neighborhood midwife. When a Catholic girl was unmarried and faced lifelong disgrace, or a forty-year-old woman with an out-of-work husband could barely afford to feed the kids they already had, Dolly would step into the breach. As a boy, Dad had to endure the other kids' taunts after his mother was once arrested.

More than a dozen years later, his abhorrence of Mom's proposal was a very personal thing.

My mother, however, was resolute. She was a pragmatic woman with tremendous backbone—hers was the grounded voice of our family, then and now. "It was hard," Mom would say, "but I knew that I was doing the right thing." She found a doctor in Los Angeles through a friend and had the procedure while my father was in Cuba. She then met Dad for a holiday in Acapulco. The doctor's prep was evident, "and he knew immediately what I'd done."

It was a terrible moment for Dad. He had deemed his brief encounters unimportant, but now they had taken from him something dear and irreplaceable.

And he told my mother, "Don't you *ever* do that again."

※

Dad made a dramatic turnaround. He kept his road trips briefer and threw himself into home life. By day he was absorbed in his children. By night he was courting Mom all over again, with dinner and dancing at Ciro's. He was really trying. He would make this marriage work in spite of himself.

Soon my mother was pregnant again, in the fall of 1947. Dad was elated and rooting for another girl. And he loved the name Tina, after Mom's sister, my Auntie Tina.

Mom had a difficult time; both she and Dad were under a lot of stress. Mayer disciplined my father by loaning him out to RKO, where he played, of all things, a priest—the most wholesome part they could find—in *The Miracle of the Bells*. (Dad called it "a silly picture.") Then he bounced back to MGM to make another forgettable film, *The Kissing Bandit*. In between, he'd take off to New York for radio broadcasts of *Your Hit Parade*. Mom tried to stay hopeful amid their separations, but she'd hesitate to pick up a gossip magazine.

By 1947, Dad's singing career began to slump. Everything seemed to be unraveling. And *then* Ava Gardner walked into his life. At the beginning, Mom didn't think that Ava would last any longer than Dad's prior affairs, but I suspect she wasn't resting easy.

When Mom was nine months along, she and Dad threw one of their regular Saturday night parties. After dinner they played charades. At eleven o'clock, my mother went upstairs to rest and count her labor pains. Shortly after midnight, she sent down word that it was time.

My father had been away when Nancy and Frankie were born; this was his first experience at the front. He behaved like the typical sitcom dad, running every red light en route to Cedars of Lebanon, where I made my debut just after two in the morning.

By whatever master plan governs such things, I was born on June 20, 1948: Father's Day. Dad had gotten his girl.

From the start, I was my father's daughter.

At around 3 A.M., when Dad returned home, the charades were still going strong. He took the floor and mimed "girl" by shaping an hourglass, then held up fingers for my vital statistics. You could say that I was born into show business.

The next day Dad took Nancy and Frankie out in the rowboat to celebrate on Toluca Lake.

Six months after my birth, we moved up in the world, from the Valley to Holmby Hills, to cooler summer temperatures and a shorter commute to Dad's workplace, MGM Studios.

And within a year after that, my father would leave us to be with Ava Gardner.

※

By her own description, Ava was a country girl. Raised in Grabtown, North Carolina, she was earthy, down-home, and totally unpretentious; she could curse with the boys and match them drink for drink. She was a defiantly free

spirit. The Hollywood star machine might mold and pro-
mote her as a sloe-eyed siren, but there was something
unyielding in Ava, and the moguls could never quite
tame her. Nor could the men in her life, from Mickey
Rooney to Artie Shaw to Howard Hughes.

It would take my father the better part of ten years to
learn the same.

In Ava, Dad had met his match. Their love affair may
have been meant to be, but that doesn't mean it was
meant to work. These were two tautly strung, ambitious,
restless people who could never quite be satiated.

My father often spoke to me about Ava. When I was
older, I would hear her side as well, and I'm convinced
that they shared a passion that neither had ever known
before. Their relationship was a melodrama of jealous
rages and tearful breakups and interloping bullfighters.
They were better suited as lovers than as spouses, but
Ava was soon pressing for marriage, for complicated reasons—to torture Dad, or to placate Louis B. Mayer (she'd
been labeled a homewrecker, which could kill a career in
those puritanical times), or perhaps to find some elusive
stability. She'd always longed, she'd reflect, for "one
good man I could love and marry and . . . who would
stick around for the rest of my life."

Dad was pushing for a marriage as well. I think that he
wanted to conquer and possess the most beautiful

woman in the world. The less grip he had on his career, the more obsessively he'd latch on to Ava and hold fast.

It would take him two years to ask Mom for a divorce, and they were two of the roughest, most insecure years of Dad's life. His career was faltering, his bank account dwindling. What money he had went to Mom to care for us. He was pursuing the highest-maintenance woman in Hollywood, and one who freely traveled the world, to boot.

My father was drowning in guilt. Over the years, he'd tell me, "I was selfish—my choices would affect you forever."

Dad told Ava that he'd left my mother for good, but that he'd always be committed to his children. As she recounted in her autobiography, *Ava: My Story*, "I was to learn that that kind of deep loyalty—not faithfulness, but loyalty—was a critical part of his nature."

My father was too obsessed to see that he and Ava were star-crossed. He didn't understand that she could never replace the happiness he had forfeited at home. He was a man who all his life looked outside for what was missing inside.

In 1950 he was playing the Paramount, the scene of his bobby-soxer breakthrough eight years earlier. But now the house was two-thirds empty. He was struggling with a bad throat and worse prospects. The music business had changed, and not for the better. The bobby-soxers now had children of their own. Dad was left with a shrinking audience and his own stubborn good taste.

From our vantage point today, we can see that he was an artist in transition—that this period was prologue to the Capitol years to come. But Dad couldn't know that at the time. He was staring into the abyss.

My father was so ashamed of himself that he couldn't turn to his one refuge, his home. ("The very sight of your three little faces would nearly kill me," he'd say.) His close friends—Manie Sacks, Swifty Lazar, Sammy Cahn—feared to leave him alone.

One night, on his way back to Manie's New York apartment—Dad couldn't even afford a hotel room—he passed a theater featuring Eddie Fisher. The lines were queued up around the block. "That was the rock bottom, the lowest of the low," he said.

Manie wasn't home. Dad walked into the kitchen, turned on the gas stove, and bent over to light his cigarette. When the pilot didn't light, he turned the burner off—and then he thought, *Hey, maybe this is easier.* He turned on all four burners and laid his head on the hissing stovetop.

Fortunately, Uncle Manie returned to find him in time. "That was stupid," Dad confessed to me. But he was a desperate man.

Something had to give, and it would be my father's most prized possession: his voice. A month later, when he opened his mouth to sing at the Copacabana, nothing came out. His throat hemorrhaged.

He would never fall so low again.

While I was too young to notice all this Sturm und Drang, my mother digested every sour bit of it. Mom had married for life, but she was coming to accept the inevitable. Her husband's future, regardless of Ava or anyone else in his life, would not include her. It had nothing to do with any failing on Mom's part. She was popular in Dad's social set and had many friends on her own. She was an attractive, intelligent, modern woman with old-fashioned values—exactly the woman Dad had wanted.

But my father was never happy with what he had when he had it.

The pressure against Mom, meanwhile, kept mounting. The tabloid winds shifted—one column compared Frank and Ava to Romeo and Juliet—and suddenly my mother was an ogre for trying to hold her family together. Dolly was seduced by Ava's glamour, and her devout Catholicism took a backseat. She'd tell Mom: *Better to let him go—better for you, better for the children. You can't keep a man if he doesn't want to be there.*

19

Mom's relationship with her mother-in-law would never be the same.

The open scandal was too much for Mom. In 1951, she agreed to a divorce. As my father would acknowledge, "I imposed it on her. She finally relented—she just gave up."

The divorce became final on October 31, 1951, and Dad wed Ava seven days later. It had taken them so long to get there that the marriage was anticlimactic; the sport had gone out of it. Though their love would be lasting and powerful, they were hopelessly ill-cast as a couple.

My mother's life was altered forever when my father moved out. His children's lives were marked indelibly. Dad himself would never feel as safe or whole again— and with all that said, thank God that he made his move. Because he had so much more to do as an artist, and he could only do it his way.

※

I was too young to see much of Dad and Ava together during their brief married life. They were on different schedules, with Ava shooting movies and Dad spending time in New York at whatever bookings he could get, or for the last hurrah of radio. And I'm not sure how comfortable Dad was facing his children just then.

When I did see Ava, it was at her sister Bappie's home atop Sunset Plaza Drive. Mom always made us available to our father, no matter what. She would clean us up and he'd collect us, and off we'd go.

I was four when I first met my father's new wife, and she made a fundamental impression on me; she seemed to stir all my senses at once. Though only five-six, she truly seemed bigger than life, a quality that can accrue to a person whose image is projected at thirty-two times life size. (Not every movie star had it, though my father did, too.) But like Dad, Ava was also gentle and accessible to children; she immediately knelt to come down to my level. I have never forgotten that gesture.

When people talk about natural beauty, I think of Ava, who had no use or need for coiffing or makeup. Her tousled brown hair was loose and soft. She had a long neck, and seemed freshly scrubbed, casual but impeccable. That first time she was wearing a shirt with the sleeves rolled up, and a skirt that was softly gathered up, perfect for twirling. And I remember that she smelled of gardenias, and that she was barefoot—and soon Nancy and I were barefoot, too.

Looking back, it was the first time I saw simplicity perfected.

Ava was not your stereotypical stepmother. (She would never have children of her own.) But she was easy to be with and seemed genuinely interested in us. She gave my sister her first lipstick; she taught me how to thread a needle and sew on a button.

I was too young to know *who* she was. Once we were watching TV with Dad in our den at Carolwood Drive—he often came over for dinner, even after he'd remarried. Mickey Rooney, Ava's first husband, was on with Steve Allen that evening, and Mickey stood on a box to approach Allen's height. "That man's so short!" I squealed. "Who could ever be married to him?" My father shot my mother a look. Mom broke up and said, "Out of the mouths of babes . . ."

By that point my father and Ava were more off than on. Their marriage was no more stable than their courtship. As Ava would note in her autobiography, there would be two abortions, repeated separations, and countless imagined betrayals. Like my dad, Ava was both compulsively flirtatious and intensely possessive. Like my dad, she needed constant proximity to the one she loved, lest her "red-fanged romantic jealousy," as she put it, lead her to assume the worst.

I think that my father was both unnerved and comforted by the combustion between them. For a man like Dad, a volatile relationship could be *easier* to sustain, because the closeness is periodically broken. Each reconciliation prefigures the next breakup, and it all *seems* terribly intimate, but it's really just drama—just going apart and coming back together.

Ava wounded Dad deeply, no doubt, more deeply than anyone else. But there was a part of him that even Ava never reached, because he held it safely distanced from the fray.

※

In *Why Sinatra Matters*, Pete Hamill explores the quandary faced by second-generation Italian Americans. He sees them as people caught between *la via vecchia*, the old way, with its lockstep rules and family-centered traditions, and *la via nuova*, the new way, a candy store of freedoms and choices. The dichotomy was hardly unique to my father. But his life was so public and his temperament so delicate that he felt it more acutely than most—he just wasn't your average bear.

To Dad, my mother represented *la via vecchia*. He was an old-fashioned guy who wanted the woman in his life to take care of him, and to be there to be cared for in return. Mom was willing to play that traditional role, to stoke my father's hearth and bear his babies. I believe in destiny, and I believe that my parents were destined to be together. Dad would surely get what he'd needed from

Mom: constancy, adoration, and total belief in him, forever and ever.

Not to mention three fabulous kids.

My father got what he needed, but it wasn't enough.

Ava was my mother's antithesis, *la via nuova* all the way. A bona fide movie goddess, she was in high demand in the early fifties, making as many as three movies a year, on location from Africa to Australia. She was living the high-wire life that had drawn my father to her—and then, once he won her, he wanted to tie and bind her to his side. It made no sense, because no one retires a movie goddess except her public. Yes, Ava loved him, but she would never be his happy homemaker—which would eventually have bored Dad anyway.

He was learning, slowly and painfully, that no one could have it all.

※

Dad's days with Ava were numbered, even before he made his comeback in *From Here to Eternity*. (In November 1953, shortly after the movie was released, they were legally separated.) To reinvent himself and revive his career, my father had to focus on his work. He couldn't do that and hold on to Ava, too. The stronger he got, the less responsible she felt for him. By the time he won his

Oscar for Maggio, a role that Ava had lobbied to get for him after Eli Wallach turned it down, their distancing was complete.

※

My father didn't hide his sadness from his children. I remember times, from when I was small, when he seemed quiet and withdrawn. The divorce wouldn't be final until 1957, but he and Ava had parted long before then.

"We just didn't belong together," he'd say wistfully, in recollection.

Sometimes he'd cancel a visit home to us at the last minute. When we asked why he wasn't coming, my mother would say he wasn't feeling well, and it would be a tiny knife into my young heart. Mom would never denounce Dad. Instead she'd make excuses for him—in her own way, she catered to him as Dolly had. Maybe she should have been more critical when he reneged on his children, because we wound up feeling expendable. I know there were times that I wanted to tell my father that he'd done something that hurt me. But I couldn't articulate the hurt. It was too much for me; I buried it deep inside.

I do remember Mom hanging up the phone from Dad in tears more than once when he was in a bad way. Then there were the calls I wouldn't know about, the ones to my mother in the middle of the night. Of Mom, he'd tell his friends, "She's the only woman who understands me." He trusted her like no other.

Was Ava the love of Dad's life? I'm not sure about that—I think he had two loves. My father was a man of contradiction. He wanted to be consistent, but his spirit was fractured. To the end of Ava's life, he'd watch out for her. To the end of his own, he'd be saddened by his failure to stay married to my mother, the woman he still called Sweetheart.

As Ava knew well, loyalty was a critical part of his nature.

Their passion was too strong to end neatly. For years after they called it off, Dad would phone Ava on the spur of the moment, and she'd wing her way out to him. They'd last a night together, perhaps a weekend if all the stars were in alignment. And then they'd blow up again, like old times.

One encounter in the early sixties ended abruptly after Ava deserted Dad at a restaurant in Spain. He turned to his friends and said, "Ain't the first time she walked out, but it's the last."

2

The Void He Left Behind

WE WOULD SETTLE into a sprawling Mediterranean with a red-tiled roof on Carolwood Drive, in Holmby Hills. The first story was brick, with an overhang that created patios and breezeways below and balconies off the second floor above. We had two basements, which provided great fun whenever the water heaters flooded. We'd take the opportunity to don our rain boots and go wading up the Amazon—to our mother's vexation, of course.

As large as the house was, we were one bedroom short, so Frankie drew the upstairs study, with built-in bookcases and a fireplace: real cozy. Nancy's room was the largest of our three—the perfect size to pitch our sheet tent, fill it with comforters and pillows (we didn't know from sleeping bags), and camp out for the night on the floor. I'd be the only one left there with a stiff back in the morning, however.

Carolwood was a place with some mystery to it. One day I accidentally brushed a small barbell off the filing cabinet in my mother's cedar closet; it rolled into the wall and disappeared! At first I thought I'd knocked a hole in the paneling, but then I saw the empty crawl space that extended behind Mom's bed. Naturally I crawled in, but the door swung shut behind me like something out of a Dead End Kids movie—*Wait a minute, I'm in the dark here!* There was no handle, and I knew that no one would hear me if I screamed, so it was no use to panic. I was about to start screaming anyway, but then I managed to squeeze the pads of my fingers underneath the door and pull it open. Crisis averted—plus I'd found the ultimate spot for our next round of hide-and-go-seek.

Our living room was the stage for Christmas and parties. But for everyday converging there was the library: leaded glass, wood paneling, two large sofas, a leather-topped partners desk, a game table, an English secretary converted into a bar, an illuminated globe of the world, a fireplace (used all the time), and most important, our

TV. This room, Dad would say, was the reason he bought the house.

One wall was lined from floor to ceiling with bookcases. My father was a self-educated man and a voracious reader, and the shelves mirrored his range of interests: novels, art books, multivolume histories of Lincoln and Truman. Dad loved to move among learned people, and many of his books were signed by their authors.

On occasion, the library would also serve as a refuge for the Crosby boys, who lived not far from us across Sunset. They were teenagers in the mid-fifties, closer to Nancy's age, and my mother would provide a soft shoulder and a hot meal after they ran away or Bing threw them out. I didn't know about Bing's tyranny then; I just saw that these kids were always miserable. I could hardly imagine what they were going through: *Running away from home—who'd want to do that?*

When I came home from school, I'd peek into the library's ground-level windows to see if anyone was inside. (On Tuesdays, I knew that Mom would be having tea with Barbara "Missy" Stanwyck, a lifelong friend of hers who was always good for a pack of Clorets gum.) If my mother was there, she'd open the window and let me step through to the wooden sill, then hop the three feet to the floor.

I was in and out a lot; the grounds were the best part of that house, as far as I was concerned. Where Beverly Hills was a flattened grid of relatively small lots, Holmby Hills felt like the country. The streets snaked through rolling hills, and the houses were set back like fortresses. The sprawling properties could hold tennis courts and Olympic-size pools, and afforded the privacy that Dad was looking for.

Our two-and-a-half acres were protected by a high wall of Mexican masonry: large red blocks with mortar oozing between them like icing on a layer cake. The wooden gate was worthy of Zorro's hacienda, and opened at the push of a button. Beyond it lay a vast bricked courtyard, complete with wishing well and user-friendly olive tree for climbing.

The back of the house was divided into sections. First, an orchard lush with flowers and tangerine and lemon trees, and a glass greenhouse, pungent with the scent of rich soil. Next came our sanctuary, a play yard complete with sandbox, slide, and swing set. The rest of the property was a trillion yards of lush green lawn, flat for a long time and then sloping down to the biggest pool ever—especially when you were tiny and didn't yet know how to swim.

The entire parcel was bordered by enormous tree beds, with bushes left to grow free and provide a dense barrier between us and the adjacent properties—not to mention a perfect facsimile of the Congo, when I got old enough to tag along on safari with my siblings. I could hear the drone of neighbors out there in the summertime, but I couldn't see them. Our lot was a self-enclosed universe.

On Tuesday afternoons we'd be visited by the Helm's Bakery truck. I'd hear its ship's whistle and run out the back door with Terry, our housekeeper, across the courtyard, out the pedestrian gate, and down the flagstone path to the curb. As the bakery man pulled out the long skinny drawers of fresh doughnuts on sheets of waxed paper, the smell of warm sugar wafted over me. We'd make our purchase and hurry back inside; I remember being tall enough to open our refrigerator, but not quite enough to reach the milk I needed for dunking.

Then there was Don Malone's dry cleaning truck. When Mom wasn't available to drive me, I could jump in with Don for a ride to my best friend Shelley Wanger's house, his next stop. Holmby Hills felt like a very small neighborhood in those days.

One of our favorite neighbors was Robert Ryan. He was a tall, gentle man who loved kids and adored my mother, and would often come over to see her. The Ryans had a daughter about my age, a real tomboy. She had a gray burro who loved apples and wore a hat with its ears poking through.

The back of the Ryans' property dropped off into a deep ravine where things grew wild. It was there that I first discovered a patch of multicolored Indian corn—I thought it was *magic* corn, since it was so different from the yellow variety I'd get at dinner. I picked the most beautiful ear, with its multitude of earth tones, and saved it for my father's birthday.

It was just an ear of corn, but Dad made a big to-do about it, as he would with all my simple gifts. Once I made him a snowman mosaic with those circa-1953 crushed rocks that you glued onto a board. Mom had my masterpiece matted and framed and wrapped, but when Dad opened it, half a dozen rocks had fallen off. Seeing I was crestfallen, he said, "It's okay, sweetheart, I can fix that." He carefully glued the rocks back in place with a tube of Elmer's—it was Dad to the rescue, just like George Bailey and the rose petals in *It's a Wonderful Life*. He hung the mosaic in his bathroom in Palm Springs, where it would remain for forty years.

Walt Disney lived across the street and up three houses from us. When Disneyland was still a swamp, he was famous in our parts as the man with the train: a perfectly scaled-down model on three-foot-wide tracks that circled the perimeter of his property. On a specified Saturday, at one o'clock sharp, the neighborhood kids would line up and wait their turn for a ride. Mr. Disney would be up front in his engineer's cap, straddling the locomotive, having as much fun as anyone. Then we'd clamber into the open boxcars behind him, and we'd clickety-clack our way at five miles per hour, a little slower around the curves. There was even a special effect: a long, dark tunnel to squeal and giggle through, with a vaulted wooden door off the pages of *Sleeping Beauty*.

Nancy and Frankie had enjoyed the train for years, and it was a great day when I was finally old enough to get on board. But by the time I'd had one or two rides, Mr. Disney had gotten busy with his Magic Kingdom. He was working seven days a week, and the little train had reached the end of the line.

☀

For the first few years after we moved to Carolwood Drive, my mother wasn't interested in making some brave new life for herself. She took her marriage vows seriously. She vainly hoped that Dad would return to his senses and come home—back to the only real family he'd ever known.

It was tougher on my mother because there was no

clean break. Even before Dad's romance with Ava was essentially over, my parents would many times consider a reconciliation. Each time my father backed away. I think he feared that his wanderlust would revisit him, and he couldn't bear the thought of hurting Mom again.

Though I had no way of discerning what was really going on, I knew that Mom sometimes cried in her room for hours. I must have felt her sadness by osmosis. Shortly after learning to write, I scrawled this message to her in pencil on notebook paper: "Dear Mama, I love you very much. And so does Daddy." Underneath I drew my mother standing still, and my father walking toward her, with his arms outstretched.

When Mom was unavailable, and I was still really small, I would find comfort in Mamie—close, affectionate, physical comfort. She had a big lap and big arms and big bosoms to lean on. I must have really relied on her, because I remember how upset I was when I came home one day to find Mom furious and Mamie packing. The gist of it was that Frankie's boyish pranks might have aggravated our nanny's blood pressure. To make matters worse, Mamie had left us to work for a family down the street; I befriended the children, just to be close to her.

Mom would replace Mamie with Matsu and Terry, a Japanese couple who would take care of the garden and the house as long as we lived there. We never had a big staff, going back to the years when we couldn't afford one. When my parents divorced, Dad was in debt. Rather than squeeze him for a stiff settlement, Mom made it as easy as she could for him. She took straight alimony in lieu of child support, which shifted the tax burden to her. And she accepted a modest annual base, plus a set percentage of his income, in good years and lean. She was mindful that he worked in a fickle business; she wasn't one to overreach.

If I sensed dysfunction in our household, it would be at the oddest times, like at breakfast, when a parent was nowhere to be found. Mom wasn't bounding out of bed to send us off to school. From the time I reached first grade, I'd follow my brother and sister to the breakfast room, where Terry encouraged us to finish our Cream of Wheat. (I loved that breakfast room, and felt terrible when, at the age of nine, I set it on fire by lighting a Christmas candle too close to the organza curtains.)

My siblings and I were comfortable, but not pampered. We were obliged to look after our own rooms and tidy our beds on the maid's day off. We left our plates in the kitchen sink and our dirty laundry in the bathroom hampers. My mother believed in order and discipline, and we complied.

Except for Nancy, who was so busy and popular that

she'd be a little messy, so I'd try to pick up after her when I could.

❈

Halloween was a big deal in 1956, and nowhere bigger than on Mapleton Drive, where my friend Shelley Wanger lived. I went out trick-or-treating that year with Shelley and her father, Walter, who'd married Joan Bennett. Shelley was a fairy princess that year and I was a clown, in a pointed hat and a baggy suit that billowed in the windy night.

(The Wanger household was the flip side of mine. Shelley's dad was always present and available; I saw her mother, Joan Bennett, infrequently, and only at dinner. Joan would sit regally at the head of the table, under a tremendous oil painting of herself. At the end of dinner, she would supervise her daughter's foot exercises. While grasping the arms of a wrought-iron chair, Shelley would curl her toes under her feet, theoretically to strengthen her arches.)

The Wangers lived near Art Linkletter, who *really* went all out. You had to crawl under a long tunnel of draped tables that wound through their house, from front door to back, where you'd get your candy. There were creepy sound effects throughout, and I remember some kids saying, "Not me—*I'm* not going in there." Boy, was I happy to see Mr. Wanger at the other end.

Once we survived the Linkletters, we crossed the street and headed back to Shelley's. On the way we came to a brick house that was set off, down a dark driveway, and Mr. Wanger told us that we'd be stopping in for a minute. We were ushered into a large tiled foyer, quite formal compared to ours, through a darkened living room, and into a small den. A smallish male figure sat in a wing chair by the fire, with this beautiful young woman resting at his feet, her light hair shining in the blaze. She was wearing a starched white shirt with its collar up, and black capri pants with side slits, and little flats, like Audrey Hepburn in *Sabrina*. She pressed up against her husband's chair as though she couldn't get close enough. And when she stood up to greet us, I thought, absurdly, *She's too young to be that tall.*

The man didn't get up; he looked tired and deeply settled, as though he might never get up. It was just after dark, but he was dressed in his robe and pajamas. I knew nothing about him, but something felt *off* to me.

Later I found out that I'd met Humphrey Bogart and Betty Bacall, whose son Stephen was in my third grade class at Warner Avenue School. Not long after Halloween, Stephen would miss a week of school because his father was very sick. The following January, Bogart died of lung cancer. It was the first time I'd become conscious of the death of a *parent*, and it must have scared the hell out of me. (Not long after that I heard about something even worse: the death of a child, Red Skelton's son, from leukemia.)

My father, a maverick born, identified with that man in the wing chair. He loved the way Bogart, and Spencer Tracy as well, seemed so natural on the screen. Dad also admired Bogart's fuck-you attitude toward the studio establishment, which would cattle-prod actors from part to part and give them no say in the process.

After Bogart died, my father's relationship with Betty Bacall turned romantic. Dad was doubtless flattered by the notion of being a worthy successor to Bogart. And Bacall, another dramatic personality who could dazzle in a simple white shirt, might have evoked Ava Gardner to him. In any case, a perfectly good friendship evolved into an unfortunate marriage proposal. When their plans were leaked prematurely by Louella Parsons, Dad panicked. I think he woke up one morning and looked at his future—two new stepchildren and a formidable, take-charge, no-bullshit wife—and he thought to himself, *What the hell am I doing?*

The relationship closed on a bitter note. They didn't speak for years, though Bacall was great to me when I met her in New York many years later. Dad had screwed up, and L.A. was too small and incestuous a town, she was mortified and justly furious. My father wouldn't talk to me about her until thirty years later, during my research for a television miniseries on his life. "I wanted to take care of her, and it got out of hand," he told me. "It shouldn't have happened."

A postscript: Shortly before my father died, my mother gave me an elegant molded silver flask. It was engraved *F.S.*, and, in the opposite corner, *Love, WITCH.* Mom told me it was a gift to Dad—from Betty Bacall. When I look at that flask, I can imagine Bacall's sly smile in *To Have and Have Not,* the arch of her brow, the sinuous way she could move through a room.

Even when Dad made mistakes, he was stepping in high company.

Yes, we had a privileged childhood, but I would have traded it all for the all-American family life that I'd see each week on *Father Knows Best.* I loved that show. The Andersons seemed like our family, only better, since Robert Young never missed an episode. I could identify with Kitten, the youngest child, and it wasn't much of a stretch to match Frankie with the mischievous Bud. And then there was Nancy, so much like Princess (played by

Elinor Donahue), the older sister with perfect hair and a bustling social life.

I thoroughly and completely idolized my big sister. I craved her time and attention more than anyone else's. She was kind, entertaining, and thoughtful—except when she'd blast the heater to kill the morning chill and then leave for school without turning it off.

When Nancy entered junior high school, I was only starting kindergarten. Our age difference was a big frustration, because I wanted to be just like her. (I'd be sixteen before we'd finally catch up with each other, and not a minute too soon for me.) When Nancy went out, I'd slip into her room. I'd sit at her makeup table, apply her latest shade of lipstick, and reorganize her drawers, which were always a mess. Then I'd clump around in her high-heeled shoes—what bliss!

Nancy even practiced her piano without Mom's nagging. She'd write new lyrics to a song from one of the big Broadway shows, then teach it—with harmony—to the girls in her school club. Baby sister, meanwhile, was a bust at the piano and self-conscious about singing; I was indisputably the least musical Sinatra of our generation. (I would trade the ivory keys for a leotard and pink toe shoes.) But I never felt competitive with Nancy. I was too busy looking up to her.

When Frankie and I were small, Nancy was quick to

stand in on Mom's behalf. She'd help me paint by numbers, or make me the perfect tinfoil princess crown. Once Nancy obtained her driver's license, she became my mostly willing chauffeur. She was even good about letting me tag along to movies with her girlfriends.

My sister and brother and I spent a lot of time playing around the house, invariably with a kid from across the street named Douglas "Bomber" Shapiro. We'd use our garage to play *Space Patrol* (a hit TV series at the time), or the pool for a game we called Florence Chadwick, after the woman who'd swum the English Channel. Nancy would swim to and fro, while coach Frankie urged her on from a nearby rubber raft, "Come on, you can make it! You're almost in France!" My job was to shuttle from the house with snacks and paper cups of lemonade for the coach, who needed nourishment to keep urging on our Florence.

My father later taught me how to swim at his place in Palm Springs, using a jumbo popcorn can as a float. (Dad was a superb swimmer himself, from all those summers on the Jersey shore.) But I wasn't supposed to go in alone when I was little. Once Nancy pursued my beachball in the middle of the pool and told me to stay back on the step. I was a daredevil, though, and the next second I was in over my head, gulping chlorine. By the time Nancy turned around and came back, I was doing my

William Holden imitation from *Sunset Boulevard*, my hair floating at the surface like a lily pad. My sister fished me out and gave me a good talking to.

At dusk we'd go exploring on a "nature walk" down the hill toward Angelo Drive, where Jack Warner lived. Our neighborhood bordered the base of Benedict Canyon, where vacant lots and rodents still abounded, and it felt like the edge of wilderness. There was barely any traffic. The only sounds of civilization were the reverberant *thwok* of tennis balls from courts we could not see.

In the summer I had to go to bed while it was still light. I'd get a sinking feeling when Mom called me in— another reminder that I'd always be the baby. I could hear my siblings, still playing outside; I felt pangs of isolation. Even now, I don't like the long summer days. They remind me of being split off from everyone else.

🔱

Dad visited us with regularity when he was in town, but it was always an occasion. Mom would fuss, "Let's clean up, Daddy's coming." She'd comb my hair and pick out a dress. (Little girls wore little dresses then, there was no way around it.) All the while I'd be squirming and fidgeting, my excitement rising till I felt like I'd jump out of my Mary Janes. Dad was always on time, if not early, but he could never get there soon enough for me.

Mom put no restrictions on my father's visitation. We were first and foremost an Italian family, and my mother was set on making our lives as stable as possible. The one thing she asked of him was to be consistent. We'd be heartsick when work would foil his plans and we'd lose out. "Your father can't be in two places at one time," Mom would say, as if that explained everything.

Mom and Nancy would be quietly disappointed, but I was different—by the time I was six or seven years old, I'd get positively cranky when Dad stood us up. I sensed that my father had a big life of his own out there. But I couldn't accept that whatever he did was more important than seeing me. I personally felt that Mom was being *too* flexible, too quick to make excuses. I'd be thinking, *No, you get him back on the phone and tell him that he should be here!*

I wouldn't say anything aloud; I knew there was nothing I could do about it. But as I look back at these experiences, I think that they molded me, for better or worse, into Frank Sinatra's most demanding child, the one who'd expect *more* from him. I know now that he was doing the best he could do—and that my standards were no higher than his own, even if he couldn't meet them.

Dad's visits couldn't have been easy on Mom, given the complexity of their relationship. Looking back, I don't know how she coped. Her heart had to break a little each time his car pulled away, and it had to tear at Dad as well. Yet we never saw a hint of friction, or heard an unkind word between them. They were remarkable people, I think—very poised and proper people, no matter what maelstrom swirled around them.

Every so often Dad would come by with his latest Capitol recording—the first pressing, in a paper sleeve. Nancy and I would curl up on either side of him on the living room couch, while Frankie manned the turntable. (My father was physically enveloping with us, and I always wanted to be next to him.) It was an adult moment, focused and still. I learned how to listen to music with the best.

Sometimes Dad would arrive with a bachelor chum like Swifty Lazar or Jimmy Van Heusen; he'd love to show us off. (Mom affectionately called these guests "the orphans.") After a ritual drink in the library, a good, simple dinner would be served. When we'd finished dessert, I might drag my father upstairs to play a game of Candyland. But the main event was back in the library, where we'd gather in front of the television until my bedtime. Often Dad fell asleep, and we'd cover him with a blanket and try not to giggle too loud. Because as long as he slept, he would stay.

For those few precious minutes, I felt as close to the TV Andersons as I ever would.

⁂

Nancy and Frankie were radio babies, but I was born into the new world of television. Dad loved clowns and comics on TV, going back to *Your Show of Shows* and to Milton Berle. Watching TV could feel like visiting family friends; Uncle Miltie would lavish us with bubble gum in real life (a giveaway from Texaco, his sponsor), and I knew Jack Benny and Lucy Ball, and George and Gracie Burns. Even my dad would have his televised appearances on weekly variety shows that ran throughout my childhood.

The Burnses were especially good to us. I remember one Christmas when my father couldn't be with us—he was in Africa with Ava, who was filming *Mogambo*—and George and Gracie invited us over for Christmas Eve. They had a present for each of us under their tree, but the best part for me was gazing at their son Ronnie, my first crush.

That absence was the exception for Dad. Holiday traditions were a big deal for him, even if he had to be back out working the next day, and Christmas was the biggest event at the Sinatra homestead. Mindful of giving Dad his due, we wouldn't begin the trimming process until after his birthday, on December 12. Matsu would team with Uncle Bart, Mom's only brother, to string multicolored lights on everything: roofline, doorways, windows, hedges, trees. It was magical. Fuses would blow and tempers flare, but what the hell, it was Christmas. Inside, lighted garlands dressed the stucco arches, mantels, and stairwell. The scent of evergreens permeated the house.

Our large silver-tip fir tree was set in the living room, in the corner window banquette, to be adorned only with lights until Christmas Eve. At some point toward midnight, long after I'd been sent off to bed, Dad would come by with his merry band of bachelors. They'd stay up into the night and trim the tree, tossing on the tinsel with something less than martial precision. But Mom and Nancy would fix it by morning.

By 7 A.M. I'd wake up, get my siblings, and run downstairs. On occasion, if my parents had hosted a party, my father and his friends might still be there, grinning and dopey for lack of sleep, waiting to see our faces. And there would be the tree, with presents spilling into the room like a horn of plenty. My father would buy and wrap our gifts himself with his featherweight's thick fingers, and they'd often be out of the ordinary. Once I got a glockenspiel right out of *The Music Man*, which seemed to me the best thing ever.

Our birthday parties weren't lavish by the standards of Holmby Hills, where people imported clowns and ponies into their gardens. Mom kept it simple: just the usual games, balloons, and party favors. Though Dad would skip the parties, he'd do everything he could to be with us for the special dinners that followed. That was my birthday bonus, beyond the presents and cake: a command appearance by my father.

※

Dad loved the element of surprise, and the best visits of all were unplanned. I'd be playing outside when I'd hear a car and look to the courtyard . . . and then I'd spy that Cavanaugh fedora, and the silver-gray T-Bird convertible, usually with the top down—*Oh cool, Dad's here!* We'd pile in and be off to Stan's Drive-in on Sunset Boulevard for chocolate milk shakes, and then to Vine Street and a quick run through Wallach's Music City, the Virgin Records of its day.

Dad was a man who delighted in the company of his children. When I was old enough for a booster seat, he'd take me out with Frankie and Nancy to dinner. After watching him record for a while at Capitol Records, we'd break for a meal at the Villa Capri before someone drove us home, so we wouldn't be out too late on a school night. On special occasions Dad would take us to Chasen's or Romanoff's. Or to La Rue on Sunset, the most special of all, because it overlooked the whole of Los Angeles.

My father rarely ate anything elaborate. I can still see him ordering a minute steak and showing the waiter how thin he wanted it, with his thumb and forefinger half an inch apart. Our only argument came over vegetables. We dreaded the gray mush that came out of the most famous kitchens of the day. (The people who make airline food must have grown up in the fifties.) I remember glaring at my father and saying, "How come we have to eat them and you don't? You don't even *order* them."

Dad cast a wary eye at the waiter, then gave the stock response: "Because you're growing."

Mom would scold us at home when we'd shove our peas or lima beans under our seat cushions, but Dad thought it was a riot. "I don't blame you," he'd say, because he detested vegetables too.

※

My father's absences said as much about his lifestyle as about the divorce. When out on the road, he might be gone for weeks at a stretch. And even when he wasn't working, he might get bored and decide to jump off to Paris with the composer Jimmy Van Heusen on a whim—why not?

The gaps between his visits could be painfully long, especially when I needed Dad to mark a childhood milestone. When I was ready for the training wheels to come off my bicycle, it felt like an eternity before he came by to witness my prodigious mastery of a two-wheeler. But just when you thought, *Where is he?* he would materialize with that rakish hat and toothy grin.

In my ninth year, when I was finally brave enough to go on sleepovers, I'd be confronted with *Father Knows Best* in the flesh. I figured out that a man could work and make money and still get home for dinner every night. That he could tuck his daughter into bed and be there at breakfast the next morning, as steady as a school bus.

It was a lot to miss, our father's physical presence. Dad was like a campfire, the point where we gathered and felt warm. He had such a big presence—he put out this tremendous energy, and we all felt more alive around him. When he was with you, he was really *with* you.

As I said, life changed whenever he was coming. But even the greatest visit is still a visit, with a beginning and an end. I could feel the end coming, and then he'd check his watch and say, "Walk me to the door." We'd each hug and kiss him good-bye. As Mom accompanied him out to his car, I'd run up to my bedroom window overlooking the courtyard and watch my father drive away.

These are my saddest memories. Each of Dad's visits was an emotional parabola: the eager anticipation of his arrival; the giddy joy of his company; a swelling apprehension as his departure drew near; the dull, aching void he left in his wake.

We were always building up to good-bye.

When the emptiness got too much for me, I'd go up to Mom's bedroom and walk into Dad's old dressing area and bath, which was laid in art deco tile, ecru with black accents. I'd never seen my father there, but I knew this was the space that once belonged just to him. It held a potpourri of smells—of Yardley lavender soap, and his box of oil paints, and his leather shoes in the cedar-lined closet with a grace note of camphor fluting through.

For years after he was gone, my father's monogrammed towels still hung in the bathroom. A few shirts remained in the closet, arranged by color. It felt as though the man who'd lived there was away on a long trip but expected back anytime.

Though I didn't witness the transition, eventually I'd find the shirts and shoes replaced by Mom's seasonal clothes and fabrics. Only the dry lavender scent, my dad's favorite, remained.

But those minutes in Dad's space must have been cold comfort, because I also remember how empty I felt. When I summon the image of that needy little girl in that abandoned room, I feel just the same today.

❋

Looking back, I was attuned to Dad's inability to nestle in with us—he was always in a hurry, always on a schedule. I felt a restlessness, a loneliness, an aloneness, and I felt bad that I could not fill him up. I wasn't enough to make him content; I must have let him down somehow.

It wasn't until I was older that I realized that it wasn't my job to fill him up, and that my father's restlessness was an organic part of who he was.

It was never something easy to be.

People talk casually about the artistic temperament, but I believe that it's something real and complex. I think that my dad was gripped by an intensity of feeling that cut him off from others, even from those he truly loved. He was different, and he knew it—not better or worse, but perhaps *more*. He lightly called himself "an eighteen-karat manic-depressive." (As flippant as Dad could be about his mental state, I believe that a Zoloft a day might have kept his demons away. But that kind of medicine was decades off.)

My father took what might have become incapacitating and made it work for him in his music. When we hear "I've Got the World on a String" or "One for My Baby" for the hundredth time, and the singing still triggers something inside us, I don't think it's just Dad's phrasing, or his timbre, or his flawless musicality. I think that we're responding to that intensity of feeling—to a man who *had* to channel his most intimate emotions into his recordings and performances, if only as a release.

There was no room for artifice in Dad's singing (or for that matter, in his living). He had more than he could handle with the real stuff, and he had to let some of it out onstage. But onstage or off, he was always exactly who he was. If that made him self-absorbed at times and led to lapses in his behavior, his family loved and accepted him, regardless. I know that he found solace in that.

My circumstances improved when I was old enough to travel with Nancy and Frankie. We'd go to Las Vegas for the weekend, or New York and Atlantic City at spring break. I would sit ringside and watch my father in his natural habitat, onstage—an indelible experience. It may be typical of young girls to place their fathers on a pedestal, but for me it was a visual reality. I'd be sitting alongside the stage, literally at his feet, my neck craned to watch him work his spell in that dark, charged space. Every light was trained on him, each rapt set of eyes. There was silence until he chose to break it, and then the sound of him was all around me—familiar as my own name, yet somehow different, and bigger, and entirely overwhelming.

By the late fifties, we were spending most vacations at Dad's place in the desert, outside Palm Springs. The house was on Wonder Palm Drive (later Frank Sinatra Drive), along the seventeenth fairway of the Tamarisk Country Club. It would be his home, and ours, for more than four decades.

The desert was Dad's lifelong passion, the place where he felt healthiest and most peaceful. Before the golf courses and their Rainbird sprinkler systems brought humidity into the area, and pollution swept in from the west, it was arid and smogless. Your perspiration would evaporate before you noticed. Palm Springs was heaven, and relatively unknown, though that would soon change.

Before Dad's property expanded into the Compound, it was just a small three-bedroom house. There was his own simple room, done up in orange, his favorite color; an adjacent guest room, which Mia Farrow would later decorate in pink; and a second guest room off the living room, where Jack Kennedy would stay in 1960, before it became a den-and-bar family room.

To accommodate his growing children and their friends, my father put up a four-bedroom bungalow (with eight baths!) west of the main house. We called it the Christmas Tree House, because it was cozy and traditional, like a New England A-frame: white with green shutters, and set on a thick green lawn. It had its own pool, and a living room with a fireplace and TV and a game table. It was like our private clubhouse.

The town of Palm Springs—a little village then, really—had a great movie theater and a renowned candy store, but those were reserved for evening expeditions. With the weather so predictable, we'd spend most days around the pool, with Dad joining in the races and chicken fights. For a special treat, he'd strap us into an authentic Army jeep, like the ones in *M*A*S*H*, and drive us across the desert. We'd swerve around the tumbleweed and fly over the sand dunes like a roller coaster, which would crack us up every time. Once we got stuck in the sand and couldn't get out, and had to walk home.

The cooking was always great at Dad's house, with

the proprietor often taking charge himself. Breakfast was a big event. We could have cereal or pancakes or anything we liked, but I also remember Dad browning a slice of bread in olive oil, cutting a hole in the middle, then frying an egg in the hole. For himself, he preferred the simple fried egg, sunny-side up, with the yolk running just enough for his toast. Or steamed white rice with chocolate bits, a comfort food from his childhood.

The dinner pot would start going by late morning, with Dad in and out checking it the rest of the day. He made a good tomato sauce, better known as *gravy* in the neighborhood. He'd drop in a dozen pork chops and let them simmer all day, till they'd fall apart, and then he'd cook the pasta to a perfect al dente.

For meatballs, though, he'd defer to Mom, with the respect one Italian cook affords to another. He also doted on my mother's secret recipe for eggplant parmesan. There was nothing like it in the world: tissue-paper-thin slices of eggplant with a dusting of cheese, best eaten cold on hot crusty Italian bread. Mom would bake it in large sheet pans and cut it into bricks, swaddle it in Saran Wrap (to protect the tomatoes) and then aluminum foil. She'd send it out to Dad in freezer bags, so he could store it wherever he might be. When you came across one of those bricks in his freezer, it was like finding a bar of gold bullion.

My father was a night person, at work or at play. We knew to adjust to his rhythms. If he'd come to the desert from a long trip on the road, you knew better than to run into his room in the morning. And since the pool was right by his bedroom, we'd keep it down until he emerged, when our day would really begin.

Once I brought my friend Shelley down for the weekend and it rained nonstop. Dad rose early with us, because he knew the weather would be gruesome, and he got out his oil paints and set us up on easels. He left us with one brief instruction: "Paint something that you're familiar with." Shelley painted a tree and some flowers that were quite convincing. But I came up with a brownstone stoop with a child's shoe on the middle step, *and* a lion in retreat—it was something Rousseau might have painted with his toes. When my father came back to check on us, he praised Shelley's work, but there wasn't much he could say about mine.

With my artwork a failure and the rain still sheeting, Dad piled us into a car and took us to a toy store in Cathedral City, where each of us could choose one game. Shelley picked one that I liked, too, so I went and got the same thing. As we reached the cashier, I explained to Dad, "I wanted to have it after the weekend."

And he said, "That's too bad, because you could have

had two different things to play with now and shared them later." We soon wearied of the one game, of course. My father never said another word about it, but I sensed that he was disappointed in me. I was filled with a child's deep regret.

That evening, lesson learned, I joined Dad on the couch and leaned into his curve as he watched the news. He put his arm around me and we sat quietly together, until the sting of that wretched day began to fade.

Sometimes I think that those are the moments I miss the most—just being with my father and knowing he loved me, without needing the currency of words.

I was mostly oblivious to my father's fame when I was young. The first movie of his I remember seeing was *The Joker Is Wild*, at a special screening at Columbia Studios. Dad played Joe E. Lewis, the nightclub entertainer who made the wrong people mad and got his larynx cut. My mother hadn't realized how graphic the movie would be. Before you knew it, I got sick to my stomach. Mom would have to drive me home, then quickly get Dad on the phone to reassure me that he was okay.

I first saw my father perform at the Copa Room, at the Sands Hotel in Las Vegas. I'd think, *Gee, it's nice that these people come to see him when he's here.* It didn't penetrate my childish skull that Dad would be drawing a similar crowd the following week in New York or Chicago or London or Sydney.

Well into the fifties, though my dad might be on the cover of *Look*, we could still move around freely in public. The press was far more reserved than it is today, and I was twelve years old before I realized Dad was *somebody*. We were driving home from a father-daughter square dance at my school, where the nuns had gone all goofy over him. We stopped at a light in his sleek Italian car on Sunset Boulevard, by the entrance ramp to the San Diego Freeway. Then a car pulled up in the next lane, to our right, and I remember four grown people gawking at me and going crazy. I was as self-conscious as the next adolescent, and I asked my dad, "Why are those people looking at me?"

And he said, "They're not looking at you, Pigeon, they're looking at me."

The light changed and we moved off. But I couldn't stop marveling to myself, *They even know him on the street, in the dark!* It wasn't just an exclusive following who applauded when he sang on stage—it was *everybody*. That night made a powerful impression on me.

Once I found out how important he was, I thought it was the greatest thing. I never resented Dad's fame or saw it as an intrusion. I took my cues from my father, who'd cordially sign his autograph with minimal fuss. It hadn't been so many years since he'd been out of fashion, and I think he was genuinely flattered by the attention, as long as people didn't crowd him.

Of course, the fans were more polite then. They wouldn't pester Dad when he was out eating or manhandle him on the street; he didn't need an entourage. I can recall just one nervous moment, when we were walking through an airport. Suddenly there was a merging of bodies, and I was too short and there was much too much going on, and I started to panic . . . and then my knight of a father plucked me up out of it, and I was okay.

Dad's company was the warmest, safest place to be. He knew where we were going, how to get there, what we would be doing when we got there—and if we didn't like it, we could always leave.

I guess that's the way fathers are. Mine just moved in bigger circles.

When we couldn't get together, Dad would stay close in touch. He'd write postcards and send us little presents, but most of all there was the telephone. He was diligent about the phone; I can't remember him missing a day, regardless of the number of time zones in between us. He'd carry ten dimes in his pocket, so he'd never be caught short at a pay phone, and when car phones became available, he was first in line. (My father always got the latest gadget ahead of everyone else, as long as it wasn't too intricate to operate.)

You could set your clock by Dad's calls. He'd wait till late afternoon, when we were home from school and just before we'd be sitting down to eat. (Once we were grown, and lived on our own, we'd still talk every day before dinner.)

I can remember hearing the phone ring and rushing to pick it up, so I could be the first to speak to Daddy. He'd want to know how things were going with you; he was a good talker and a better listener.

Mom kept my dad informed about our grades and doctor's visits. But knowing this man and his limits as she did, she tried to spare him the burdens of fatherhood. She would tell him about a problem only if she couldn't handle it on her own, and even then she'd wait for "the right time."

But Mom had a breaking point like any other mother. If one of us (usually Frankie) *really* got out of hand, she might say, *If you do that again, I'm going to tell your father!* That threat, used sparingly, would be enough to set us straight—for a little while, anyway. Not because we feared our father, but we'd been raised not to bother him. He was so busy, after all.

As I got older, though, I remember feeling, *But he's my dad—why* can't *I go to him?* I was his headstrong kid, and I wanted less buffering.

Like many men of his generation, my father was a halfhearted disciplinarian. A soft touch, he never raised a hand to his children. The only time he took issue with Mom's parenting was when she gave us a spanking; he wanted no part of it. His strong feelings might have stemmed from the indignities of his own childhood, when Marty, the ex-prizefighter, would bop him if he got out of line. But Dad was more afraid of his mother, who'd slap him upside the head as an endearment. Once Dolly went after him with a broom and whacked him. He accidentally fell backward down the cellar stairs, hit his head, and was knocked unconscious. Dolly thought he was dead. Dad said she was so upset that she hovered over him for a week, like a chastened mother hen.

At worst, Dad would lecture, but usually he'd try to reason with you. He liked guiding more than scolding. But he let me know when I'd let him down, and I'd feel so small that I'd rarely repeat the offense. I couldn't stand that look of disappointment; I hated being out of my father's favor. There was already too much distance between us, through no fault of my own, and I couldn't bear to create any more.

Once I went to play at a girlfriend's house, and she had the most beautiful china tea set with a pink rosebud design. I was seven years old, and I really wanted that tea set. So I took it. Later on, in my rebellious teenager years, analysis would teach me that the tea set was symbolic. My friend's father had sat down to have tea with us; I was yearning for my dad to do the same. My mother made me take it back and admit what I'd done, and *then* she told my father.

A few days later, Dad came over for dinner and took me aside. He said, "I understand that you took something that didn't belong to you."

"Yeah, I did," I said, uneasily, "but I gave it back."

And he said, "Okay, that's a good girl," and the case was closed.

On the next big occasion, my father gave me my own tea set. I'd learned my lesson, and he'd rewarded me, but for some reason I still felt dissatisfied. Something was missing.

I'd gotten my tea set, but I never had tea with my dad.

"I'm not home much, but I'm a pretty damned good father," my dad was once quoted as saying. It's no surprise that he sounded defensive. He'd wanted so desperately to have children, and then to do right by them. He did the best he could, but he'd never feel it was good enough.

If our broken home was hard on us, it was even harder on Dad—he could only blame himself. (Which leads me to wonder: did he come less often because it was so tough on him to leave?)

He'd compensate by giving us "goodies," as he called them. Dad was by nature a generous man. Maybe that's why he had kids, for the chance to indulge them. Sometimes a gift would be jaw-dropping fabulous, like Nancy's seventeenth birthday present: the pink Thunderbird with the detachable hard top and portholes, and a gargantuan red bow that Dad had tied around its hood. Other times, upon returning from a trip to Las Vegas or Europe, he'd shower us with souvenirs and such. Mom was the practical counterweight to Dad's extravagance, and she'd dole the booty out over time.

I particularly remember a suede pouch with the Sands Hotel logo stamped on it in gold, and a hundred silver dollars inside. I started saving money at a very young age; I kept my loot in a wood-and-brass chest out of *Treasure Island*. My father, who lived like there was no tomorrow, must have found my prudence hilarious. He took to calling me Miss Moneybags, and found me a plastic satchel with MONEY BAG stenciled across it. And he'd tease me, "How about a loan?"

In 1957, the hot item among the nine-year-old set in Holmby Hills was a battery-powered Thunderbird Junior, big enough for two small kids to sit inside. The T-Bird itself was a new phenomenon, compact and racy, the most desirable object on four wheels. I'd fallen in love with Nancy's convertible, and I'd been longing for a Junior for months—even more so since the previous July, when we'd previewed Disneyland before it opened to the public. I was particularly looking forward to a car ride called Autopia, but I flunked the height requirement. I had to stand there, simmering with envy, and watch Dad and Nancy and Frankie ride without me.

The Thunderbird Junior would be my recompense, my chance to finally take the wheel.

I didn't ask for the car in so many words, but I was vocal enough in my admiration for my parents to get the picture. And when I didn't get one on my birthday, I felt deflated and ashamed of myself at the same time. Especially since Dad had bought me my first real diamond necklace, with a tiny fifty-point stone set in a heart-shaped bezel, and he was clearly thrilled to be giving it to me.

The upshot came the following Christmas, when I *did* get the car: powder blue, with two-toned vinyl interior and those audacious flared fins. By then, unfortunately, I'd sprouted to the point where I could barely fit inside. I had to straddle the center console, leaving no room for Shelley to be my passenger. A few months later, I wound up pushing the car's pedals with my hands, with my legs hanging out over the sides. That's when I learned the meaning of that miserable adage, *Be careful what you wish for* . . .

Whenever he could swing it, my father would go above and beyond the call. I will always remember my first trip to New York, when Dad was brave enough to take the three of us without Mom. The weather was chilly, and I was still small, and Dad endured all the mundane tasks that baffle any bachelor father. Buttoning my coat was a challenge, and he'd literally break out in a sweat putting my gloves on; the fingers never seemed to match up. He'd be patient, never exasperated, but it was quite the ordeal.

When Dad bought me a gold charm bracelet with the city's famous landmarks, it instantly became my dearest possession. Just hours later, as the lights dimmed for a Wednesday matinee of *My Fair Lady*, it slipped off my wrist, Empire State Building and all.

"Oh, Daddy, I lost my bracelet!"

"That's okay, Sweetheart, we'll get it at intermission."

"No, Daddy, I want it *now!*"

My father spent a good part of the first act on his hands and knees, periodically flicking his lighter, until he retrieved my prize.

When I was twelve, my friends and I thought that *Soupy Sales* was the greatest TV show ever, much hipper than *The Mickey Mouse Club*. Dad did a guest spot on the show in New York with Frankie. After Soupy moved to Los Angeles, I pleaded with Dad to do it again. It wasn't that tough a sell, as my father loved slapstick. I can remember him watching the Three Stooges with Frankie, and the two of them rolling off the sofa together.

Dad escorted me and my two best friends to the studio. We watched him get hit with a whipped cream pie, which was the funniest thing I'd ever seen. It turned out that Dad was a pretty fair country pie-thrower himself— he practiced at the Sands, where he'd order two dozen pies to the steam room for wars with Joey Bishop and Sammy Davis Jr. Soupy got his comeuppance that day.

I left the studio with Soupy's signature red-and-white checked tie and a confirmed appreciation for the coolest dad in the world.

When Nancy was fourteen, she joined Dad on a trip to Australia for a two-week tour. They were having a great time—until my sister found a pair of ladies' stockings in my father's room. Nancy was undone, terminally upset. To make matters worse, Dad was having trouble with the Australian press, so he cut the trip short.

As young as I was, I remember the day they came home. Mom and I rushed out to greet them, but Nancy marched straight into the house. She didn't even say good-bye to Dad. I was sidetracked by a boomerang he'd brought for Frankie, but I remember thinking, *Uh-oh, something's wrong.*

Years later, when I learned the full story, I could understand why Nancy was so upset. It hurt my sister to find Dad gallivanting on her time, on a trip for just the two of them. It had to feel like a betrayal.

And I believe there was something more. Of the three Sinatra children, Nancy had held longest and hardest to the hope that our parents would reconcile. But now I think she began to realize that some things would never change.

For her part, Mom was doing better by then. Four years after the divorce, she had a full social life, with no want of beaus for a night on the town. She had a circle of prominent women friends (including Jane Wyman and Missy Stanwyck and Edie Wasserman), and regained her love of entertaining. Sometimes Dad would attend and sometimes he wouldn't. Mom would have a good time either way.

But there were also other signals, mixed signals, if you cared to look for them. From my bedroom over the courtyard, every so often I'd wake in the night to the sound of two taps on a horn. I'd puzzle over this at breakfast, until Nancy clued me in: "It's *Daddy*, goofy." My knowledge remained sketchy, however, because my parents were too discreet to let me find them together the next morning.

Maybe I was just too young to share Nancy's wistful dream; I thought it could be wonderful, but not likely. I didn't fantasize about the notion that my father could or should or would remarry my mother. I just didn't think about it.

At the very end of my day, as I went to brush my teeth, I'd pass a pair of silver-framed studio portraits: Mom and Dad. They were just two feet apart, but the distance was constant; they would never get any closer.

Separate pictures, separate parents, yet one very close and complicated family.

3

Turmoil and Transition

WHEN MY FAMILY lived on Toluca Lake, Frankie was my father's little appendage. If my father was showering instead of taking a bath, Frankie wanted to shower. If Dad was shaving, Frankie would insist on lathering up, then shave with an empty razor. Sometimes they'd head out for a fishing expedition on the lake—"Come on, son"—and Frankie would trudge lockstep with Dad to the rowboat, then ape his technique: same stance, same pose, same expression.

They were, Mom and Nancy tell me, just adorable.

It was a full and happy house for a little boy—and then the only other male left. Gone was the man who gave

Frankie bowl haircuts, or tickled him till he couldn't catch his breath for laughing, or pulled him off his big sister after he'd conked her in the head with a toy train and she'd punched him in the nose. (They'd been dressed up for dinner in their summer whites, and Dad walked in the door to find two screaming kids covered in blood.)

Frankie was four years old when Dad left, the worst possible time. My brother understood just enough to draw the loss inside. He felt bewildered and abandoned and quietly traumatized.

I think that his world just fell apart.

In the ensuing years, Frankie would grow up surrounded by women. In addition to Mom and Nancy and me, my aunts Tina and Julie frequented our home; they were our mother's staunch companions. The consistent males in Frankie's life were pretty much limited to Uncle Bart and Matsu, and a nice man named Johnny who ran a weekend day camp in Culver City.

And then there was Dad, who would come and go en route to his next commitment. His schedule left little time for male bonding, or a simple game of catch.

※

Frankie was my playmate and protector, a great older brother. On Saturday mornings I could hop into his bed and he'd read me the latest comic books. Once, when I was very small, I locked myself in the bathroom. Terrified, I screamed and pounded on the door. Frankie had to go to the second-story balcony and manipulate the security chains on the bathroom window to get inside and get me out.

That's the kind of thing a girl doesn't forget, believe me.

When I'd make him crazy, my brother would get his revenge by dumping my drawers out in the middle of my room. (Frankie had my number; I was a born anal-retentive who couldn't stand anything out of place.) But in peacetime, my brother would include me in the neighborhood games of catch or war or cowboys and Indians, whether the other kids liked it or not. He'd tell them, "If she doesn't play, I don't play," and mean it, because we were pals. (I was a real tomboy, in my blue jeans and plaid shirts, so I fit right in.)

Grandma Dolly would call Frankie her pride and joy, and regularly reminded the rest of us of her preference. "When I die," she'd say, "Frankie gets everything."

My brother was treated affectionately by Milton Berle and Danny Thomas and so many of our parents' friends. He was cute, smart, and funny, the life of every party. When he was ten or eleven, he'd perform for anyone who'd listen, and mimic Dad's latest TV appearance word for word.

Frankie's performance would bring the house down, but it also had a poignant side. Our guests wouldn't see Frankie building a model airplane alone in his room, or rocking himself to sleep while listening to Dad on the radio. They wouldn't think of all the evenings when a television screen was as close as the son could get to his father.

As he lurched into adolescence, the lonely boy was becoming more and more insular. Frankie loved to tinker—he'd rig a strip of rawhide to lock the folding doors to his den-turned-bedroom, then take a radio apart and put it back together. (Or catch hell from Mom if there were any pieces left over.)

My dad truly loved Frankie. But he was also perplexed by his introverted middle child—much as Dad must have puzzled his own simple, honest father back in Hoboken in the 1920s. My grandfather Marty was an acutely shy man, an immigrant who'd never learned to read or write his own name. He struggled with his limited vocabulary, though he got his point across when he got mad enough. When a rival who owed Marty money opened a drinking establishment down the block from the Sinatras' saloon, Marty visited the local glue factory and bought an old gray horse. He led the swayback into the offending storefront—and put it out of its misery with a shot between the eyes. Rigor mortis set in almost instantly, and the competition had to dismantle the front of their building to get rid of the carcass.

Grandpa didn't believe in things that came easy, like Dad's singing. He wanted his son to go to college and become an engineer; he couldn't endorse Dad's lofty dreams. When young Frank refused to knuckle under, Marty took to calling him Mr. Big Shot, and ultimately kicked him out of the house. Even after my father made it, Marty found it hard to praise him, because he was so unsure of the larger world and of his son's place in it.

After Dad had won some renown, he paid a surprise visit to his father at the firehouse. As Grandpa stood shaving, Dad glanced at his open locker door. It was lined with Dad's photos and newsclippings. When Marty noticed his son, he slammed the door shut.

With his grandchildren, Marty was a sweet little bull-dog of a guy. Despite his raspy voice and gruff exterior, he was all marshmallow at the core. He was really bash-ful, and would blush over shows of affection, but you could tell that he loved us. When Grandpa hugged us, we were *hugged*.

But there was an awkwardness between Grandpa and Dad, and it seemed to echo with my father and Frankie. They shared a certain shyness with one another. That wasn't so unusual for fathers and sons of the time, but I think that Frankie needed something more.

It was Dad's job to reach out and find a way past Frankie's hardening defenses, but the things the boy required were precisely what the man couldn't give. I think that we all needed *more* from Dad; I know that I did. But due to gender or birth order or the random draw of temperament, Frankie would feel the deficit most.

※

I guess I was at that age where nothing suited me, least of all my school life. Nancy had soared through school, and Frankie did fine without killing himself, but I struggled from the start. I had terrible astigmatism, which no one was testing for then, so I couldn't properly see the blackboard. I got my glasses at age eight, but by then I'd lost a lot of ground and confidence.

Mom thought the solution would be smaller classes and more attention, and she enrolled me at Marymount Junior School in Brentwood. She liked the Catholic affiliation, and the uniforms, and the fact that the school was all girls—which added up to three strikes in my book. Plus I'd be losing the schoolmates I'd had since kindergarten at Warner Avenue.

If I had to move, I would have preferred St. Martin's, a

coed school where Shelley Wanger was headed. Dad and Nancy lobbied hard for me, but Mom wouldn't be swayed. So I donned my navy blue felt beret and white gloves each morning. I put on my white scalloped blouse with the puffy sleeves, and my blue jumper, in which the nuns made me kneel to see that my hem touched the floor. I folded down my white socks, but only once, since a flash of anklebone put you on the express lane to hell. I'd slip on the blue-and-white saddle shoes that I had to polish each night.

I was a two-toned picture of misery.

They made me repeat fourth grade, which was embarrassing, but I had to admit that my schoolwork improved. What I resented most was that daily catechism business, and going to confession—what could a ten-year-old have to confess, for heaven's sake?

My father was an Easter Sunday Catholic. If he was tooling down Fifth Avenue in New York, he might tell the driver to stop so he could duck into St. Patrick's for ten minutes. Faith was important to him, but whatever you believed was your business; he didn't like the church pushing people around. (When Dad asked Morris Stoloff, the head of Columbia Studios' music department, to be my godfather, and the priest rejected him because he was Jewish, Dad boycotted the ceremony.) Frankie and I must have felt the same way, because we ducked out of Sunday school every chance we could when I was younger.

Marymount was like Sunday school five days a week. When Dad called, I'd plead with him to get me out of there. He sympathized, but he wouldn't buck Mom; that wasn't his style.

The school was snobbish and exclusive, and you had to be the right kind of girl to get in. My schoolmates included Bridget O'Brien (Edmond's daughter) and Pam Powell (Dick's daughter), but there were far more celebrity kids at the public schools in West L.A. or Beverly Hills. It carried no weight at Marymount to have a famous father; if anything, it made you a little suspect. Especially if that father was neither married nor famously chaste, and a fixture in the local gossip columns.

I don't think the nuns liked me, and the feeling was mutual. Judging from some comments the kids made, I got the feeling that the Sinatras weren't too popular among some parents, either.

Dad always tried to give us fair warning when the newspapers were about to break an item that was even faintly controversial. But in 1960, when I was eleven, we were blindsided by the uproar over *The Execution of Private Slovik*, a provocative book by William Bradford Huie that my dad sought to bring to the screen.

Back in 1945, my father had asked Albert Maltz to

write a script for *The House I Live In*, a short film that attacked intolerance and won a special Oscar. Two years later, Maltz refused to cooperate with the House Committee on Un-American Activities. He was blacklisted and imprisoned, and then he moved to Mexico. His career in movies appeared to be over.

My father had stood opposed to McCarthyism from early on. He considered the blacklist to be shameful, and counted a number of friends among the Hollywood Ten, including Maltz. Dad was automatically for the underdog, going back to his Hoboken days, when he'd been one himself. He once went so far as to say, "I'm always for the little guy, and if that makes me a communist, then I'm red through and through."

So Dad was doing what came naturally when he hired Maltz to adapt *Private Slovik*, which told the true story about the first American since the Civil War to be executed by the U.S. Army. As producer-director, Dad had bought film rights to the book with his own money, and set up Steve McQueen to star. Maltz was the best writer for the material, and that's all there was to it. And if Dad could poke a hole in the blacklist along the way, all the better.

But that wasn't all there was to it. Larger forces were at play, notably the Kennedy presidential campaign, which counted my father as one of its most vocal and visible supporters. After the Maltz story came out in the *New York Times*, Hearst's right-wing columnists went to town. They labeled Dad a communist, or at very least a "subversive." Along with Hollywood right-wingers like John Wayne, they used his association with Maltz to attack the Kennedy campaign. (Dad would soon channel his creative juices into another serious film: *The Manchurian Candidate.*)

Both Joe and Bobby Kennedy told my dad flat out to fire Maltz. I suppose they expected him to do the expedient thing without a second thought—which was, after all, how the Kennedys had made their way in the world. They hadn't banked on my father's stubborn Sicilian streak. He was willing to compromise, but not to compromise himself in the process. And he resented being told what to do, even by the father of the next president of the United States. He told the Kennedys that he'd stick by Maltz, whether or not it jeopardized his role in the campaign.

I was minding my own business in the fifth grade, meanwhile, when a girl at Marymount walked up to me and said, "My dad says your dad's a communist. Does that mean you're a communist, too?" She was confused and curious, not trying to be cruel, but I didn't take it well. I was fuzzy about communists, but I knew they were anti-American, and they came from China, and they were bar-

baric enough to make us duck and cover once a month in the halls, as far away from the windows as possible.

I went home in tears that afternoon. I ran off the bus and told my mother what had happened, and she got Dad on the phone right away, while I was still in my blue blazer with the white piping. "I'm sorry that this happened, Pigeon," he told me. "This whole thing is very complicated, but I'm telling you that I'm not a communist, and neither are you. Don't cry, please. I'll take care of it."

Private Slovik had become a nightmare for Dad. He was being pressured and middled from every side. On the day I spoke to him, he'd already been flooded with calls from the highest political and Hollywood circles, all squeezing him to back down. Through it all, he'd dug in his heels. Up to the moment I'd called, he'd considered the discussion closed.

Yet where Dad wouldn't bow to the mighty Kennedys, he buckled before his troubled child. After saying goodbye to me, he turned to Guy McElwaine, his publicist, and said, "Get Albert a check, and tell him I'm very sorry." He paid Maltz the full $75,000 for the job, which he didn't have to do. "It was my problem, not his," Dad said.

Dad would never mention *Private Slovik* again. But my father's loyalties would remain suspect in certain flag-waving circles for years. And I'm sure that the gossip didn't help my standing with the nuns, who knew that red would never be a school color at Marymount.

*

Where Nancy idealized our father after he left home, and I just forged ahead without him, Frankie struggled for Dad's attention by acting out. By his early teens, my brother was seeking out the wrong company, notably an older kid from outside our neighborhood. He was the black-leather-jacket type—the complete opposite from Frankie, which must have made him compelling. There was no one to keep my brother on the straight and narrow, and soon Frankie and his new friend were shooting out street lamps. The next thing we knew, Frankie had broken the local curfew with a BB gun in his pocket, and Mom was bailing him out of jail at two in the morning.

For my mother, this was the last straw. As farfetched as it sounds, she imagined Frankie's mug shot plastered all over the post office. In her hysteria, she decided there were only two options for my brother—he'd either go to boarding school or to live with his father.

The second choice, of course, was no option at all. Mom wasn't wrong in thinking that Frankie needed more structure and male influence in his life. But my father was on the road forty weeks out of fifty-two; he wasn't equipped to be a bachelor father. Dad simply couldn't come to the rescue this time, and I only hope that Frankie never bought into the flimsy idea that he might.

Which left us with boarding school, a popular solution for all sorts of kids in the Stone Age 1950s. Frankie was shaken by this unexpected turn of events, but he was brave about it. He chose a coed school in the San Jacinto Mountains, near Dad's place in Palm Springs. (He might have hoped that he'd see Dad more often, but that didn't pan out, since Dad was rarely home.) In the months before my brother left us, life settled down at Carolwood. Mom and Frankie got along a little better. Everyone put a good face on the decision.

But I cried my eyes out the day my brother left.

Once I saw the Desert Sun School for myself, I felt better about Frankie. Its alpine setting was spectacular—green and lush, with air like glass. To this day, however, Frankie describes the school as Stalag 17. The central heating was less than state of the art; my brother was allergic to the horses, and didn't like to ski. He was homesick at the beginning, but he survived it. (And stayed until he graduated.)

Frankie and I would still get together at the Compound for holidays and at home for a chunk of the summer, but our childhood was interrupted.

We would, inexorably, grow apart.

It seemed to me that Frankie was just fine; I was the one who was suffering. My brother's closet was empty. His room was still. I didn't have anyone to share my bathroom anymore.

It was just a bad, lonely time for me. The summer before Frankie went off, Shelley moved to New York.

On September 11, 1960, when Nancy married Tommy Sands, my misery became complete. I'd lost my best friend, my hero, now my idol; I was bereft. I sobbed at that wedding until Mom had to shush me.

We'd had our share of disappointments, my brother and sister and me, but we'd gotten through them together. Now we were all split up; now there was void, void all around. With my siblings gone and Dad as scarce as ever, it was just Mom and me rattling around in that cavernous house. My one consolation was to move into Nancy's larger room, where I inherited the dressing table.

Though the upkeep on Carolwood was expensive, Dad would have wanted us to stay there forever. But Mom was always looking to alleviate Dad's financial pressures. She'd tell him, "Frank, we've got to move, it's just too big for us"—a practical explanation that he could accept, even if he didn't like it. When I was thirteen, we sold Carolwood and moved to Nimes Road in Bel-Air. Our new house was a sleek, contemporary three-bedroom with a pool and a cantilevered deck, but no grounds. (It is now home to Elizabeth Taylor.)

I suppose it was a good fresh start for Mom and her youngest. But our move didn't alter the fact that I'd become an only child, and I didn't like it any more than my father had before me.

❋

My father was a lifelong Democrat, staunchly pro-union and for the little guy. His involvement in presidential politics dated back to Franklin Roosevelt. He supported Harry Truman and Adlai Stevenson, but Jack Kennedy was something different, someone special.

With Kennedy, it was personal. Dad had known Jack for years, through Kennedy in-law Peter Lawford, and had put the candidate up at the Compound for two proud nights in November 1959. (For someone like me, who wore her *JFK* button like all the other good Catholic girls at Marymount, this was heady stuff.) My father even made Jack an honorary member of the Rat Pack, alongside Dean Martin and Sammy Davis Jr. They knew him by a less than reverent moniker: Chicky Baby.

The singer and the senator were contemporaries who

shared the same interests, particularly the extracurricular ones. The difference was that my father was single at this time and Jack was not. As time wore on, I think Dad became uneasy with their exploits, because he had enormous respect for Jackie.

Much has been made of the story that my father introduced Judith Campbell Exner to both Jack Kennedy and Sam "Momo" Giancana, the dapper Chicago crime lord. Dad never discussed this triangle with me. (He wasn't one to gossip about such things, especially with his daughter.) But in our interviews for my miniseries, he divulged a more significant story: that he had served as a liaison between Joe Kennedy and Giancana on a mission that may have swung the 1960 presidential election.

When Dad was summoned to Hyannis Port early that year, he assumed that Joe Sr. would be asking him to sing at a fund-raiser or two. But the Kennedy patriarch had a more ambitious plan in mind. The campaign had entered a critical phase. Jack needed to win the primary in West Virginia, a state with few Catholic voters, to knock out Hubert Humphrey. The Kennedys would need strong support from the mob-infested unions—which was where my father came in.

As Joe Sr. cryptically explained, "You and I know the same people, and you know the people I mean."

"Sure," my father said. He didn't need to have the dots connected.

"I can't go to those people," the old man went on. "It might come back at Jack. But you can. The best thing you can do for Jack is to ask for their help as a personal favor, to you. Keep us out of it."

Dad had never done anything like this before, but he didn't hesitate. He nodded his assent, and with a smile and a wink from Joe Sr., he was on his way.

My father was familiar with this kind of alliance. He'd come of age at a time when politics, show business, and the underworld formed an overlapping triumvirate. The people in them had a lot in common; they were all looking for money and power.

Later on, when Dad's career was at ebb tide in the early fifties, people like Skinny D'Amato kept him booked in their clubs. As Dad once said to Ava, who was allergic to gangsters, "These are the guys who gave me a job when nobody else would." From Atlantic City to Miami to Las Vegas, mobsters controlled the nightclub industry, and virtually every top entertainer in the country worked for them. That went for George Burns and Danny Thomas, too. It was just a part of Americana, and no one ever called them to task for it.

But *their* names didn't end with a vowel.

That said, my father had known people like Willie

Moretti and Johnny Formosa all his life. But contrary to folklore, I think that Dad was interested in the wise guys because they were so *different* from him, just as Frankie had looked up to the boy with the black leather jacket.

Dad openly cultivated a cozy acquaintanceship with Momo Giancana, as though oblivious to its implications. His more lawful friends were aghast—including my mother, who admonished Dad after a national magazine published a picture of him with the crime boss. (Although Mom worried about the fallout, she actually liked Giancana when they met in Nevada, before she knew of his reputation. "He was a gentleman of the first order, very soft-spoken," she recalled. She also appreciated that Giancana, along with other friends of my father's in Chicago, had repeatedly counseled Dad to go back to her. "To those people," she noted, "family is everything.")

But my father was loyal to people who were loyal to him, come hell or federal subpoenas. When Louis B. Mayer brandished the MGM morals clause after my father was photographed with Lucky Luciano back in 1947, Dad was unmoved. "I don't kiss ass and I don't sell out my friends," he'd say. When I asked him in the early nineties how he could befriend a known murderer like Giancana, he responded more politely, but his attitude hadn't changed.

"I never reacted beyond how he treated me," Dad told

me. "I wasn't unaware of what he was, and I didn't bring him to your First Communion, but he was always decent to me."

After returning from Hyannis Port, my father called Giancana and made a golf date, where they couldn't be bugged. Dad said, "I've never come to you for a favor before, Sam, but this time I have to." When he conveyed the Kennedys' request for help in West Virginia, Giancana must have been scratching his head. He went way back with Joe Sr., and he knew how the game was played. What was my father getting out of the deal?

And Dad said, with wholehearted conviction, "I believe in Jack Kennedy. He's a good man."

Giancana looked him in the eye and said, "It's a couple of phone calls. And tell the old man I said hello."

The rest is in the history books. Kennedy won the West Virginia primary and fended off Humphrey's challenge. He then squeaked by Nixon in the general election, thanks to a phenomenal turnout in the mob-controlled wards in Chicago, Giancana's home turf.

A favor was paid, and a favor was owed.

There is no larger celebration than an inaugural gala; it is the ultimate comingling of entertainment and politics. In

January 1961, the coproducers for Jack Kennedy's big party were Frank Sinatra and Peter Lawford. Dad was working triple-time on every detail of the affair, from transportation and scheduling to special song lyrics.

The night before the inauguration, he was having dinner in Lawford's hotel suite at the Statler Hilton with other members of the organizing committee. Dad laid out the program he'd put together: "Mahalia Jackson's going to open with 'The Star-Spangled Banner,' and then Milton Berle's going to come on, then Harry Belafonte, and I'll close the first act with 'The House I Live In.' "

Peter might have been feeling his oats as the president-elect's brother-in-law, or he might have been several sheets to the wind. In any case, he said something he'd later regret: "Well, I don't think that's right."

As Guy McElwaine would observe, "Frank Sinatra was the most powerful person in the entertainment industry from 1954 to 1965, and powerful people aren't accustomed to hearing, 'That's not right.' Frank was badly insulted, really steamed."

Dad's relationship with the Kennedys was already fraying around the edges. He'd been perturbed by their position on Albert Maltz. He was angered when they asked Sammy Davis Jr., another willing campaigner, to postpone his wedding to the Swedish actress May Britt until after the election, for fear that the intermarriage might alienate Jack's redneck constituency. And my father was appalled when Peter told Sammy that he'd been disinvited to the gala—now because he'd married May. For Dad, who'd been Sammy's best man, and had busted more than one color line on his friend's behalf over the years, this had to be hard to swallow.

In short, there was a little tension in the air when my father looked at his coproducer and said, "Peter, what the *fuck* do you know?" They got into a loud argument, and Dad stalked off. He was still dressed at five the next morning when he knocked on McElwaine's door, patted him on the cheek, and said, "Pally, I'm going home. Let the fucking Englishman sing 'The House I Live In.'"

McElwaine followed my dad into his suite and found him packing, a sight that threw him into a panic. The publicist knew that Jack Kennedy planned to surprise my father with a major award at the gala. If Dad left now, he'd be standing up a president on the eve of his first day in office.

McElwaine had been sworn to secrecy about the award. He was just twenty-one years old. He knew it was no easy task to change my father's mind when he was fighting mad. So he tried a different tack, based on their mutual love of baseball: "I said, 'Frank, people are coming here for two reasons: one, to honor the President; two, to see you. Let's say I'm pitching for the Yankees in the

World Series tomorrow. You're asking me to pitch without a shortstop.'

"There was this incredible pause, and I didn't know what he was going to do. It probably lasted a minute, but it seemed like an hour. And he turned around from his suitcase and looked at me, and he said, 'I feel like rehearsing.'"

About eighteen hours later, swathed in his satin-lined cape and swallowtail coat, my father escorted Jackie Kennedy into the biggest evening of his life. And the show, as always, went on.

As soon as the polls closed in Illinois and Dad saw the numbers, he knew what his mission to the Mafia had accomplished: the securing of the presidency. He'd gone to Giancana out of friendship for Jack Kennedy and expected nothing back. What he did *not* expect was to be set up like a blindsided innocent, like a fool to take the fall.

Which was exactly what happened.

Within months of taking office, Attorney General Robert Kennedy became the most zealous antimob crusader in town. He launched an all-out investigation of some of Giancana's closest associates, and Giancana himself was being tailed wherever he went. Dad was stunned when the administration began to prosecute the very people it had enlisted for help just the year before. And he thought to himself, *What have I done?*

My father ultimately mollified Giancana by performing, along with Sammy and Dean, at the Villa Venice nightclub in Chicago. I don't believe he did so out of fear of repercussions in low places. (Though the FBI wiretapped a thug proposing a hit on my father, the idea was immediately squelched by Giancana.) I think that Dad offered his services because that's what you did when you came from the neighborhood. You paid your debts. You kept your word.

I know that my father would have loved to bring us to visit the Kennedys at the White House, an invitation he'd receive from nearly every sitting president thereafter. But he got in to see Jack only once, alone, a number of months after the inauguration. Joe Sr. and Bobby plainly did not want Dad around; he personified a page of history that they'd rather have erased. His relationship with the Kennedys had gone south, and fast.

Dad's spirits were high, nonetheless, after Peter Lawford arranged for the president to stay with my father in the desert in March 1962. The news fed Dad's fondest fantasy: that the Compound would become the western White House, Jack Kennedy's home away from home.

As it happened, work was already under way on the Christmas Tree House, the four-bedroom building designed for the Sinatra children. Now it would be needed to house the Secret Service. Dad pushed the construction schedule to seven days a week, to finish the building before the president arrived.

As JFK day neared, the crunch of activity accelerated. A concrete helipad was poured. A blue and white telephone with a red handset and a blinking light was installed for the famous hot line, just in case the Soviets chose that day for a nuclear strike. While his men friends were out playing golf, Dad gathered Roz Russell and Ruth Berle and the rest of the wives, and took them into town to help him shop for lamps and paintings.

Two days before the visit, workmen were still hammering round the clock. My father and his friends were having a blast getting the house ready, right up to the eleventh hour—right up until the president withdrew, as a matter of fact. As usual, the Kennedys made Peter Lawford their bearer of bad news. It was the Secret Service, he told Dad. They thought the Compound was too open and unsafe, too big a security risk.

But Kennedy wasn't canceling his visit to the desert.

He'd be staying instead with Bing Crosby, whose house backed up against a mountain. They might as well have stuck a poker in Dad's eye, because he knew as well as anyone that Bing was a Republican.

The cancellation made a big splash in all the papers, of course. Had the Kennedys sought deliberately to humiliate my father, they couldn't have done a better job.

I'm sure that Dad threw a tantrum that day, though he didn't tear any walls down or take a jackhammer to the helipad, as the yellow journalists would have it. (With Jimmy Van Heusen as his pilot, in fact, Dad would continue to use the helipad for years, until the local enactment of noise abatement laws.) There was no consoling him. He wouldn't voice his disappointment to his family, but his fervor for Camelot was plainly waning.

Dad cut off his close friendship with Peter Lawford. You could say that he was shooting the messenger and that Peter was inconsequential to the scheme of things. But my father felt betrayed once too often, and blamed Peter for not standing up for him.

My father had never trusted Bobby Kennedy, and now he viewed the president's brother as an out-and-out fink. But Dad couldn't bring himself to blame Jack, who professed not to know about the snub, just as he'd stood outside the fray in the Giancana affair. No one else could have gotten away with such a breach of loyalty, but Jack enjoyed a sort of presidential immunity with my father. Dad still considered him to be his friend, and I suppose it would have hurt too much to look at the great man more clearly.

The hot line phone remained in the house for years, along with the plaque that commemorated Jack's stay there before he became the most powerful man in the world. They were bittersweet memorabilia now, tokens of Dad's fall from grace.

The Kennedys used a lot of people, of course. In my father they found an ideal mark: someone who craved to be loved and accepted, who'd do anything for the people he cared about.

Dad's relationship with Jack and Bobby Kennedy was not the first time he'd be taken advantage of by the people he trusted—nor, from my perspective, would it be the last.

⚜

By the fall of 1962, everyone seemed to be building a bomb shelter in their home, except us. But we had something even better: a dad with a plan. He was by nature the organizer, the leader, and we all knew the family civil defense drill. If something happened, we would get back to Carolwood, then out to the desert, far from the vulnerable coast.

On the day the Cuban missile crisis broke, fear and chaos ran through the halls of Marymount. But I felt safe, because I knew that my father would be strong. I knew that he would never let anything happen to his kids.

I think it was Sarge Weiss, my dad's right-hand man in his music affairs, who picked me up from school and brought me home. Mom had already packed, and she drove us out to the desert in her Buick Riviera, a nice big car if you're worried about Armageddon.

Dad flew in and met us at the Compound. Nancy and Tommy were in from back east. We spent most of the weekend watching Huntley and Brinkley or Walter Cronkite, and I remember how somber Mom and Dad seemed for those few days. My father was calm but strictly business, as if gauging our next step.

I could hardly fathom all the ramifications; I felt swept away by events. To tell you the truth, though, I was having a good time. I was happy just to be hanging out with my parents and sister, together again.

It was a strange sort of crisis, building and then dissipating so quickly. It fizzled so fast that we had no need for the stores of canned food and water that had been laid in. Nancy remembers Dad showing her a map he'd drawn of the region's deserted airstrips, just in case we needed to use his plane. But I never got to see it. Maybe he didn't want to scare me.

And when things had cooled off, and our family broke apart in its different directions, I felt a little regretful that Khrushchev had caved in so quickly—and that Marymount was still standing.

※

In November 1963, when I was fifteen, my mother took my boyfriend, Roger Reynolds, and me to the Coconut Grove to see Johnny Mathis—my favorite singer, to my father's chagrin. We were out late, and for an extra treat I was allowed to stay home from school the next day. At eleven o'clock, a telephone call from Roger woke me up with the news: Jack Kennedy had been assassinated.

Like tens of millions of others, I was stunned. Though I'd begun to awaken to politics, my reaction was purely emotional. I'd never met the president, but I felt somehow connected to him through my father. And he had that beautiful wife, and children younger than me.

When Dad got the news, he left the set of *Robin and the Seven Hoods*, went back to the desert, and locked himself in his bedroom for three days. My father was a private man, and never more so than when he was grieving. He wasn't good alone, but he healed alone.

The following weekend was Thanksgiving, and Mom and I spent the holiday with my father and Frankie at the Compound. As usual, Dad invited his favorite strays, people who needed a surrogate family. Mom did all the cooking, which was traditional and out of this world: two tomasina turkeys (more tender than the toms), with yams and mashed potatoes, cranberry sauce, and pumpkin pie. My mother happened to make the best stuffing in the world, with pecans and apricots and celery, and the top burnt a little bit to give a crunch to it.

Thanksgiving was a jovial holiday for our family, but that year my father was subdued. Dad ran through my bloodstream; when he hurt, I hurt, too.

He hadn't been invited to the president's funeral, which would have been too painful and awkward for him anyway. Still, he had a soft spot for Jack, and now his friend was dead. Political violence deeply disturbed Dad, upset his sense of the order of things. "This shouldn't be happening anywhere," he kept saying, "but certainly not *here*."

(The year before, United Artists had wavered in distributing *The Manchurian Candidate*, perhaps Dad's best film, because the story involved a presidential assassination attempt. Dad mentioned the problem to Jack Kennedy, who pooh-poohed the studio's qualms.

Kennedy called Arthur Krim, the president of United Artists, and gave the movie his blessing.)

By contrast, Frankie was in great spirits that weekend. He'd quit college to do what he always wanted: his music. At the age of nineteen, he was singing with Sam Donahue and what was left of the Tommy Dorsey Orchestra, Dad's alma mater. I thought he was very courageous—if a little crazy—to pitch headfirst into the eye of the hurricane. Though it isn't so strange for sons to want to be their fathers, it was a loaded choice for Frankie. The comparisons would be as inevitable as they were unfair. But my brother was proud to be performing, and he loved it, and he happened to be very good at it, too.

While he wouldn't have admitted it, I think that singing was a way for Frankie to try to get closer to Dad, to win his approval. Deep inside, I think he was still the little boy in front of the fireplace, mimicking his hero for all he was worth.

It wasn't the future that Dad had envisioned for his son, as he knew just how tough his world could be, particularly for a singer named Frank Sinatra Jr. But once Frankie set his course, Dad supported him all the way.

It was around this time that my brother taped an NBC radio program as a birthday greeting for Dad. When asked about their father-son relationship, Frankie said,

"He was, shall we say, strict with me, but always open-minded. . . . But my really great experiences with him came in the late years. He's never been too busy that he couldn't talk with me about the movie industry, about religion, about philosophy or anything."

About anything, that is, except their feelings for each other.

Frankie drove me back to Los Angeles the day after Thanksgiving, because I was anxious to get back to my boyfriend. My brother was working at the Ambassador Hotel, where Roger would be waiting. Frankie escorted me through the front entrance that day, rather than the artists' entrance in the back—a small deviation in routine that would have large repercussions.

On December 8, 1963, around ten o'clock on a Sunday evening, my mother and I were bedding down at Nimes Road when the phone rang. I could hear Mom pick up and exclaim, "Oh my God!" The raw horror in her tone was something I'd never heard before, and it struck me—*Something's happened to Dad!*

I started down the hallway, where Mom took hold of me and said, "Your brother's been kidnapped!"

The call had come from Tino Barzie, Frankie's manager. My brother was at Harrah's Club in Lake Tahoe, appearing with the Dorsey band. He was having dinner in his room with a trumpeter named John Foss when two men in ski parkas, one of them armed with a .38, pushed their way inside. They blindfolded Frankie and John, then took my brother—clad only in slacks, T-shirt, and loafers without socks—into the snowy night.

Mom and I got dressed, the one thing we knew we could do, and the vigil began. My mother was pacing the hallway like a deranged cat, back and forth, back and forth, until I thought to myself, *Am I going to have to slug her?*

Mom reached Dad at the Compound. He'd already called his lawyer and manager, Mickey Rudin, and they chartered a plane to Reno to meet with an FBI agent on board. Within ninety minutes of Tino's call, my father came through the door at Nimes Road. In his face I saw a mix of barely contained emotion, of grief and rage . . . and something else.

Dad felt helpless. It was a foreign sensation for him, and sheer torture.

And for the first of many times, I broke down and cried.

Because the kidnappers had apparently taken Frankie across a state line (and in all likelihood, because the victim was my father's son), the case quickly escalated into a top federal priority. One moment there were two scared little women in our house, and the next a small battalion of people: Dad and Mickey, and the publicists Jim Mahoney and Guy McElwaine, and Jilly Rizzo, my father's best friend, and George Jacobs, his valet. In addition, Dad had brought in a private security force to patrol the perimeter of our property.

And, not least, there were three young FBI men in their white shirts and skinny ties, just like on TV.

Dad hadn't been there long before J. Edgar Hoover called to say he'd put his best agents on the case. Bobby Kennedy checked in with similar reassurances. Though my father had little use for either Hoover or Kennedy man to man, he was ready to trust them as professionals on this night. Their calls must have meant a great deal to him.

I was bewildered and overwhelmed—very alert and focused, yet feeling horribly impotent. There would be no sleep that night for any of us. I remember sticking close to my parents and avoiding dark rooms. If one of us got up to move, all three of us moved; we clung together like lifeboat survivors.

For the next fifty-four hours, the FBI took over our home and our lives. They told Nancy to stay put in New Orleans, where it would be easier to keep an eye on her. They set up taps on our phones, and expropriated Frankie's small bedroom for their surveillance equipment, which they'd man in shifts around the clock. They told us to act normally when the phone rang, to wait three or four rings before answering—not an easy thing to do, under the circumstances.

I took a nap Monday morning, then was up for the day. For the duration we would sleep at off hours, catching catnaps when we could—except for Dad, whom I never saw sleep at all. There was too much commotion for resting, anyway. Our house had turned into a law enforcement nerve center. People gathered nonstop in our kitchen or living room. The den was reserved for conferences between the FBI and my father.

We got to know the agents by their first names. They were young and very kind, and all had kids themselves. They did their best to stay supportive and positive, though at times they seemed lighter and at other times grave. We took our cues from them, our hopes rising and falling with their latest analysis.

Suspense mounted through the morning as we waited fruitlessly for the kidnappers to make contact. We'd hold our breath each time the phone rang, and then my dad would pick up—only to hear the voice of Roger, my boyfriend. When you're trapped in a nightmare, you look for levity where you can find it, and each false alarm gave us a chance to laugh. But only for that moment, and then the tension cranked up again.

A few more people were allowed into the house,

including the gossip columnist Rona Barrett, then a close friend of Nancy's. It was a decision we would later regret.

The night before, I'd moved in disbelief of Frankie's danger. But as Monday wore on, it became more believable. I felt impatient and very scared. I remember thinking, *It's broad daylight now. Wouldn't somebody have seen him? Where do they have him that he can't be seen?*

Our main concern was for Mom, who'd refused any sedatives and was just this side of hysterical. Dad and I decided to keep her busy cooking, which would also do wonders for the general morale. Tray loads of meatball sandwiches were soon streaming out of the kitchen. But my mother could be distracted only so far.

"They wouldn't let him put on a coat!" she moaned.

My dad said, "He'll be okay—"

"There's a *snowstorm* in Tahoe, Frank."

But it was Dad who made me most nervous. I'd seen him truly frightened just once before, on a very bad flight to New York. Now I saw the same chilly look in those blue eyes, and it chilled me in turn. My father did his best to conceal his emotions. He wanted to lead by example, not exacerbate the problem. But he couldn't fool his daughter, and it was tough on me to watch him wrestle with his fear.

"Why haven't they called?" he kept muttering through the afternoon. "Why haven't they *called?*" He was getting angry, which was good, because it made the rest of us a little stronger.

Finally, just before 5 P.M., Dad picked up on the fourth ring. His face froze. "Speaking," he said flatly. "How's my son?"

A pause, and then: "Let me say hello to him."

I could see Dad getting frustrated when they refused to put Frankie on. "Look," he said, "I'll switch places with him. You bring him back and take me. You don't want him—you want *me*." The dam had burst, and Dad was flooded with guilt. He knew that he hadn't given his son enough of himself. And now, what he *had* given him—Frankie's last name—might just kill the boy.

The kidnapper hung up. It was contact, but with no specific instruction—the first indication that we might not be dealing with professionals.

I'd begun to calm down, but that call shook me up again. Darkness came, and had it ever felt so sinister? My fear redoubled; I could see Mom going through the same thing.

That day blurred dimly into the next. The telephone, our only lifeline to my brother, fell silent. The hours crawled. (We found out later that the kidnappers were busy moving Frankie around.) By Tuesday morning, December 10, we were in anguish. That's when they made their second call, and Dad cut to the chase: "Look, let's get this show on the road. It takes time to get money together. Why don't you tell me what you want so I can work on it?"

The men who had Frankie might be holding the cards, but Dad sensed weakness; he was beginning to intimidate them. (As the lead kidnapper later acknowledged, "He started telling *us* what to do.")

They instructed my father to go to a phone booth at a service station in Carson City, Nevada, for further directions. He left with two of the three agents who'd been camping with us.

Dad was flying in a major blizzard, and the wait for his return was endless. I knew that I mustn't think dark thoughts, but I lost my moorings without him around. The FBI was now convinced that the kidnappers were amateurs, a gang that couldn't shoot straight. The good news was that amateurs might be more easily outsmarted. The bad news was that they might panic at Frankie's expense, even if they weren't violent types to begin with. (We didn't know then that the one supposedly in charge was high on painkillers.)

I couldn't stop rewinding what I'd heard on the radio news: that most kidnapping victims didn't come home, even when the ransom was paid, as it was for the Lindbergh baby. You never imagine that such a thing could happen to your family. And yet now it *was* happening, and people were betting that the boy who called me Squeaky would never make it back.

Finally Dad returned. There was progress. The kidnappers had demanded a ransom of $240,000 in small denominations. The FBI thought the amount was strange, too low. But it looked like a lot of money to me after Al Hart, the president of City National Bank, brought it into the house. He opened a leather pilot's bag to reveal thick stacks of bills in rubber bands; I was wide-eyed.

At around nine-thirty Tuesday night, my father was instructed to go to another phone booth, this one in Beverly Hills. Once again Dad asked to speak with Frankie, and this time the kidnappers relented. My brother said he was fine, but just hearing his voice seemed to set Dad off. When the kidnapper came back on the phone, my father said, "You son of a bitch, you hurt my son and I'll kill you!"

The Sinatra temper was alive and well.

Events were moving rapidly toward the endgame. The kidnappers asked that a courier deposit the money in a trash can at a deserted gas station in West L.A. They said Frankie would then be left at the Mulholland exit off the San Diego Freeway, a few miles from our house.

The money was dropped. At 2 A.M., near the designated time for Frankie's release, Dad took my face in his hands and said, "I'm going to bring your brother home." I trusted him absolutely, because my father had never let me down, not when it counted. He went off in his car alone, as instructed, though tailed by the FBI.

When Dad came back, half an hour later, the look on his face alarmed me. I had never seen a face like that: stunned, angry, wired, and terminally tired, all at the same time. "I'm sorry," he told us. "He wasn't there." It was the day before my father's forty-eighth birthday, but he suddenly looked old to me.

Had they taken the money and kept Frankie? Had they panicked and killed him? One of the agents quickly said, "This isn't good, but it's not necessarily the end."

My mother and I broke down, just fell apart. I felt wrung out; I had nothing left. It was dark and late, and I fell into bed with my clothes on. Though it felt like a few minutes, it must have been at least an hour later when I heard a car pull up outside and someone yelling my name.

I ran to the front door. Standing just outside were Mom and Dad—and their pale, skinny, but very much alive and breathing son. I thought it was a dream. I just grabbed on to Frankie and cried.

As we pieced together my brother's story, we learned that he'd been dropped on the wrong side of the freeway. When he didn't see Dad's car, he started walking toward Bel-Air, then flagged down a neighborhood patrol. The

Bel-Air patrolman, George Jones, backed his car close to our front door, with Frankie in the trunk to avoid the reporters who'd congregated in our driveway. Jones rang the bell and said, "Mr. Sinatra, I have something for you."

Dad followed him out to the trunk, and Frankie popped out. He looked at Dad and said, "I'm sorry."

Frankie wolfed down an overdue meal and then was questioned by the FBI. After they were done it was family time. We were exhilarated just to be safe and together again. At some point Mom opened a magnum of Dom Pérignon. She drank the entire bottle by herself and never got a headache.

We'd all caught a second wind, and it was close to dawn before Dad left with Mickey Rudin. Mom called out after him, "Frank, button your coat, it's drizzling." And Dad turned to his lawyer and said, "That's my girl—that's Nancy."

The rest of us went to bed. Since Frankie's room was still crammed with FBI men and surveillance equipment, he bunked with me. I had twin beds, but I climbed in with my brother and stayed for a while, just like when I was small and heard things go bump in the night.

The vigil was over, but our world still felt turned inside out. My father had been sick, off and on, since Kennedy was shot. Now his immune system was in shreds, and it would be a while before he could resume his tour.

Mom wouldn't be herself for a long time. She'd go out on a simple errand and turn the wrong way; she was discombobulated.

When I made it back to Marymount, my school friends treated me as though I were made of porcelain. We had an affluent student body, and they all knew that it could have happened to them.

I'd move more cautiously in the world for a while. I changed my route to school and had security following me for several weeks. Roger was warned to be careful; we went out in big groups. My parents wouldn't say it in so many words, but I knew what they were thinking: *If it happened once, it could happen again.*

I knew it, because I felt the same way.

The FBI stayed in our house for three days after my brother was freed—until December 14, when all three kidnappers were in custody. The ringleader, Barry Keenan, was a young drug addict who'd attended University High School with Nancy. It was a large school, and she didn't remember him.

Keenan had first considered seizing Nancy, but then reasoned that a male hostage might be less volatile. He'd planned to grab my brother at the Ambassador Hotel the day after Thanksgiving, until Frankie crossed him up by going in the front way with me. (The running joke at our house was that if they'd taken me, instead, they would have returned me with a rebate.)

I believe that Frankie could have recovered from the abduction with minimal harm. What hurt him more was the trial, where Keenan pulled a typical addict's gambit: he tried to absolve himself by blaming the victim. He contended that the kidnapping was a hoax, and that Frankie had conspired with the defendants in a play for publicity to jump-start his career.

Never mind that the theory was ridiculous on its face. (As Dad noted, "This family needs publicity like it needs peritonitis.") Or that the jury dismissed the defense in forty minutes flat, and found the trio guilty on all six counts.

The newspapers were not about to let facts get in the way of a good story, and they ran with it, with huge head-lines in the *Los Angeles Times* and the *Herald-Examiner*. In her book *Miss Rona*, Rona Barrett recaptured the willful idiocy of those days: "In my heart of hearts I always felt Frank Junior had his own kidnapping. Not for money. Not for publicity. But for the attention of his father."

With friends like that, who needs kidnappers?

(After serving an absurdly small portion of his original life sentence, Keenan became a developer. In 1998, to add outrage to insult, he sold his story—which acknowl-edged that he'd lied about the hoax—to Columbia Pictures for $1.5 million. He was blocked from taking any profit, however, after an appeals court ruled that he was bound by California's Son of Sam law. We are confident that the California Supreme Court will uphold this decision.)

Frankie was utterly blameless, but he couldn't unring the bell. He'd get heckled at his shows, and it hurt him deeply; he'd be dogged by public stigma for years. Nancy will tell you that this incident soured his life and ultimately hurt his career. I'm not so sure, because my brother was also swimming upstream in the music world. By the mid-1960s, tuxedo singers with big bands were an endangered species. Frankie might have been a victim of bad timing and his own stubbornness as much as anything.

As for the two men in my family, and their choked and halting relationship . . . Our family crisis didn't forge a breakthrough, as it might have in the Hollywood version. Dad and Frankie went on as they had in the past, not quite connecting. They loved each other and knew it, but it had taken a near-death experience to bring them close and together. When the trauma was over, the connection was broken.

They were two men who shared a name and a history and a pure passion for music, and all of that wasn't quite enough.

4

Generation Gap

"THE RAT PACK" was a label applied to them by the press. Frank, Dean, and Sammy referred to themselves as the Summit, the name of their act at the Sands. To me, they were simply the coolest grown-ups I knew: my father and some of his closest friends, notably Dean Martin and Sammy Davis Jr.

Even after he left Jerry Lewis, Dean remained the perfect straight man. Where Dad could be tightly wound and extravagantly emotional, Dean was easygoing and kept to his own business. I had the sense that he would disappear when anything displeased him. (He veered away from the Kennedys early on, before things went sour.)

The Sinatra children knew him as Uncle Dean. He

was warm and reliable, a big man with big hands, and he hugged like a bear. Though he had an air of authority, he was never intimidating—just the opposite, in fact. He loved to kid around. He approached young people at their level; he wasn't your typical patriarch.

As Dean was also born in June, Nancy and I began celebrating our birthdays together with him at Chasen's, along with another Gemini, James Darren. Those parties became legendary. The guests—and performers—routinely included Milton Berle, Jack Benny, Jimmy Durante, Joe E. Lewis, George Burns, and Sammy.

The Martins lived in a huge house on Mountain Drive in Beverly Hills. They had seven children under their roof, four from Dean's first wife and three with his second wife, Jeannie. Their home was laid out like a dormitory. It was full of action and fun, and there were always people on their tennis court—a stark contrast to the quiet at Nimes Road. I'd spend many an afternoon with them after school, hanging out.

I was closest to Deana. The youngest child from Dean's first marriage, she'd been in my class through fourth grade, before I was sentenced to Marymount. She was a pistol, as big as a minute and invariably laughing. Later I got to be friends with Dino, who was four years younger and the apple of his father's eye. I'd hear him rehearsing with Desi Arnaz Jr. and Billy Hinsche in the

Martins' garage, before they became teenage heart-throbs.

Dino was quite the young romantic. He was all of sixteen when a group of us went to see Zeffirelli's *Romeo and Juliet*. When I glanced at him during a love scene, Dino looked hypnotized by Olivia Hussey, the fifteen-year-old British actress who played Juliet. He literally couldn't close his mouth.

"What is it?" I whispered.

And Dino said, "I'm going to marry her."

I said, "What are you talking about? Hello, Dino? Are you in there?"

A few years later, Dino met Olivia Hussey and was true to his word: he married her. I wouldn't doubt anything he said after that.

🦋

Where Dean marched to his own drummer, Sammy would follow Dad anywhere. My father had put Sammy on the map in the late forties, when he insisted that the Will Mastin Trio (with Sammy as lead dancer) open for him at the Capitol Theater in New York. He thrilled to Sammy's talent and loved helping him. No friend gave Dad greater joy—or, when Sammy went on one of his self-destructive binges, greater pain.

Their friendship was entwined with my father's ingrained hatred of bigotry. His feelings were rooted in his Hoboken boyhood, where neighborhoods were divided by ethnic allegiances. "There weren't gang wars," Dad told Walter Cronkite in 1965, "but there were beefs and battles about position and who should cross the line. There were many times when I had to go on an errand where I skirted certain areas of the town, because the cry would go up, 'Kill the dago when he comes to the corner!'"

Dad would carry the memory of that experience for his entire life. He wanted our world to be different and did what he could to change things. His fight against prejudice went beyond singing "The House I Live In." My father also walked the walk. Back in the early forties, when integration was a radical idea, Dad demanded— and got—a hotel room key for the Dorsey band's arranger, Sy Oliver.

Dad stood tallest where he cast the longest shadow— in Las Vegas, which was strictly segregated through the 1950s. At that time, the same black performers who packed the showrooms at white hotels would have to sleep elsewhere. After Lena Horne's child waded into a pool at the Sands, a manager had the pool drained. The next time Dad performed there with Sammy, he went on strike. A born rule breaker, he announced that he would not go on unless Sammy was given a room. *If my friends are good enough to play here, they're good enough to stay here.*

Dad exerted tremendous pressure to the point where it was do-or-die, and management blinked. Sammy could stay, and gamble if he chose. The rules had changed for good.

As Sammy would say, "Frank cared when nobody else did—before it became popular." He later told me that Dad had helped him buy a house in an exclusive part of Beverly Hills: another color line broken.

(It was always clear to me that the Summit's ethnic humor—however incorrect by today's standards—was meant to poke fun at bigotry, not endorse it. In real life, Dad was offended by racial jokes and epithets, and wouldn't stand for anyone using them in his presence.)

Sammy was younger and smaller than my father's other friends, more *boyish* in a wonderful way, and we were on a first-name basis from the start. After losing his eye in an auto accident, Sammy recuperated with round-the-clock nursing care at the Compound, where Dad could oversee things. When Dad took us to the Disneyland preview a few months later, Sammy came, too—he was like one of the kids. He snapped pictures left and right, undaunted by his new eye patch.

Sammy was a wind-up toy, a firecracker, always ready to join in our fun. He would come and go from our lives over the years, but whenever he walked through our door, we'd just pick up where we'd left off.

I miss him . . .

I wasn't conscious of color until I was four years old. Late one night Mom returned from dinner with guests. She woke me up and carried me downstairs to see someone who wanted to meet me. Still dopey with sleep, I took her hand and toddled toward the living room. I was just fine as far as the archway, until I saw the man who sat very straight in the wing chair. He was also very dark—and I screamed and tore out of the room. He was the scariest thing I'd ever seen.

The man who'd scared me was Nat King Cole. Mortified, Mom came back up to my bedroom, calmed my little nerves, and asked me to come down again. I gave it a second try, and ended up on Nat's lap. I remember that he spoke as softly and gently as he sang.

In the years to follow, we'd often share holiday meals with musicians who were working with Dad, including Duke Ellington and Count Basie. But it was Sammy, along with our dear friend Quincy Jones, who must have made me realize that we're all the same, because they were truly part of our family.

Looking back, that was quite a gift.

Predating the tower architecture that now dominates Las Vegas, the Sands was a sprawl of one- and two-story buildings, all named after racetracks. When we went to see Dad perform, we stayed at the Churchill Downs, in a two-bedroom bungalow with its own little garden and pool area. And its own kitchen; Dad always liked to have a kitchen. If friends or relatives joined us, we'd spread out to any number of adjoining rooms—it was like going to camp, with everyone staying together. Once Nancy and Frankie had moved on in life, I could bring a girlfriend for company.

In its day, the Sands was the most glamorous place in Las Vegas. The high rollers camped there because it marqueed the biggest names in show business, beginning with my father. Entertainment came under the purview of a nice man named Jack Entratter, whom Dad had met years earlier in New York. No one was better at catering to talent. (I remember that he wore thick-soled, wedge-shaped shoes, which I thought were funny; Dad said it was because he had feet like a duck.) As you might imagine, the Sinatra children were also treated exceptionally well at the Sands. I was introduced to room service and became a quick convert. To stay in your pajamas and have any variety of food come to you—now *that* was living.

Las Vegas was a dusty Western town in those days.

Is he cute or what?

F.S. and the Sinatra matriarch

Already had the look.
Major Bowes tour, 1936

Like his music, his sense of style
is timeless. 1942

Dad loved to shop. 1941

F.S. at the Jersey shore, 1939

Mug shot, Bergen County, 1938 7.

Marty, F.S., and Dolly 8.

Mr. and Mrs. Frank Sinatra dance,
February 4, 1939.

With his dreams set on a singing career,
Dad dallied as a sportswriter.

Mom dressed to the nines with my
sister under all that fur.

Frank shows off his expectant bride as
Manie Sacks looks on. 1940

Dad and Mom with little Nancy, 1941

13.

14.

Crosby boys, Peggy Ann Garner,
Elizabeth Taylor, Roddy McDowall,
Margaret O'Brien, and little Nancy

15.

Dad and Mom with little Nancy, 1943

The last family Christmas card,
1948

Nothing could stop the inevitable,
Not even me! 1948

The Sinatras in the Carolwood Drive play yard,
1949 (last photo as a family)

The Sinatra kids in the Carolwood Drive library, 1952

19.

20.

Mom and Dad step out (the last dance).

21.

Mr. and Mrs. Mickey Rooney and friend (I thought this was a hoot.)

I'm certain Ava got the message.
F.S. imitates a bullfighter.

22.

23.

Frank and Ava, Washington,
1951. They were somethin'.

Academy Awards ceremony,
1954

24.

The notorious Australian trip,
1954–55

25.

Portraits of parents kept in my nursery

Dear Mama,
    I love you very
much. And so does daddy.

Mama when she
was a little girl.
N.S.   F.S.

Love,
    Tina.

*Notice the arm positions;
Mom's open—Dad's outstretched*

Frankie does an F.S. show. 1954

*Dad and me at Nancy's high school
graduation, 1955*

Frankie, 1955

Nancy does an F.S. show. 1954

*Marymount Junior School
graduation, 1963*

Fathers and daughters:
Deana Martin and Tina;
Dean and Frank,
Christmas TV special, 1968

34.

Just after the kidnapping, 1964

35.

Father and son at work, 1969

Mom and me, 1964
(shot at Nimes Road)

F.S. and Michael Romanoff at the
Compound, 1972

*Nancy, Dean, and Tina support F.S.
as he leaves his footprint at
Grauman's Chinese Theatre. 1965*

*Frank and Mia,
Beverly Hills, 1965*

Dad's fiftieth birthday party, Beverly Hills, 1965

Downtown was really seedy, and there were maybe a dozen big hotels on the Strip. Diversions for children were sparse. Dad would arrange outings for us, like boat rides on Lake Mead or tours of the local ghost town, but mostly I'd be happy to hang out by the pool. At night I'd get dressed up and sit ringside in the Copa Room, and I'd smile when Dad winked at me in the middle of a number. Of all his songs, my favorite was his signature closing number, "Put Your Dreams Away," which sounded like a lullaby to me.

That was the best part of Las Vegas: just being with my father for whole luxurious days at a time.

When the Summit convened at the Sands in the late fifties and early sixties, it was the hottest ticket in town. Show business was more casual then; the rooms were smaller, and most of the big names had started out around the same time, from the same humble beginnings. Whenever we went to see Milton Berle, my father would get up and join in Milton's routine, for better or worse. He did the same with Jack Benny and Bob Hope, and especially with Danny Thomas, who was godfather to Frankie and like a brother to Dad. As they traded banter and insults, you knew that these men really liked one another.

The Summit's flashy repartee came off like the height of spontaneity. In fact, they'd polished and refined the act on the road, in Miami or Atlantic City. Though they were free to improvise, the act was thoroughly plotted, including Dean's turn as a drunk. Dad and his friends were consummate pros who never drank during the day of a performance. The "bourbon" in Dean's glass—and in my father's as well—was usually iced tea or apple juice, at least at the first show. (The second show, however, could be a different story.)

With the possible exception of *Soupy Sales*, the Summit was the most exciting thing I'd ever seen Dad do. When he and Dean and Sammy were at the top of their game, nothing was sacred. But they were never mean-spirited, and the show went every which way but blue. (Well, maybe a *little* blue.) They could entertain people by basically being themselves, and they knew it; they had as much fun as their audience.

The energy on that stage was indescribable. By the end of the second show, the entire hotel would be abuzz. The headliners would head for the lounge to unwind, then move to the casino, where Dad and Dean might commandeer a blackjack table and make every pretty girl a winner. As a player, Dad had a preference for craps. When I came of age, he tried to teach me the rules, to little avail. He'd risk thousands of dollars on a roll of the dice. I'd get nervous when Dad was losing, but he'd take it in stride, and for the most part he knew when to leave the table. (Once, when he should have left and didn't, they cut off Dad's line of credit. Fisticuffs ensued with a casino executive, and it was all over the newspapers the next day.)

If my father and his pals were shameless practical jokers onstage, in real life they were incorrigible. Whenever they got together, the pranks flowed nonstop. Some were simple and obvious, like short-sheeting or cutting off someone's pajama legs. Or the stylish silver lighter Dean gave to Dad, with his initials engraved on one side and a heartfelt message on the other: FUCK YOU VERY MUCH.

Sammy was a popular mark, but the greatest target of all time was Michael Romanoff, the legendary Los Angeles restaurateur who imagined that he was Russian royalty. (In reality, he was a Jewish orphan from Illinois.) Michael was a tiny, meticulous man with a salt-and-pepper crew cut and a regal manner of speech. He was very dear, and he loved my father.

Dad in turn was drawn to older men with whom he could exercise his curiosity. He would talk to Noël Coward or Bennett Cerf for hours at a stretch, and he'd fly Mike and Gloria Romanoff all over the world with him—which also conveniently kept Dad's favorite victim close at hand.

It wasn't enough to nail Michael's shoes to the floor

of his closet, though my father was happy to do that, or to cut his cigarettes to three-quarter size and reseal the pack. The best jokes were more elaborate and required long-term planning. Each week, wherever he might be, Michael would pack his fine laundry—from dress shirts and silk pajamas to his shorts and handkerchiefs—in a strapped metal box, and ship it to Sulka in London. Dad intercepted the box, replaced Michael's clothes with rags, and sent it on to Sulka. It came back to its owner with each rag perfectly pressed.

On one extended road trip, Dad and Dean got hold of Michael's walking stick after the "prince" had gone to bed. Each night they shaved off a quarter inch of the stick. After a few days, Michael began hunching over. He was just about falling down when he finally caught on.

"You know, old boy, I think I'm still growing!"

My father fit the mold of the classic overachiever. He had his own void inside, the product of his emotionally meager childhood. As long as he kept working, kept moving, he might outrun his loneliness.

The void gaped widest when he lacked a special woman in his life, as in the early sixties, when Dad and

Ava moved permanently from turbulent romance to entitled friendship, and no one had replaced her. From 1960 to 1965, Dad worked at a phenomenal pace. In addition to upwards of two hundred club dates per year, he released twenty-six albums and made eleven movies (not counting three cameos); launched his own record label, Reprise; and became part owner of the Cal-Neva, a charming, rustic hotel and casino in Lake Tahoe.

(After thirty years of working for others, Dad wanted to work for himself. He loved the Cal-Neva but was led to divest after Sam Giancana—banned from all casinos by the Nevada Gaming Control Board—paid a visit to his girlfriend, Phyllis McGuire, who was appearing there.)

Dad's career was so mammoth by then that I don't think his family much entered into the equation. Like his own parents, he would do what he felt he needed to do, regardless of how it affected the people around him. And like his own parents, he wasn't prepared for his children to pass judgment on his priorities. We were to trust him.

I was a shy if precocious teenager through the most prolific phase of my father's career. With no brother or sister at home to divert me, I felt chronically short-shrifted and dissatisfied. I was missing my father more than ever. The older I got, the more I felt that he wasn't seeing me enough.

At fourteen, I was spending a lot of time with my girlfriend Joanie Glick, the middle child of a drop-dead gorgeous clothes manufacturer and his zany, stylish wife. While I'd take Joanie along to the Compound or Cal-Neva, it was even better to sleep over at her house, when I could immerse myself in her "normal" household, a sixties version of *Father Knows Best*. Joanie was like the girl with the tea set; she had something I'd always wanted.

I have fond memories of my dad around this time. Overnights at his Japanese-modern bachelor pad on Bowmont, with its 270-degree view of downtown L.A., the Pacific Ocean, and the San Fernando Valley . . . a driving lesson on the flat, straight roads of Palm Springs . . . a visit to Dunhill's, where Dad kept his own humidor, and the pungent musk of all those cigars . . . an afternoon at the Tamarisk golf course, where I got to drive the cart.

They were all great times, but they apparently weren't enough for me. In the interminable weeks or months between them, I was stuck at home with Mom, and all I wanted was to be out *there*, with Dad. I was in a terrible hurry to grow up, with no one telling me what to do. (Sound familiar?) Mom bore the edge of my impatience, and countered by tightening the reins. I had the earliest curfew in West L.A., and lagged a year behind my friends in graduating to high heels.

I felt hemmed in on all sides. I'd moved on to Mary-mount Senior School, in Westwood, and though we no longer had to curtsy to the nuns, I found its restrictions insufferable. In warm weather we'd take our lunch out-side and gaze over the wall, across Sunset Boulevard to the UCLA campus. We were tantalized by all that free-dom, so close and yet so far. I remembered how my sis-ter used to sail through forty-five minutes of high school homework, then pin-curl her hair and be on the phone for the evening. Eight years later, it was taking me four hours to get through my work, and then I'd fall asleep, totally spent, in my dowdy school uniform. I got so overwhelmed that I stopped caring, and cadged my algebra answers over the phone from Christine Cuddy, now an entertainment lawyer.

I was angry all the time, a ticking time bomb with braces. Having grown up in a home with older, talented siblings and a lovingly dominant mother, I was striving to find an identity. But I couldn't find one in an environ-ment that squashed me—not in a blue-and-white uni-form, not among nuns who tapped you on the shoulder if you danced too close with a boy. Mom knew I was unhappy, but my improving grades made her loath to move me to a coed school. Dad tried to intercede but could do only so much. It went back to the understanding he had with Mom; he would defer in matters of schooling and discipline.

When you come down to it, my parents were confounded, like parents everywhere in the sixties. They'd raised us to be respectful and obedient, never aggressive or confrontational. Their methods had worked well with Nancy, somewhat less well with Frankie (who had the excuse of being a boy), and not at all with me. My sister was more like Mom, very caring and concerned about everyone else; I took after my self-involved father. Nancy dressed like one of the girlfriends on *Ozzie and Harriet*, down to the poodle skirt; I was headed for tie-dyes and love beads.

Though my rebellion was mild by the standards of the day, it shook my parents up. We were fighting over limits: where I could go, when I could go, and with whom. Mom took the brunt of it, day to day. It was easier for Dad to overlook some of the superficial things. He'd laugh at my bell-bottoms, which were long enough to cover my four-inch-wedge corky sandals—"My daughter has no feet!" he'd say. But even Dad didn't go unscathed.

In the middle of one argument, I remember throwing

his bachelor lifestyle back in his face: "You've got to be kidding—look at the way *you* live."

And Dad said, "You'll do as I say, not as I do."

And I shot back, "You don't *really* think that's going to work with me, do you, Dad?" (I was such a smart-ass.)

"Well, yes, I do," he said, with those big blue eyes at full attention. I think that he saw his young and willful self in me, and it flustered him. It was more than he thought he'd have to handle with a girl.

I remember one weekend at the Compound with three girlfriends, and only Dad as a chaperone. Feigning fatigue from a day of sun and sports, we retired early. When we thought the coast was clear, we snuck out a side gate to a waiting car for a night of dancing at the El Mirador Hotel. I suspect that Dad made a bed check, because the next morning he said to me, "Have a good time last night?" His look belied his casual remark. I froze speechless, and he quietly added, "This house has rules, too. If you take advantage, you'll ruin it for both of us." I burst into tears and ran to my room. I knew Dad was right, and I still hated disappointing him.

(When I tried a similar stunt at home and Mom caught me sneaking back through my bedroom window, I'd be grounded for a season. Different parents, different methods—but a lesson learned well in either case.)

Dad let me have it just once in my life, when I was fifteen years old and—unbeknownst to my parents—had agreed to ride a motorcycle with my boyfriend, Roger. He was inexperienced, and helmets were unknown. (I knew I was wrong to go, but this was a taste of *freedom*.) Roger moved slowly onto the shoulder of Sunset just as a car unexpectedly turned right onto Hillcrest, cutting us off. The bike crashed and Roger and I were airborne, flying over the car. Roger tore his groin, while I landed on the right side of my face and went skidding on the asphalt, passing out along the way. I wound up eighteen feet from the point of impact, in the middle of the intersection.

When I came to, as luck would have it, I saw Uncle Dean standing over me. He'd been on his way home from a golf game, and stopped as a good Samaritan for these two kids smashed on the street. When he saw it was me, he knelt down and said, "Oh, *God*," which scared me.

I said, "I know you're going to call somebody, but could you please make it my mother?" Dean agreed, but we both knew that Dad would have to be told, and sooner rather than later.

Treated and released and back safe at home, I feared that the worst was yet to come. Dad drove straight from the studio and checked in with Mom; I remember hearing their muffled voices in the hallway. With the right side of my face one huge abrasion, I'd hoped that the sight of me might soften Dad. But by the time he'd entered my bedroom, Mom had convinced him there was no permanent damage. His fright and worry had boiled down into pure paternal wrath. He knew that I could have been maimed or even killed, and all for a stunt that *I* knew wasn't safe from the start.

After kissing me hello, Dad distilled his anger into a few words: "Not smart, Tina. I thought you were brighter than that."

I was feeling weepy and sorry for myself, but I had to concede his point. And I've never been on a motorcycle since.

※

By my late teens, I would come face-to-face with my anger—and confront Dad with it, as well. He understood, as he'd grown up with a fair ration of the stuff himself. He'd sit and hear me out, and then we'd attack the issue of the moment together.

He'd say, "Don't be a pain in the ass to your mother. When you feel these things, come to me." There was a warmth and constancy to my father that made baring your soul a lot easier. He wasn't threatened by emotions, light or dark.

While it was my idea to go into analysis, Dad heartily supported me. He saw how I'd been wasting my energy by digging in against the forced conformity at Marymount. He thought I needed a place to vent my resentments and, he hoped, release them.

Therapy gave me a way to investigate the issues I'd filed away for sixteen years. When I rebelled against Mom's rules, I came to see that I was misplacing my rage. The real source of my anger was an event from long ago, when I was much too young to absorb it.

I was angry because I felt abandoned by my father. And because I hadn't been old enough when he left to comprehend all that I'd missed.

I'd be in and out of analysis for years, but the first stage was devoted to coming to terms with my parents. I went in resenting their choices and mistakes, and came out with understanding and forgiveness: a big step toward adulthood.

To ease my way, Dad joined me at several sessions, knowing he'd be taking it on the chin. He gave himself fully to those discussions and readily accepted a parent's responsibility for whatever our relationship lacked—for all the times I needed him and he was not there. His sorrow was deep and genuine, and freely expressed.

Dad and I came out of our sessions a lot closer than when we'd gone in.

We didn't have it easy as the children of divorce. But we were also the lucky ones, because our parents tried all the harder to make us feel secure. Though he didn't live under our roof, Dad taught us that our family was impenetrable. He nurtured the most precious part of us, our deep-seated trust in one another. We knew that he would never intentionally do anything to hurt us.

We'd laid a groundwork for the turbulent years to come, when I'd need all the courage and trust I could muster to confront Dad when I thought he was wrong. When my father's choices would jeopardize everything we stood for, and all that we meant to one another.

※

Just as I thought I'd burst out of my navy jumper, life started to get a little better. When I turned sixteen, Dad presented me with a new, powder-blue Pontiac Firebird convertible. (He thought new cars were safer, and got a kick out of buying nice ones.) Once I had my wheels, I no longer felt like a prisoner of Bel-Air.

The following spring, Tommy Sands abruptly walked out on my sister. Devastated, Nancy found safe harbor with us on Nimes Road. I remember coming home from school on a Monday and finding Nancy in Frankie's old room, with Dad sitting at her bedside and holding her.

They were shooting a movie together (the unfortunately titled *Marriage on the Rocks*), and Dad came by after work each day for the next week or so, until Nancy felt strong enough to rejoin him on the set. He was there as much as she needed him; he was a rock whenever one of us felt forlorn. No one understood emotional breaching better than Dad.

Nancy stayed with Mom and me for a while, and for the first time we could be more than sisters. We could be girlfriends. After she recovered her high spirits, we were double-dating all over town. Often Dad would take us to dinner or some function, a daughter on either arm. After all these years, I'd finally caught up to my big sister.

Once Nancy was home and saw for herself how truly miserable I was at school, she and Dad geared up their campaign to spring me. Even my therapist joined the anti-Marymount lobby. After I finished tenth grade, making it seven years without parole, Mom finally relented. I followed Deana Martin to Rexford, a tiny private school with a dozen kids to a class. I regained the year I'd lost and enrolled as a senior. Now I could go to lunch off campus. I could wear culottes with boots if the spirit moved me. And I could keep my confessions to myself.

Nancy was Mom's confidante, and I'd overhear them discussing the prospects of my father coming home—to stay. I'd say, "You guys are crazy!" It sounded like a fairy tale to me, and I couldn't honor or respect it. Mom was waiting for a man who was never coming back, and I started resenting her for it: more grist for analysis. As I saw it, Dad had done what he needed to do, and it was time for my mother to follow suit.

Mom would laugh and dismiss my ambitions for her. "I married one man for life," she'd say, "and with my luck it had to be your father."

She was Catholic, and she'd had her three kids with Dad, which counted for just about everything in her book. But what I wouldn't understand until much later, after a giddy girls' night out with Mom and Nancy, was that Dad actually *was* coming home to her on Nimes Road, just as he had at Carolwood. Sporadically, but very romantically. He'd encourage Mom just often enough to make waiting for him seem almost reasonable.

My parents were deeply, irrevocably connected, and there was no changing either one of them.

❃

After I graduated from high school, Dad and I took a trip to Europe via New York. We landed in Newark on a warm summer evening, and I asked to stop in Hoboken, because I'd never seen it. Dad had been offended at some ceremony in his hometown years before and had never gone back, but that night his nostalgia ran deep. He pointed out Stevens Institute, on the Palisades, where Grandpa Marty had longed for Dad to study engineering. I saw the four-story house on Garden Street where Dad grew up, and nearby the site where he was born, marked by a plaque after the house burned down.

We drove down to the wharf and he told me, "We'd swim here with our shoes tied around our necks, so they wouldn't be stolen." This was the place where he'd sit as a boy and look across at the glitter of New York. And promise himself, *I'll be going there someday.*

We stayed for a few days at Dad's apartment on East Seventy-second Street, which overlooked the East River. We'd sit on his walk-out terrace in the evenings and gaze at the splendors of Queens. After dinner one night, we strolled through Times Square. We passed the site of the old Paramount, where Dad once did eleven shows on a single Saturday, and the bobby-soxers lined up all the way down to Eighth Avenue and back around the block to Broadway.

On my last night in the city, heading out to the airport, Dad took me to Patsy's uptown, in East Harlem. The street was deserted on our way in, and the restaurant protective, so no one approached us while we were eating. But ninety minutes later, we walked back outside . . . and found five hundred people awaiting us! I guess word had gotten out. It was like a cut in a movie where you go from a silent hallway into a room with a big party, but you don't hear a sound until the door opens to the blast. I felt overwhelmed, and just a wee bit nervous.

The crowd packed the sidewalk and the street, and there were more people behind them, hanging out the windows of their brownstones. I saw a sea of scooped T-shirts—it was a very Italian-looking crowd to me, and they appeared ready to love my father to death.

Dad still moved around without security in those days, and it was just us and the driver. When you were with him in public, you adapted and moved *with* him; you didn't dare fall behind. *Stay close, stay close to me, let's go*, he'd keep telling you.

That night was definitely one of those stay-close situations. As we jumped into our Town Car, the crowd spilled around it like the Ganges overflowing its banks.

I was relieved to be inside and safe . . . and then I felt the car *rocking*. I couldn't believe it.

My father was as claustrophobic as the next fellow, only more so. "Go, go, *go!*" he urged the driver, but there was nowhere to go. We were surrounded. So Dad bowed to the circumstance, and even lowered his window partway to shake a few hands and touch a few babies.

I relaxed. After Dad explained that we had to catch a plane, the crowd gradually parted to give us a narrow lane. Dad was waving as we left, and I could tell he was pleased—he'd made a triumphant return to the kind of people he'd grown up with.

"This," he said proudly, "is where I came in."

❦

On December 12, 1965, Mom and Nancy and I threw a black-tie party at the Beverly Wilshire Hotel for Dad's fiftieth birthday. Sammy Davis and Tony Bennett performed with an orchestra. Sammy Cahn wrote several memorable parody lyrics, including one sung by Nancy to the tune of "Titwillow":

Who in the forties was knocking them dead?
My daddy, my daddy, my daddy.

The rug he once cut he now wears on his head.
My daddy, my daddy, my daddy . . .

Just about everyone who was anyone to my father was there, with one conspicuous exception: twenty-year-old Mia Farrow, the star of TV's *Peyton Place*, and now the love of Dad's life.

Mia and Dad would unavoidably revive that awful Freudian cliché: she found a father, and he found youth. Mia's dad, the film director John Farrow, had died two years earlier. Frank Sinatra was just what the doctor ordered: an exciting, attentive lover, and at the same time a strong shoulder for the leaning. (In *What Falls Away*, Mia's autobiography, she notes that our fathers wore the same cologne.)

Mia needed nurturing, and Dad had a crying need to nurture. He'd recovered from his emotional stupor of the early sixties, when he'd been buffeted by Jack Kennedy's assassination and my brother's kidnapping and the last pained chorus of his romance with Ava. A forty-three-day engagement to Juliet Prowse notwithstanding, he hadn't settled in with anyone since. The definitive swinger was aching for some stability in his life. He was ready to stop floating and settle down. He was primed to try again.

As they say, timing is everything.

I think that Dad looked at Mia and saw this frail little waif, and thought, maybe *this* one would be more malleable. Only later—too late—would he realize that Mia's frailty was all on the surface. She was just as career-driven as Ava, and probably more independent.

Dad and Mia saw each other privately and very quietly for some time. I sensed something was going on with him before I knew the details, if only because Nancy and I were suddenly seeing him less.

When I found out, I was surprised, because Dad hadn't dated anyone nearly so young before. From what little I knew of Mia (she'd been a few grades ahead of me at Marymount, and I'd met her once in passing), I thought that she might be good for him. But their age difference led me to take them less than seriously.

Despite Mia's urgings, my father was reluctant to put her together with his kids. My curiosity would go unsatisfied until early in 1966, when I stopped by to play tennis at the house he'd rented in Holmby Hills, at Sunset and Delfern. Dad was puttering around with George Jacobs, his houseman, and he said to me, "If you stay long enough, Mia's coming over."

He didn't need to ask me twice.

When Mia came through the door in her sundress and sandals, I thought to myself, *She's perfect.* Porcelain skin, with no makeup. Flawless hair, short as a boy's.

She'd come straight from work, with a script in her bag, and looked surprised and nervous to see me there. I tried to put her at ease, because that's the way we'd been raised; I'd met a lot of women with Dad over the years, if none so close to my age. Besides, I wanted him to be happy.

Mia and I became fast friends. We'd socialize when Dad was on the road, which meant that I probably saw more of her than he did. We were three years apart, a big difference at the time, and I found her impressive. Mia was more eccentric than I was. She had a diverse group of friends, most of them older mentor types, like Salvador Dalí and Yul Brynner. But we had other interests in common, like music and clubbing and clothes. We had a playful relationship that didn't run all that deep, not in the beginning.

I really liked Mia. I just never thought that she and Dad would last.

⁂

I think that Mia would have been willing to live with my father indefinitely, no paperwork required. But as we've seen, Dad was the marrying kind. He was a traditional man who felt that Mia would be compromised without a wedding ring. And he was always reaching for what he didn't have.

Shortly before they eloped, my father told Dean Martin, "If I could have one or two good years, that's all I can expect." (He'd repeat the sentiment to Nancy and me after tying the knot.) That's how very lonely he was. Dad knew the odds were against the marriage. He knew that it would read like a soap opera and that he'd be held up to ridicule if it failed. (His mistakes were always public ones.) But he was willing to accept the relationship on its own terms—and once he made the commitment, he gave it his best shot.

On the afternoon of July 19, 1966, I'd pulled into the Martins' driveway to drop off Deana and Dino, when Uncle Dean beckoned me inside. He took me into his little den, where he'd retreat to watch his golf on TV. He sat me down on his sofa with an Indian blanket, and said, "I want you to know that your dad is marrying Mia as we speak." The ceremony was taking place in Jack Entratter's living room at the Sands.

All I could muster was, "You're kidding." I was surprised—no, I was shocked. And I felt hurt that Dad had shut us out of this central event.

Uncle Dean said, "I think you should go home and tell your mom—it's going to break any second."

By the time I got home, Mom had already received a

call from her friend Dorothy Manners, who'd assumed the writing of Louella Parsons's influential column. The happy couple had posed for pictures, which had gone out on the wire. My mother was stunned, and insulted that Dad had failed to confide in us. It was the first time we'd been excluded from something important in his life.

An hour or so later, Dad left his reception and called us at Nimes Road, because he hadn't wanted Mom to find out about the wedding on the news. I happened to pick up the phone, and he could hear how angry I was.

He said, "I want you to be happy for me—I want you to wish me well."

I said, "I'm too busy resenting you for not telling me." I wouldn't give him my blessing; it was not a pretty conversation. (I'd apologize to him and Mia later.)

Looking back, I can't blame Dad for keeping his secret. He couldn't trust his family because he didn't want to hear what he already knew: that he was nuts. He could go through with the marriage only by living in denial. "I just didn't want anyone ruining it for me," he'd confess to me long afterward.

I won't speak for Mom, but once Nancy and I got over the shock, we came around and rooted for the marriage to work. My father was a youthful fifty, after all. And Mia was a very precocious twenty-year-old. Like a number of Dad's previous flames (Ava, Betty Bacall, Kim Novak), she was a voracious reader with a sprightly intelligence and an active imagination. She was interesting and interested in what was going on around her. If anything, Mia brought something extra to the table: a firm set of politics.

Mia could also be silly, and Dad loved silly. She possessed an intriguing physical dexterity; rather than simply walk through a room, she'd dance through it. And she had a flair for being part of a group—she was both entertaining and easy to entertain. Mia could make you feel like you were the only one in the vicinity worth listening to.

It wasn't hard to see how Dad could have fallen in love with her. (As a bonus, my father got a dream mother-in-law: Maureen O'Sullivan, one of the world's warmest and most gracious people.)

They were model, adoring newlyweds. There wasn't anything Mia wouldn't do for Dad, or he for her. She brought out my father's gentlest, most caring side: the fireside Frank. To his new bride, Dad wasn't "Ol' Blue Eyes" or "the Chairman of the Board." She called him "Charlie Brown," after the sweet-natured cartoon character, and coming from Mia it suited him.

I didn't feel threatened by Mia. I felt grateful to her, because she made my father happier than I'd ever seen him. When I spent time with them in the desert, Dad's old restlessness was missing in action. As we passed the time playing word games, he seemed quiet and relaxed. Mia was so proud of how she'd converted the guest room into her dressing area, and Dad glowed along with her. She'd had it done all in pink, which didn't quite blend with the earth tones in the rest of the house, but neither of them cared. They were making up the rules as they went along.

Dad and Mia were at their best when they were isolated, when they stopped the world and got off for a few days. But they could also have fun stepping out in public. I remember joining them at the Daisy, the Beverly Hills nightclub of the moment, and Dad wearing a Nehru jacket and love beads, or silver-studded denim—he got downright funky, as cute as he could be. He'd sit and smoke and drink with us, and he loved to get up and dance to the latest tune from Motown. Dad moved just enough, mostly with his upper body, but he had great rhythm. (Gene Kelly, who made three movies with him, always said that Dad was a damn good dancer.)

Though we'd all joke about the age difference between Dad and "Mama Mia," as I sometimes called her, I wasn't conscious of it when with them. My father was truly young at heart, a man adaptable and *alive*, with a strong interest in what was current in music. Though

Dad wasn't a fan of rock 'n' roll, he made some important exceptions. He enjoyed the Beach Boys' harmony and had tremendous respect for the Beatles' songwriting. (After the Beatles came out with the "White Album," and then with *Abbey Road*, Dad asked Nancy and me to help choose the Lennon-McCartney ballads he might adapt for his own recordings.)

Not long after the wedding, Nancy and I met Dad and Mia at the Sands and took connecting rooms to their suite. That weekend turned into one long pajama party. I can remember Mia's fuzzy slippers; she wasn't a negligee kind of girl. In the early evening, while Dad was preparing for his performance, Nancy and Mia and I indulged in two of the great things in life: girl talk and room service.

In the Copa Room, Dad would introduce us in order of appearance: "My Nancy, my Tina, and my Mia."

As I look back at them, the Mia years were some of the very best for my father and me. Mia didn't get in the way of our new closeness—if anything, she enhanced it, because we'd grown as close as sisters.

I'm not sure when I got the first inkling that Dad and Mia might be in trouble. Maybe it was the afternoon I dropped by their new place on Copa d'Oro, the English Tudor-style house they would barely have time to decorate before parting company. Dad was out, no doubt working, and I found Mia in the loft over her dressing area. It was a bright, beautiful day, but she was content to stay inside reading a book, cuddling her puppies at her side.

Here, I thought to myself, was a woman who could live very quietly.

Coming from a family of nine, like my mother's, Mia owned a rare social grace, but she didn't *need* people around all the time, as Dad did. She treasured their days alone together in the desert; he invited armadas of houseguests. She disliked big, boisterous gatherings; he threw her a twentieth birthday party at Chasen's with a cast of thousands, most of whom she didn't know. She wasn't eager to get dressed up and go out *every* evening—Dad's regimen when he traveled, which was 85 percent of the time. Mia was more of a day person, while the only dawns my father saw were on the back end of a hard day's night.

Through her parents, Mia had a number of older industry friends in common with Dad, including Ruth Gordon and Garson Kanin, and the playwright Leonard Gershe. She was less comfortable with Dad's rough-and-tumble cronies in New York or Las Vegas, the Damon Runyon types who'd lay in for a siege of big talk and bigger drinking. I happened to get a kick out of those lounge-table assemblies. They were a cross section of real life, and uproariously funny in small doses—especially when Jackie Gleason, one of Dad's dearest friends, joined the party. Then again, I loved being anywhere with my dad, and could leave when I got tired. Mia likely had to take too many doses for too long, and she didn't belong there in the first place.

There were other tensions, too, not the least of them political. The first year of Dad's marriage to Mia coincided with a massive escalation of the Vietnam War, and their generation gap was showing. My father thought the war was senseless, but he took the position that we had to back our boys. When Jane Fonda went to Hanoi, he was irate. He'd say, "We've got human lives over there—how *dare* you not support them?"

Though Mia wasn't an activist, she had strong feelings against the war, and I know that she and Dad had a big row about it. While I was hounding him, too, it was par for the course to line up against your kid over Vietnam. It was something else to be at such bitter odds with your wife.

But while friends and politics might have been flash points, Dad's third marriage was doomed by the same forces as his second one. The fact is, my father had an unresolved dilemma in the girl department. The vacant starlet type bored him. The woman who rang his bell would be high powered, independent, with a real life of her own—someone who would give him a run for his money.

But the same qualities that sparked Dad's interest would eventually drive him away. He'd want his vital professional woman to change her whole existence and stay tethered to his side. Ava was too talented and driven to meet my father's specifications. Mia was softer on the surface, but she, too, was an *actress*, and just beginning to explore what she could do.

Dad was willing to give all he had to Mia. His mistake was to expect her to give everything back.

In fairness, I believe that Mia had no idea where her ambitions would lead when she fell in love with my father. They both agreed that she should leave *Peyton Place*, and she did. Dad had a vision of them working together in movies, to avoid the long separations that had poisoned his life with Ava.

It was a pretty picture, except that their careers were winging in different directions. In the fall of 1967, Dad wanted to cast Mia in *The Detective*, a film he'd be producing and starring in. Mia was game, and committed to him, but then she got another offer that she could not refuse: Roman Polanski's *Rosemary's Baby*, her first starring feature role.

Polanski was supposed to finish shooting before Mia was due on Dad's set. But the director, a notorious perfectionist, ran late, and then later. My father stalled for time and postponed Mia's scenes, but the delay was costly, and he wouldn't do it twice. Dad had an obligation to the studio. He felt professionally embarrassed in front of his crew. The gossip sheets, meanwhile, were taking odds that Mia wouldn't be his wife much longer. It was one big, sticky mess.

When Dad called me, I could hear the gloom in his voice; I could tell that communication between him and Mia had collapsed.

Just as Dad neared his boiling point, I had some business in New York and asked Mia if I could bunk with her at the East Side apartment. I wasn't going on my father's behalf, but as a friend who'd known this woman's husband a lot longer than she had.

We spent the weekend together and sat up talking for hours; I found out a lot more from Mia than Dad had been willing to tell me. It opened a new and deeper phase of our friendship, and I said to myself, *She's really changing.* In New York Mia was hanging out with Liza Minnelli, dressing in caftans, delving into Eastern spirituality when it was way ahead of the curve. (Just a few months later, she'd travel to India to join the Maharishi Mahesh Yogi and the Beatles.) At the same time, she was showing less tolerance for Dad's lifestyle in Las Vegas, where he was booked indefinitely. Mia certainly wasn't going to walk off *Rosemary's Baby* and risk her reputation in such a competitive business. Dad had given her an ultimatum that she could not possibly honor.

Just sixteen months after their wedding, they'd arrived at a cul-de-sac. If Mia stayed tight by Dad's side, in Dad's world, she'd be miserable. But if she followed her own path, she couldn't be the wife that he needed. They'd been separated for weeks already, linked only by long distance, and Mia was picking up on Dad's displeasure. But she still hoped she could somehow finesse the conflict and hang on to the marriage.

It was fast becoming a war of wills, with neither side about to relent.

After a night on the town, Mia and I changed into our pajamas and examined her shooting schedule. "*Look* at this," she said. "How can I possibly work this out?" In fact, she couldn't. I could see that there was no way for her to make Dad's deadline.

I decided to level with Mia. She needed to understand how dug in Dad could get, how needy he was for companionship. And how serious the repercussions if he concluded, rightly or wrongly, that she was more loyal to Paramount than to him.

"I think this is a real problem," I said. "I don't think that he's going to accept this."

I sympathized with Mia, who was losing weight from

the stress, but I also had the feeling that she'd be strong enough to survive, however it played out. I was more concerned about Dad, because I knew how much he adored her, and how much he needed someone in his life.

My father had learned from hard experience that a clean break was best, that he'd better cut his losses while he could. "She thought she could have it all," he'd say, "but I knew better."

But despite his deep affection for Mia, Dad lacked the stomach to end it face-to-face. Not long after my November visit to New York, without advance word, he sent Mickey Rudin to Mia's movie set. They moved to her dressing room, where Mickey opened his briefcase and set the stack of divorce papers in front of her.

Mia signed on the spot, without complaint, and they were legally separated.

The following August, Dad was preparing a TV special. They had just finished taping the dress rehearsal when Mickey Rudin phoned in the news: the divorce was complete. Without a word, Dad went home.

It's not always easier to leave someone than to be left. Given Dad's guilty underpinnings, for him it was probably harder. He knew that the marriage should never have happened, and that the responsible party was wincing at him in the mirror. His friends—and his enemies—had been right all along. He'd screwed up, one more time. He'd followed his romantic heart and set himself up for a fall, not to mention a double helping of ridicule.

Rosemary's Baby aside, Dad and Mia were at cross-purposes from the start. Mia was a very young woman who would want to have babies—lots of babies, as it turned out—even while she continued acting. She never could have had that family with Dad. He was beyond that point in his life, and I think that he and Mom both understood that his fathering days were over—it was one of many unspoken things between them.

If I could have one or two good years, that's all I can expect.

Once the divorce was finalized, Dad closed the chapter with Mia. He went through none of the grinding agony that followed his breakup with Ava. He'd learned to move on without looking back.

Though my father made it clear that he was ready to take care of Mia, she would take no alimony. All she wanted, she'd say, "was his respect and friendship." They would, indeed, be friends for life.

Their brief marriage, Mia wrote, "was a little bit like an adoption that I had somehow messed up and it was awful when I was returned to the void."

Mia had never been closer to my father than in that bleak return.

5

My Father, My Friend

IN JANUARY 1969, after years of fighting emphysema, my grandfather's heart was giving out. Dad had him flown to Houston for an emergency operation by Dr. Michael DeBakey, the eminent cardiologist, but Marty was beyond help.

Dad would have the time to tell Grandpa he loved him, and to say good-bye, and then he would have to fly his father home.

A good portion of eastern New Jersey turned out for the funeral. Hundreds of citizens came through the receiving line, many of them just to see Dad and shake his hand, until he was worn down and had to step away. On our motorcade to the cemetery, the route was lined with miles of people, from local families with children to uniformed Elks and Rotarians. Every time we passed a firehouse, we'd see the firemen standing outside in full regalia, hats over their hearts and Dalmatians by their side. Some were saluting the fallen captain.

At the burial Dad stood with a daughter's hand in each of his own. He was silent and grief-stricken as I'd never seen him before, and he'd mourn for a long time. "My old man was a helluva guy," he'd say. "He was tough on me, but a helluva guy." Dad so respected his father, who'd had nothing to offer his family but his labor, and did the very best he could do. Marty was quiet, unassuming, never overreaching. It would have been hard to convince him just how much Dad admired him.

Grandpa's death had brushed Dad with mortality. He became a little more quiet, a little less ebullient. It was as though a piece of him had been chipped away. He was the first one to tell me how tough it was to lose a parent, and I remember thinking, *He'll never know how tough it will be on me.*

My father was adrift in other ways, as well. For the second time in his life, his career had reached a crossroads. The Beatles were outselling him in the record stores. The nightclub era—*his* era—stood in eclipse, and he'd yet to plot his next move.

As an added aggravation, Dad would require hand surgery. Not long after Marty died, a painful condition called Dupuytren's contracture left him unable to hold a microphone, barely able to shake hands. As my father hated hospitals, Nancy and I and his best buddy, Jilly Rizzo, made a field trip out of it. After we took Dad out to the Pacific Dining Car, Nancy burrowed in overnight with him at Good Samaritan. She stayed with him until his release, which was considerably sooner than the doctors would have liked. Dad's convalescence was slow and painful. It was the first time I would see my father suffer, a helpless feeling that I would come to know too well.

After his last divorce and the publicity circus surrounding it, my father was ambivalent about matrimony, to say the least. But he gradually returned to dating. He never stopped longing for a substantive relationship, though he must have doubted whether he'd ever attain one. In his stoic way, he felt hapless and defeated. It was a time when I made a conscious effort to be with him, because I knew how much he needed the company.

In March 1971, I found Dad poolside one day at the Compound, pen in hand. I assumed he was busy with his daily ritual, the *New York Times* crossword puzzle, which he could do in ink.

In fact, he was sketching a statement for his retirement. He was fifty-five years old. It was time, he wrote, "for reflection, reading, self-examination . . . for a fallow period, a long pause." His throat was tired, his soul was tired. He needed time to recover, reenergize.

A few days later, he called to tell me what was going to be in the papers the next day. He'd been thinking aloud about retirement for a long time, but I found the reality unbelievable. Literally inconceivable. I knew that Dad had been sad and quiet of late, and needed a stretch of solitude, but I hated the finality of his statement. I asked him, "You're *never* going to appear again?"

"I'll be freer," Dad said, attempting to soothe me. "I won't have my schedule to worry about anymore, and we'll have more time to be together. Maybe I'll even teach."

His farewell performance would be at a benefit for the Motion Picture and Television Relief Fund. The event was such a sellout that it overflowed onto two adjacent stages; each act opened at the Ahmanson Theatre, then crossed a courtyard to the Dorothy Chandler Pavilion. The performers were among the biggest in the business, including Barbra Streisand and George Burns.

Rosalind Russell introduced Dad and cried. I cried; I think everyone cried.

Dad performed for twenty-five minutes. He'd hand-picked his songs with special care; they would be his parting gift to his audience, and to himself. Those eight numbers telescoped the whole of his rich career, from "All or Nothing at All" to "My Way" and "That's Life." Dad's final selection was "Angel Eyes," the saloon song he sang like no one else. All lights were doused, save for one pin spot on his profile. As he sang the last line (*'Scuse me . . . while I disappear . . .*), Dad stepped out of the spot. When the lights came on, he was gone. The audience leapt to their feet, screaming for more, but he never came back.

It was one of the most memorable exits in the history of popular music. My father was a master of stagecraft because he understood human emotion; he was brilliant that way.

At Chasen's, following the concert, I felt like we'd had a death in the family. The one person who seemed content and carefree—as happy as I'd seen him in a long time—was the one who'd just slipped from the stage. Leaving the rest of us in darkness, with no promise of an encore.

He wouldn't sing for pay for the next eighteen months, nor would he seem to miss it.

As Dad reassessed his life, I was out seeking my niche. Of the three Sinatra children, I had long been the reluctant performer. My first big opportunity was a TV special for Valentine's Day. I was eight or so, and all I had to do was sit inside a big lace heart in a new white-and-red dress, just *sit* there, while Dad sang "My Funny Valentine" to me. The dress rehearsal went fine, but when I heard the rumble of the audience filing in, I froze. I refused to go out, and Nancy had to sub for me in her school clothes.

But in this family, you'd perform whether you liked it or not. Some years later I'd join my siblings and Dad to record *The Sinatra Family Wish You a Merry Christmas*. (That's me straining for my high note on "O Bambino.") I was also pressed into service for a Martin-Sinatra holiday songfest on Uncle Dean's TV show. The kids were paired off to sing with their dads, in descending order of professional experience: Nancy and Gail Martin; Frankie and Dino; and finally Deana and me. We knew we had to do it right because our dads weren't keen on second takes. My knees knocked all the way through.

I was proud of my sister and brother; I thought they were sensational and brave to do what they did. But I didn't covet their musical talent—or the pressure that faced any singer with our last name. I never dreamed of following in Dad's prodigious footsteps; I was more afraid of failure than my siblings. It would be safer to make my own way, on my own terms.

Marymount had killed any interest I might have had in further schooling, and it was a great day when I found out that I didn't *have* to apply to college. As usual, my father was one step ahead of me. Dad was dying for me to become the first Sinatra college graduate. He reached out for the best opportunity he could find for me, the first coed class at the Yale Drama School. It was a sly move on his part: *You want to act, here's a place you can learn to act.*

Offered a priceless opportunity, I promptly declined. Though Dad was miffed, as usual he kept his cool, and suggested I give it more thought. But I was eighteen and knew what was best for me: financial independence, my ticket out of Nimes Road. I successfully auditioned for an acting class given by the inspirational Jeff Corey, a blacklisted actor who was still feeling the effects of the McCarthy era. And I began looking for work.

I've been asked all my life about the advantages of being a Sinatra, and whether the climb to success came easier by way of favors. I can only say that for me it did not—though it certainly opened some illustrious doors. I was taken on by Dick Clayton and then by Stan Kamen, two of the very best theatrical agents. But that's where the favoritism stopped. In the absence of real talent, à la Jane Fonda or Candice Bergen, those doors don't stay open for long.

A case in point: At nineteen, and with virtually no experience, I was meeting with Otto Preminger about a small part in a film, rather than being glanced at by some assistant casting director. Mr. Preminger was sweet in his Teutonic way, but both of us knew I was in over my head. He told me, "You have baby fat in your face— get rid of it. You must continue to study. You're not ready for this part . . . and please give my regards to your father."

I hadn't respected the craft enough, as Jeff Corey would say. I had much to learn and investigate. I also needed to leave Los Angeles and break away from Mom. In 1968, when offered a part in a European TV miniseries, I jumped at it. I moved to Germany, my base for the next two years.

Though our family was more dispersed than ever, birthdays remained sacrosanct for Dad. He loved to surprise us. For my twenty-first I came home to visit, and Nancy threw me a party. At the last minute I was told that Dad had been called out of town on an emergency. I understood, but it was a big disappointment, as I hadn't seen him for months.

As we sat down to an alfresco dinner, a line of ten violinists snaked out of the house and into the garden to serenade us. They were all wearing tuxedos—except for the fifth in line, who seemed strangely out of place in a suit and tie . . .

Just a few people had known Dad was coming; he didn't want to risk any leaks. I stood to greet him, and we hugged and cried for a very long time.

A year later to the day, back in my Munich hotel room, I answered a knock at the door expecting the housekeeper. But it was my father, who'd managed to slip off our familial radar screen for a day. (He would have made a fine spy.) When he joined me at a restaurant for a cast-and-crew party that night, his appearance sparked mass adulation and chaos—Dad was the biggest thing to hit there since the Allied invasion. But I was used to that. What impressed me was how Dad could pull off such a surprise from a continent away, between our nightly phone calls.

(My father was so resourceful that I thought he could do just about anything. On another occasion he invited me to meet him in Monte Carlo for the weekend, adding, "I have a big surprise for you." On our landing approach into Nice, I looked down—into a brilliant display of fireworks. I was awestruck: *My God, that is a surprise. How on earth did he do that?* But when I bubbled over to Dad about his wonderful present, he smiled and gently said, "It's Bastille Day, Pigeon.")

I returned to California for good in late 1970, not feeling very well. Mom took me to see our family friend Red Krohn, gynecologist to the stars. A pioneer in hormone replacement therapy, Red was known for his discretion—and for his love of gifts from his affluent clientele.

After a battery of tests, Red discovered a mass on my left ovary that would have to be surgically removed. My mother and sister accompanied me to Cedars of Lebanon and saw me off into surgery. We didn't tell Dad. He'd been through so much of late that I didn't want to worry him.

We were always trying to protect him, I guess. Old habits die hard.

By the time they'd wheeled me out of recovery and back into my room, it was light again the next day. As I emerged from anesthesia, I heard a creaking noise. Disoriented though I was, I could tell that I was not alone. I looked over to the window . . . and there was my father, silhouetted by the light, rocking in a chair and doing a crossword puzzle.

Our eyes met, and I sensed something wasn't quite right. As he leaned over my bed to kiss me, I said, "Hi, Pop, is it over?"

He said, "Yes, Sweetheart," but there was something about his tone that lingered with me as I drifted off again.

In the course of my abdominal surgery, Red Krohn had discovered an added complication, something he hadn't anticipated: a pregnancy, already past the first trimester. To make matters worse, the doctor had betrayed my trust and taken it upon himself to bring my predicament to Dad.

When I found out, I felt foolish and embarrassed that I hadn't realized what was going on—and that Dad knew about my condition before I did.

It was three years before *Roe v. Wade*, and Red Krohn took the position that he couldn't simply give me an abortion. Instead, he performed a surgical procedure and induced me to miscarry at home. It was the most grueling experience of my life: a five-hour labor with a sutured abdominal wall.

Left to my own devices, I was really sick for a few weeks. Thank God for Mom, who was strong and steady through it all. Dad came by Nimes Road to visit me each day. He came without a word of judgment, not a single second guess. He may not have been the perfect husband and father, but he was the best friend a girl could have. The older I got, the better friends we'd become.

But behind their brave fronts, I knew that my parents

were deeply upset. They were paying for my careless-
ness, and I couldn't abide it. I vowed that I'd never hurt
them like that again.

A postscript: when Dad noticed that my bedroom
had a black-and-white television, he replaced it with a
color set, just to make my recuperation a little more
pleasant.

Then I later found out—*thank you very much*—that he'd
given a similar TV to Red Krohn.

✺

Dad set me up in my first apartment in Century City,
across from Fox Studios on Avenue of the Stars. No
bohemian downtown loft would do for his daughter. Dad
insisted on a good neighborhood and a doorman for
security. He paid my lease until I could take it over.

My neighbors included George Raft, Phil Silvers, and
David Janssen—my three godfathers, I'd call them, as
they were all old family friends (and probably kept a discreet eye out for me). I felt buoyantly independent,
nonetheless, and the move did wonders for my relationship with Mom.

I'd returned to my studies with Jeff Corey, among
others, and found periodic work as an actress. I could
earn $1,000 a day for episodes of *It Takes a Thief* or *Man-*

nix, and was cast by the producers for the *Fantasy Island* pilot. (As a result, I got to spend ten enjoyable days with Peter Lawford, whom Dad hadn't spoken to for years.) My reviews were generally good. But I gradually came to see my limitations—they may have been inhibitions and insecurities, but they amounted to the same thing. I lacked the confidence and ambition to become an actress; I wasn't driven enough.

On the other hand, I was intrigued by the creative side of the business. I liked the idea of working with writers and following a project full circle, from inception to completion. To make up for my missing business background, I became an agent under Arnold Stiefel. I cut my teeth on the likes of Robert Blake, star of the cop show *Baretta*. The joke was on me, because Robert was notorious as the most difficult client in the industry. One day I made a ninety-minute drive to the San Andreas National Forest to attend to his latest tantrum. When Robert saw me instead of Arnold, he broke up, and the crisis passed. But I still had to drive the ninety minutes home.

It was an exciting and unsettled time for me. I was searching for whatever would give me the drive to succeed, and learning all the time. (I was also debating whether to marry Wes Farrell, a record producer.) With an assist from my friend David Begelman, I'd move on to a production company under contract with MGM Studios.

I knew that Dad was in my corner regardless of what I chose to do. He got a kick out of my curiosity, and encouraged me to keep seeking my calling. He'd say things like, "You won't succeed if you don't enjoy the journey. You're young enough to experiment and explore—if you're not happy, move on."

As we've seen, Dad was more grasshopper than ant. He wasn't given to planning for our future. *Today is today,* his philosophy went, *and I'll be there for you always.* But he was also eager to launch his children into the world with some financial basis. As each of us reached maturity, he would gift a million dollars out of the proceeds of the sale of Reprise to Warner Records.

At the same time, Dad wanted us to be self-reliant and happy in ourselves. He never set us up with trust funds and vast stock portfolios; we wouldn't be clipping coupons each month. He just didn't think that way.

My father's retirement was an introspective time for him, when he walked away from everything but family and friends. He fell back on his twin passions of painting and art collecting; he especially liked Andrew Wyeth, Edward Hopper, and Childe Hassam.

I'd often accompany Dad to dinners and parties at friends' homes. Baseball games were a family affair, when we'd all limo out to Chávez Ravine. A diehard Dodger fan who'd been given his pick of seats, Dad chose a front-row box over the enemy dugout. He enjoyed interacting with the visiting players, and I became an accomplished baiter in my own right. I'd give Lou Piniella such a bad time that Dad would say to him, "Don't look at *me*—I've never seen her before in my life."

I was spending more time with my father than ever before, and I had a ball.

In the summer of 1972, Dad was in France while the latest publicity-seeking congressional committee dug into his alleged ties to the Mafia. He'd invited Mom and Nancy to fly over and join him. (I'd made my own summer plans with friends.) On the morning of their departure, however, Dad called my sister and said, "I wish I were coming the other way." Feeling weary and homesick, he'd decided to confront the committee and get it over with. He knew that he could be himself with his family, and that we'd give him an out. Mom and Nancy kept their disappointment to themselves, as usual.

The federal inquiry was just one of a long and fruitless series. Over the years, Dad would be scrutinized by the Nevada Gaming Control Board, the New Jersey State Commission on Investigation, the House Select Committee on Crime, the U.S. Justice Department, and the FBI. He would become, as Pete Hamill put it, "the most investigated American performer since John Wilkes Booth."

(I recently obtained Dad's 1,275-page FBI file through the Freedom of Information Act. Among its many gems: a 1945 letter from some good citizen in Topeka, Kansas, asking "if rumors were true that Major Bowes, Kate Smith and Frank Sinatra were German agents"; a 1947 article in the *New York Daily Mirror*, in which Dad denied that he sympathized "with Lenin and the Marx brothers"; a 1961 entry noting that Dad had come to Carnegie Hall "to pay tribute to the king of mass resistance struggles against racism and segregation, Martin Luther King"; a 1971 memo from the Bureau's New York field office to J. Edgar Hoover, stating that my father had been "diagnosed as having terminal cancer, and estimates of life expectancy vary to as little as two months.")

Yet none of these distinguished governmental bodies ever tied my father to a shred of illegal activity or criminal behavior. Dad was never indicted, much less convicted of anything. As far as I can tell, his crime lay in being Italian, and not giving a good goddamn about appearances—neither one of them hanging offenses, the last I checked.

※

Many famous people are famously cheap, but Dad wasn't one of them. He believed in living large, but also in giving large—and not just to his family. Even early on in his career, with a baby to feed, he was so compulsively charitable that Mom had to caution him to be careful. She knew he was capable of handing over his topcoat to a homeless man on the streets of New York. (She knew it because once Dad actually did it.)

Some might twist Dad's generosity to reflect some insecurity, or a drive to overcompensate for the things he'd missed out on as a boy. But what I can tell you is that my father simply loved to give and to share—and that he was far more comfortable giving than getting.

At times he'd be impossibly extravagant. At one dinner at Chasen's, even I was stunned by the party favor awaiting each woman at her place setting: a small box from Van Cleef & Arpels.

And inside each box, a diamonds-by-the-yard bracelet.

At other times Dad impressed with simple thoughtfulness. One evening, while preparing dinner at my home, he couldn't find an adequate strainer for the pasta. The next day a colander arrived at my door, big enough to strain linguine for the city of Hoboken.

After a party at the Gregory Pecks', Dad spied an empty wall in their foyer. He pointed and said, "You need a painting there, and I know just the one." Within a few days he'd *painted* them one, an abstract in harmony with the Pecks' terra-cotta tile floor.

I saw similar incidents repeated many times over, until I wondered if Dad kept a pad and pen in his pocket to make notes. (But I knew better, as he abhorred any bulges in his suits' clean lines. He never carried a wallet, or used a credit card. The only items in his pockets were a set of folded C-notes, held by a rubber band or a gold money clip; a house key on a bob; a few Kleenex tissues, individually folded; ten dimes for phone calls; and maybe a pack of Beeman's chewing gum or a roll of cherry Life Savers.)

A number of Dad's friends were elderly and very much alone in the world. They would depend on his help for food and shelter—people like Swifty Morgan, an old-time street vendor with rows of watches lining his jacket, or Joe E. Lewis, the comic who'd turned to drink and lost everything. During one of our trips to New York, Dad and I took Joe E. out to dinner. Dad watched him as you would an older parent—wiping his chin, making sure he ate enough. After a night of play, Dad and I walked him up to his tiny apartment. I watched as my father put his friend to bed with loving tenderness.

I would witness a similarly poignant moment one

summer in Biarritz, when we were poolside with a group of people including Bruce Cabot, the actor. Bruce looked very thin and frail. (Unbeknownst to me, he was dying of cancer.) The Atlantic coast of France is typically sunny from noon to three, at which point the fog rolls back in and brings a chill to the summer air. As the sky darkened, people grabbed towels for covering. But Dad saw that Bruce seemed unaware that he was shivering. Without a word, my father draped his windbreaker over his friend, so Bruce could hold it closed himself. I was the only one to notice the simple kindness.

Dad was acutely aware of his surroundings; if something needed to be done, he would do it. That instinct ran deep in him, even with complete strangers. It's been estimated that he raised more than a billion dollars for charity, for the most part through benefit performances worldwide. (Beyond contributing his services, Dad would go out-of-pocket to pay all expenses, including the cost of the orchestra.) But he also worked on a smaller scale. I remember sitting with him in our den in the desert, watching a news report of a Hispanic family whose home had burned in a Christmas tree fire. All their presents were destroyed. He picked up the phone and asked Sonny Golden, his lifelong friend and business manager, to find them and "send them a nickel"—anonymously, of course.

In Dad's parlance, a "nickel" was $5,000.

Then there was the day that Dad took me for ice cream sodas at Rumpelmayer's, off Central Park. As we sipped away, we saw a mother and small daughter at the toy counter, in heavy negotiations over an ornate Madame Alexander doll. ("Mommy, *please*." "I'm sorry, Sweetheart, but no, it's too expensive.")

As the two of them left the shop, Dad smiled at me and said, "C'mon." He paid for the doll and lit out down the sidewalk. As Dad caught up to them, he tapped the little girl on the shoulder and presented the doll in its opened box. With eyes large as saucers, she grabbed it. The mother was so startled that at first she didn't see who it was.

Dad was like the Lone Ranger; he didn't wait around for thanks. We jumped into our car and were gone in a flash, though not before I caught the mother's stunned look of recognition. And oh, the expression on that little girl.

❈

The Compound had by now expanded to ten bedrooms, and when Dad was resting at home, there were usually no vacancies. With no one relationship to center him, he filled his time with friends. He moved through life with a fraternity of chums, from the Rat Pack (a term to which we'd reluctantly succumbed) to his New York street guys to the Hollywood A-list. His guest list was amazingly diverse: from Cary Grant to Averell Harriman, from Yul Brynner to Dr. DeBakey.

I met the world around Dad's dinner table. It was a phenomenal experience, perhaps his greatest gift to me.

Dad's hospitality would often start with his private plane, the *Christina*, which shuttled guests from L.A. to Las Vegas or to his desert retreat. Repeat visitors to the Compound would stay in the same room, with either a king bed or two twins, depending on their needs. Each room would be stocked with robes and hair dryers, and a medicine cabinet with every toiletry item known to man: toothbrushes, razors, shaving cream, aspirin, and so on.

The Compound was like a luxury bed-and-breakfast, only better. The kitchen never closed, and Dad was always ready to share a bottle from his vast collection of the best French Bordeaux. For dinner, he might fly in pizza or fresh clams from New York. When Ruth Gordon confessed that she'd never tried a Maui onion, a sackful arrived the next day from Hawaii. And then there was the time Dad promised his guests a Mexican dinner—and flew them all to Acapulco.

Of my dad's countless friends, none was more devoted than Jilly Rizzo. With his fireplug build and glass eye and tortured English ("Don't *ax* me, I can't go dere!"), Jilly was a Soprano come to life. He was best known for his renowned nightclub in New York, which became Dad's favorite watering hole. Later he moved to Miami and lived on a houseboat with his second wife, Honey, a woman famous for her azure hair coloring. (She was known to Jilly's friends as "the blue Jew.")

The world was changing by the early seventies, and Dad felt safer keeping someone by him in public at all times. For many years that someone was Jilly. He provided protection and insulation, onstage or at dinner. I never saw him hit anyone, but I can testify that where Jilly went, crowds parted.

My father and Jilly were cut from the same cloth. Like Dad, he was impulsively generous, a street guy who never forgot his roots. And like Dad, Jilly was a hopeless prankster. He habitually carried a few cherry bombs in his pocket and would drop them in the oddest places, like the lobby of the Hotel de Paris in Monte Carlo.

One night at Chasen's, the comedian Pat Henry brought a date who'd had too much to drink—to the annoyance of my father, who frowned on sloppy imbibers. Dad and Jilly huddled. Twenty minutes later a private ambulance arrived, complete with stretcher, and they had the woman removed. (She went willingly.)

More than anyone I've ever known, my dad could mix with princes and paupers, and get them to mix together, too. Dad joked that Jilly would "clean up real good." Flawlessly pressed and manicured, he'd accompany my father to Buckingham Palace or the most elegant private homes in the south of France. He was a remarkable dancer, and could deliver an unforgettably fractured recital of "Gunga Din." Jilly mixed in any social circle just by being himself. People loved him. Women couldn't get enough of him. He eventually moved out to Palm Springs and opened another bar called Jilly's, just to stay close to Dad.

These two men shared a great comfort and cama-raderie. They'd relax by the pool through the day, read-ing the papers and talking sports and politics. They especially looked forward to Monday Night Football, when Jilly would place their bets with a bookmaker friend.

Jilly belonged to the whole family. He was crazy about Mom, and he'd referee between Dolly and Dad when they periodically locked horns. There wasn't anything he wouldn't do for any of us; he was always energetic and available. He didn't seem to need to sleep—a great quality for someone whose best friend is an insomniac. (Later we figured out that Jilly slept more than we'd thought. We'd be fooled by his glass eye, which often stayed open even when he was snoozing.)

At twenty-four, I would be voting for president for the first time. I'd been inspired by a Tom Hayden lecture on Vietnam and aligned myself with the McGovern campaign. At the suggestion of campaign organizers, I put together a group of actors—Jane Fonda, Jon Voight, and Cicely Tyson, to name a few—to take the voter registrar's test. Our goal was to register and rally people in the inner city, but first we needed to gain the community's acceptance.

As part of an event keyed to Ted Kennedy's appearance in South Central L.A., I was elected to present our voters' initiative at a Baptist church. As I spoke, I couldn't help but notice a ring of six large young men at the perimeter of the congregation. They stood at attention with arms crossed, their eyes locked on mine.

After I finished my presentation, two of the young men followed me into a private room. "You'll have our cooperation," one of them said, and I thanked him.

"Who were those guys?" I asked Jim Mahoney outside the church.

"You don't know?" he said, incredulous. "That was the Black Panthers."

I'd been auditioned, and the Panthers evidently liked what they'd heard. They would show up on all our street corners over the following weeks to help our initiative succeed.

I was bent on doing everything in my power to unseat Richard Nixon, whom I considered a hopeless hawk on the war. In the middle of the campaign, I drove down to the Compound for a weekend. I found myself by the pool with Sammy and Altovise Davis, Irving and Mary Lazar, Bill and Edie Goetz . . . and none other than Vice President Ted Agnew! He and his wife, Judy, had become regular visitors, to the point where our guest house was renamed Agnew House. "Never prejudge," Dad had warned me.

With my McGovern button proudly pinned to my bikini, I walked around the pool with my registrar's clipboard of duplicate forms, hawking my wares: "Who wants to register?" I wasn't expecting much of a response, but four or five hands went up, including Sammy's. With each new voter, I'd let out a yelp across the patio. Dad would say, "She got another Democrat," and Ted Agnew would howl with laughter. Whatever else he might have been, Ted was a good sport.

(Postelection, Ted invited me to a nonpartisan event in Baltimore, followed by a visit to the White House. He said, "I'm going to win you over if it's the last thing I do." Yet on the same trip I was entertained at a cocktail party by Pam and Averell Harriman. All of these people were friends of the family; I could venture anywhere along the political spectrum and find a warm reception.)

When I look back at that weekend in the desert, it reminds me of how my relationship with Dad was expanding. Our daily phone calls now featured political talks. I can't recall a week when I didn't get a packet of newspaper articles he'd ripped out for me, with his self-reminder—"For Tina"—handwritten on each one. I'd also get copies of his letters to the editor. Dad respected the printed word, and he liked to be the average Joe who'd write in with his two cents.

I knew that my father was no great fan of Richard Nixon (who, after all, was a Joe McCarthy protégé). For months I'd wheedled him to tell me which way he'd be voting. All he would say is, "I haven't decided yet." But given Dad's friendship with the Agnews and his deep reservations about McGovern, I should have foreseen what was coming on the five o'clock news one Friday. My father had endorsed Nixon, and it was all the more newsworthy because he'd been such an outspoken Democrat all his life.

My hair was on fire. I called him at the Compound and vented my spleen: "Damn it, Dad, I've been killing myself for McGovern, and now you come out for *Nixon?*" I couldn't believe what he'd done. While I'd been stationed for hours at shopping malls, registering fifty people in a day, he'd just swayed a trillion votes in a blink.

And Dad said, "That's the way it goes, kid—it's a free country." *Like I didn't know that.* Hearing how upset I was, he wisely suggested that I come down and talk it out. I huffed into my car, loaded for bear. One speeding ticket later, I arrived at the Compound in time for dessert. Dad had warned his houseguests that his liberal daughter was en route; it was cute the way he set it up.

We spent the weekend in earnest discussion, and I saw how much he respected and enjoyed my interest in the political process. He was never a parent who squelched you into following his lead. He wanted you to find your own voice. (The one time he got upset with me was when I didn't vote at all, in the '76 presidential election. "You can't *do* that," he reproached me. "That's not the way this country works.")

I decided to forgive him his appalling lapse in judgment, and we agreed to disagree. Some weeks later, when the Thomas Eagleton crisis paralyzed McGovern's campaign, Dad called me to see if I was okay. When I was hurting, he'd be more paternal than partisan, every time.

❧

In April 1973, three months after Nixon began his second term, the president invited my father to sing at a state dinner for Prime Minister Andreotti of Italy. After all those Democrats Dad had gone to bat for, dating back to FDR, it was the first time he'd ever sung at the White House.

Dad earned another perk that I especially appreciated. For years I'd kept track of his globe-trotting schedule through a monthly itinerary issued by Dorothy Uhlemann, his girl Friday. Now I had access to something better. Whenever I wanted to reach him, no matter where he had flown, I had simply to call the White House switchboard, identify myself, and ask them to find my dad for me. Within moments he'd be on the line. I tried it several times, and it worked like a charm.

Years later, Dad confided why the White House tracked his whereabouts: he served as a courier for the CIA and the State Department, a not uncommon practice for citizens with private planes and the ability to slip in and out of places. Sometimes he carried papers, other times people. "It's no big deal," Dad told me. "I'm never in any danger. But you cannot tell anybody about it."

And I never did, until now.

Ted Agnew's disgrace and resignation had no effect on his friendship with Dad. My father shielded the Agnews—who'd become sapped and old overnight—and made them welcome any time. He never froze them out.

What I came to see, once again, was that Dad cared nothing about a man's public reputation or popularity. As long as you were his friend and stayed loyal to him, he would repay you tenfold. He had stood by Albert Maltz, and now he would stand by the beleaguered Ted Agnew.

As Dad's politics shifted, he upset his old Hollywood liberal friends. Burt Lancaster, Gregory Peck, Warren Beatty—each would approach me and respectfully inquire, "What is he *thinking?*" For those who knew Dad when, it seemed almost a betrayal.

But from his own perspective, my father hadn't changed all that much. He was still an incorrigible maverick. Even as he took a right turn in electoral politics, Dad remained stubbornly left wing on many issues. He was pro-choice and against the death penalty. He supported handgun reform before the Brady bill made the gun control movement more popular. He was a patriot who proudly flew the nation's colors on his fifty-foot flagpole, but he was also the immigrants' son who believed in open borders.

Down the road, my father would stage Ronald Reagan's inaugural gala—twenty years after he'd done the same for JFK.

Onstage and off, he moved to his own beat.

In 1973, when Dad told us he was going back to work, I don't think anyone was surprised. He ended his sabbatical with a vengeance by moving his act into oversized venues, from Madison Square Garden to a soccer stadium in Rio de Janeiro before 175,000 people. It was all a far cry from the intimate Copa Room.

Twenty years earlier, the crooner had grown into the saloon singer nonpareil. Now, at an age when many popular artists wear out their voices or their welcomes, my father was reinventing himself once more: as an international icon.

In January 1974, I married Wes Farrell in a penthouse apartment at Caesars Palace. No sooner had I donned my wedding dress, with the help of Dolly, Mom, Nancy, and my dear friend Suzanne Pleshette Gallagher, than I broke out into an all-over nervous itch. As Suzanne scratched me in places I couldn't reach, all in attendance were laughing hysterically. The moment was broken by Dad's knock on the bedroom door, signaling it was time. As my very pregnant sister began the procession and the others took their seats, Dad and I had a moment to ourselves. I took his arm and said, "Oh Daddy, I'm terrified."

He was fatherly and comforting: "Don't worry, Pigeon, it's normal. You're going to be fine." As we stepped up to the doorway to the living room and into our guests' view, Dad added, sotto voce, "Besides, you can always get a divorce."

Already caught between terror and tears, now I had to hold back nervous laughter. With my mix of unruly emotions, I somehow made my way to the minister.

Less than four months later, Nancy gave birth to her first child with Hugh Lambert: a blue-eyed girl named Angela Jennifer, whom we'd all call A.J. As Nancy and I grew busier with our own households, Dad had to look elsewhere for social partners—not that he ever lacked for female companionship. My father was a gentleman of the old school, a man who genuinely loved women. He loved to entertain them, indulge them, share quiet and high times alike. He prized his female platonic friends for their keen minds, their sly humor and social grace. And they returned his admiration in full measure. (In the words of Marlene Dietrich: "He is the Mercedes-Benz of men!")

Four years after parting from Mia, Dad was starting to rethink his stance that he'd never marry again. My father might have been the consummate bachelor, but he was never really good on his own. Now he was staring straight at the furrowed face of sixty, looking to the rest of his life and to his dread of finding himself alone at the end of it. "There's nothing worse," he once told a writer, "than being an old swinger."

Enter Barbara Blakeley Oliver Marx. I'd had one or two passing encounters with Barbara at our tennis court in Palm Springs. Tall, blond, and athletic, she'd play with her friends Bea Korshak and Dinah Shore, or enlist as a doubles partner for Ted Agnew. I knew that Barbara lived across the seventeenth fairway at Tamarisk with her husband, Zeppo, the unfunny Marx brother. She was known as a good mixer, an excellent hand at gin rummy, and a social fixture at the Palm Springs Racquet Club. (Her friends dubbed her "Sunshine Girl" for her dogged cheeriness.)

I didn't really meet Barbara until the summer of 1971 in Monte Carlo, when I found her at my father's side.

Her presence didn't seem so important; Dad had neglected to tell me that she would be there.

Through our four days together, I saw nothing to give me pause. Barbara had a fetching energy about her, an ability to enjoy herself that is invaluable when you're with someone in close quarters. We got on just fine. True, she was a bit gruffer and tougher than his norm. On the other hand, a number of people I trusted, including Dinah Shore and Robert Wagner, thought she was perfectly swell.

In any case, I assumed that Dad knew better than to be serious with a married woman. I sensed no real affection between them. Though constantly smiling and eager to please, Barbara was also quite demure. She and Dad stayed at arm's length from each other. They behaved like casual companions; they just didn't seem smitten to me.

On instinct, I didn't trust the type, but it was nothing personal. What could I hold against Barbara? She was just passing through; Dad was still seeing Eva Gabor. I couldn't take Barbara's relationship with him seriously— I couldn't even see a relationship. And while I might have wondered about Barbara's marriage, I had no cause to suspect that Zeppo would soon be *zippo.*

As things turned out, of course, I wasn't the first person to underestimate Barbara Blakeley Oliver Marx.

6

The Climber

$\mathcal{B}$ ORN IN 1927, Barbara Blakeley grew up on the prairie in Bosworth, Missouri, a wheat and corn center where her grandparents owned the general store. Her father worked as a Safeway butcher in nearby Wichita, the big city to which young Barbara longed to move. "I was that proverbial toe-headed [sic] tomgirl who dreamed of faraway places," she confides in an unpublished memoir. "I vowed to pursue a life of excitement, no matter what." (Years later, to show how far she'd come, Barbara would delight in telling the squeamish how they killed the chickens back on the farm.)

After moving to Long Beach as a teenager, she met her first husband, a college student named Robert Oliver, while leading a parade as Miss Fiesta Queen. Before their brief marriage broke up, she bore her only child, Robert Oliver Jr., to be known to all as Bobby. Mother and son migrated to Las Vegas, where the Riviera hired Barbara as a showgirl "to float around and smile." This is where her life story took wing: Horatio Alger in a headdress.

To earn her $175 a week, Barbara was asked to repair to a swank piano lounge after the second show and "dress up" the room, to perch prettily on a chair and mix with the high rollers. It was there that she learned how to make a little extra at the craps table. (When her gentleman friend of the moment gave her hundred-dollar chips for gambling, an unwritten house rule allowed her to stash half of them in her bodice.) And it was there that she met Herbert "Zeppo" Marx.

"He was a lousy actor and he got out as soon as he could," Groucho Marx once said of his younger brother. But Zeppo parlayed a shrewd eye for talent into a small fortune as a Hollywood agent, then retired early to the desert. He presented Barbara with an offer "that seemed irresistible. He was lonely in Palm Springs. If I agreed to move there and be a part of his busy social life, he would pay for an apartment for me. . . . I thought, why not?"

Zeppo covered the costs of Bobby's private schooling, and Barbara quickly cottoned to the good life. But Zeppo was also twice her age, and Barbara got bored. So she left him and returned to Los Angeles, to work as a lead model for the notorious Mr. Blackwell. Observing her from ground zero, the designer was duly impressed.

"Barbara Blakeley was one of the most striking women I'd ever seen," Blackwell recalls in his autobiography, *From Rags to Bitches*. "Little did I realize that hidden beneath her soft smile and honeyed voice lurked a mind as cunning as [Anne Baxter's] in *All About Eve*. . . ."

Now past thirty, Barbara knew that her modeling days were numbered. And while Zeppo wasn't getting any younger, he was starting to look better and better. As Blackwell notes, "She was very ambitious. Not for a career, because she really didn't want to work. . . . [Barbara] bluntly stated that she was absolutely determined to marry a man of means. Zeppo Marx was her target; she'd succeed in landing the comic—or die trying."

Her boss helped Barbara borrow top-shelf jewelry and minks for her dates with Zeppo, so as not to seem transparently mercenary. As Blackwell puts it, "No one knew better than Barbara the power of illusion in catching and keeping a man, as she later proved so clearly. . . ."

Zeppo never knew what hit him. He proposed at Chasen's, and Barbara accepted before the old vaudevillian's knee could touch the floor. "Someone to take care of me," she considered. "Real security. It sounded like a nice life."

They were married in 1958.

Thirteen years later, Barbara was primed to move on. Her first romantic encounter with my father, breathlessly recounted, came one spring evening at the Compound. Barbara arrived unescorted; Zeppo, pleading fatigue, had stayed home with the television.

"I am a rather terrible flirt with nearly every male," Barbara admits to us, "and for a while that night Frank and I cruised each other—innocently, I thought. All of a sudden, he took me aside and led us into the kitchen. Wrapping his arms around me, he delivered a slow, hard kiss that almost made my ears fly off."

In June 1971, Barbara met my father for a tryst in Monaco, the trip where we intersected. Her timing was impeccable. It was just two weeks after Dad's farewell performance at the Los Angeles Music Center. He had no work, and no woman to revolve around—had he ever been more vulnerable?

Back in Palm Springs, Barbara and Zeppo showed up with increasing regularity for card games and dinners at the Compound. No one seemed to find this significant or suspicious—until December 1972, when Barbara filed for divorce from her seventy-two-year-old husband. Not long after, she moved into a nearby condo, which my father paid for. Zeppo, Blackwell concludes, "was a good launching pad to get Frank later on." The youngest Marx brother had lent Barbara the legitimacy she needed to move up in class; the Riviera receded to a vague and distant past.

With hindsight, the match seems as fated as a car crash. On one side we have the relentless strategist, a professional survivor to make Pamela Harriman proud.

And on the other side? Just the loneliest, most guileless man in the world.

As an ornament on Dad's arm, Barbara did nicely. She was nearly as tall as he was, and had good fashion sense; she'd passed a dozen summers in Europe for finishing school, with Zeppo footing the tuition. Once Dad started paying the freight, her taste only improved—the more money, after all, the finer the ensemble. And no one worked more overtime than Barbara (now well past forty) to stay as young looking as she could.

I didn't judge her on those counts. Nor did I begrudge my father this radical change of pace. I knew full well the frailties and demons that threaded through this accomplished man. He wanted an equal partner, was bored by anything less, yet he needed to be taken care of—and, no less, to have someone to care *for*. The older he got, the more he required his life's partner by his side.

Which brings us back to Barbara. She was accessible and enthusiastic, content to stand on the sideline and cheer on her man. Whatever Frank wanted was fine with her—and make no mistake, my father called the shots in those early days.

Barbara worked hard to mix with my dad's inner circle. She was an animated listener, and shared laughs with everyone from Henry Kissinger to Jilly Rizzo. If Barbara liked you, you saw nothing but smiles and clear skies.

From what I could see, Barbara also made for a good buffer against the irritations that could get under my father's skin. On one of our days together in Monte Carlo, Jilly was charged with renting a yacht for a catered picnic lunch and a ride around the harbor. No, he hadn't seen our boat, but it sounded great—it had some imposing, exotic name, like *Venus of the Seas*.

Our directions took us to the far end of the docks, past a string of enormous yachts, each bigger than the one before. One of them even came with a helicopter. But as we got farther from the yacht club, the boats began to get smaller. At the very end of the very last dock, we found this beat-up fiberglass fisherman's slip that smelled faintly of bait. It was all of about twenty-five feet long. The catered lunch was sitting in cardboard boxes on a cramped, turquoise-painted deck.

"This can't be right," Dad said.

Jilly didn't argue the point: "I've got ducks bigger than this in my bathtub."

"You big dope," my father said, "what the hell were you thinking?"

I was tempted to suggest that we skip the boat ride and make for a beach club instead, but I bit my tongue. Then Barbara caught my eye and whispered to me, "Let's just do this."

"Absolutely," I said, because neither of us wanted my father to be embarrassed, or to beat up on Jilly too much. So we circled the harbor for fifteen minutes, which appeased him, and Barbara was all smiles. She never skipped a beat; she knew how to neutralize a bad situation.

But some of the people closest to my father were less than charmed or disarmed by Dad's new love interest, even then. Jilly had reservations. So did Ruth Berle. And so did my sister, Nancy. With hindsight, Nancy thought it strange that Barbara had invited her and Mom over for margaritas—chez Zeppo—when her affair with Dad was still a secret. (Mom would say that Barbara was pursuing a classic military strategy: *Keep your friends close, keep your enemies closer.*)

While others looked on with quiet suspicion, Dolly, our salty-tongued grandmother, made her feelings plain. "I don't want no whore coming into this family!" she'd blurt out. (She'd pronounce the epithet *whoo-er*, the way they did back in New Jersey.) She and Dad had some huge falling-outs.

After I came back to the States and spent more time around Dad's new interest, I began to understand people's skepticism. Barbara's high gloss notwithstanding, Dad was working with less material here. She didn't bring out Dad's best side, as Mia had. He didn't show her his tenderness or good humor. He was hard on Barbara. He knew that he could behave any way he wanted and that she would still be there.

From Jilly came a story that worried me. Late one night in 1973, Dad and Barbara joined a bunch of his pals at Jilly's after-hours spot in New York. Barbara could drink with the best of them; she'd keep right up with my father, shot for shot. The men began talking politics, and then Barbara jumped in to voice her opinion. In slow motion, the whole table turned and gaped at her, as if she'd said the dumbest thing they'd heard that night.

My father laid into her: "What the hell do you know about anything? When I want to hear something from you, I'll ask you a question. Until then, you just *sit* there."

And Barbara sat there. Perhaps her tenure in Las Vegas had hardened her to men's contempt.

Why was Dad acting out like that? I wondered. *And why would she tolerate it?*

As the months passed into years, I kept making a big effort with Barbara. I genuinely felt for her, though I could tell she wasn't any pushover—there was steel inside those black-label cocktail dresses. I knew that Dad had broken it off with her more than once; Barbara seemed unsure of him, and rightly so.

I didn't foresee what she would become if given the chance. I didn't foresee my father *giving* her that chance. She felt to me like a substitute, a stopgap, a one-night stand with an extended visa.

I was still selling Barbara short.

☸

In honor of Dad's sixtieth birthday, Wes and I threw a party at our house at Sunset and Whittier Drive. The guest of honor looked especially youthful that day in a salmon shirt and brown jeans suit, Western cut. What we'd all remember is Dad's gift from Gene Kelly: the USC marching band, at full blast, advancing up the sidewalk from my driveway in perfect formation in the dark December evening.

Four months later, just before Easter 1975, I called Dorothy Uhlemann, Dad's secretary, in search of my mother. I hadn't heard from Mom in two days, a long gap for us. I spoke to my sister, who told me that Mom had called the day before to say she was "off on a little holiday with Dad" at a summer retreat we called the Mountain House, not far from the Compound. *That little trollop,* I thought. My parents were presumably not playing Parcheesi, and I was sure that Dad had put the word out to keep me uninformed.

I called them, and my father picked up the phone. "Hi, Pop, can I speak to my mother?" I asked sweetly.

"Why don't you mind your own business?" Dad growled.

Mom and Dad stayed up there for four or five days. It wasn't quite headline news, as they'd remained the closest of friends for the past twenty years—and something more than friends when my father was between marriages. (Three years after Barbara divorced Zeppo, my father was still resisting the charge to the altar.) Though Mom sustained a full social life, she'd never remarried and rarely dated seriously.

Shortly after my call to the Mountain House, we joined our parents for our traditional holiday gathering at the Compound. With four generations of Sinatras, from Dolly to A.J., Nancy's baby daughter, it was an especially close-knit time for us. I'd never seen my parents dearer with each other.

My mother had taken the guest cottage nearest my father's bedroom in the main house. They were discreet around their children, even then, and it was only after the lights were low and the kids safe in bed that Mom stepped out to be with the only man she ever loved.

It would be their last romantic interlude.

Two months later, in June, we reconvened for Amanda's christening at Nancy's home in Beverly Hills. The gossip had it that Dad and Barbara had broken up for the umpteenth time, and so my father arrived with a double surprise. He'd brought Barbara, who had a brand-new profile and looked ten years younger. She was wearing a gorgeous purple tweed suit—I remember it well, because it was almost identical to one I owned, except that she looked better in it.

But no one else was looking at Barbara's suit. Their eyes were locked on the new ring on her finger, the one with a diamond the size of a quail's egg.

They were engaged, but Dad had lacked the nerve to tell us. (He'd sent Mickey Rudin, the only courier in southern California with a six-figure retainer, to break the news to the glowering, cursing Dolly.) The whole family was agape. Heedless of the shock waves he'd created, my father took off early for a recording session—leaving his fresh-minted fiancée behind with Mom's sisters. It was very awkward for all concerned, especially for Barbara, and Mom and Nancy and I rallied around her.

For my sister and me, the secret engagement echoed Dad's elopement with Mia. He'd avoided us then because he knew that we'd panic about their age difference. But this wedding, this marriage, would be different. Rather than shut us out, my father would engulf us in the whole melodramatic saga. He was not going to do this one alone. He wanted us around him.

As it turned out, he would need all the support he could get.

The wedding was set for July 11, 1976, at Sunnylands, the Walter Annenberg estate in Rancho Mirage. Frankie was on the road and unavailable, but my sister and I stayed over at the Compound the night before. By breakfast the house was abuzz: The wedding might not take place after all. Barbara was balking at the prenuptial agreement, and Mickey Rudin was calling her bluff. The ceremony was off unless she signed.

That afternoon we made the short trip to Sunnylands. Nancy and I were mixing with the usual suspects—Ronnie and Nancy Reagan, Sammy and Altovise Davis—in the Annenbergs' living room, which was slightly smaller than a basketball court. Then Dad motioned us over to a remote corner of the room. He wanted a private word with his two daughters, and he didn't care if it was five minutes before the ceremony, or a mere twenty feet from where the judge was setting up. He was determined to come clean.

"I want you to know," Dad began, "that I've thought this over very carefully. I've thought a lot about Mother, and I really tried to make things work again with her, because it would have been great for all of us. I'll always love her, but this is the right thing for me right now. This marriage is best for me."

As my father leveled with us, as Gregory Peck and Ted Agnew patiently waited for the leading man to take his mark, my mind flashed to the previous December. My parents' liaison had been more serious than I'd assumed; Dad was still deeply ambivalent about Mom. He'd had only three children, only one spouse who'd known his name before it went up in lights. We were his nucleus, his home base, and he knew that his life would be blessedly simple and whole if he could figure out a way to stay with us.

My dad's inner life was a maze with no exit. What could you tell a man in such turmoil that he hadn't told himself a thousand times over? There was nothing to say, and I was glad when our family huddle was over. I felt queasy in the moment. I wanted to get out of it as quickly as possible.

I barely heard a word of the ceremony. My mind kept replaying what Dad had just revealed to us, and how nervous he'd seemed. I'd have expected him to be a little preoccupied, because he was a stickler for every detail at events big or small. But this went beyond that. Dad seemed pensive, even troubled.

When the judge asked Barbara, "Do you take this man for richer or poorer?" my father interjected, "Richer, richer." Everyone laughed, but Dad's face stayed straight. As he completed his vows, he sounded to me like a man who knew the terms of a deal and was determined to see it through. He would try like hell to make this marriage work.

The reception moved back to the Compound. Amid the festivities, I saw Nancy and Dolly huddling in a corner of Dad's projection room, welcoming guests in their vicinity, working hard to smile through their distress.

When someone in my father's position brings a new wife into a very bonded community, there is always an audition period. My father was prized by his friends, and they wanted to believe he'd be happy. At the reception I was approached by a number of wives, all of whom asked me more or less the same thing: "Do you think he'll be all right?" By which they meant, *Would Barbara take good care of him? Would she be up to the task—and instant stature—of being Mrs. Frank Sinatra?*

And I replied, "I can only hope so."

For my part, I wasn't panicking. I was willing to trust Dad's judgment. I figured he'd stay in this as long as he stayed happy. If the marriage didn't work out, Dad had the capacity to end it. He'd always known when to move on, without wavering.

In between calls to Mom, to make sure she was okay, I remember talking to my sister and trying to put a brighter face on things. "Look," I said, "we're all involved in our own lives, and it's probably going to be easier on everybody that he has a wife." I meant it, too, but Nancy was inconsolable. Her toast to Dad—"I hope that with Barbara you'll be less vulnerable"—was less than a ringing vote of confidence.

I felt more heartened later that evening, when I went outside for some air, arm in arm with Kirk Douglas. We strolled toward the oval swimming pool, and sat and talked for ten or fifteen minutes. It was a balmy summer night. The moon was big and brilliant in the desert sky. I felt I could breathe again.

As Kirk and I chatted, a tall, reedy, silver-haired man came out and approached us. It was Sidney Korshak, the legendary (and absolutely charming) attorney who'd cut his teeth with Al Capone, a man who could fix the bitterest labor dispute. Sidney had a unique perspective on the day's big event. He'd once courted my mother, in the late fifties, before marrying Bea Korshak, Barbara's matron of honor. He knew Dad's new bride better than any of us.

After settling into the next chaise longue, Sidney retrieved a black Flair pen from his breast pocket and handed it to me. "Keep this as a memento," he said amiably. "It just saved you a *lot* of money and aggravation."

Kirk and I traded quizzical glances. "I don't get it," I said.

It was the pen, Sidney explained, that Dad and Barbara had used to sign their prenuptial agreement. Just in time to seal the deal.

〰

My father's appeal to Barbara was obvious. At the age of sixty, he was still near the top of his considerable game. Sure, Frank had an edge about him. But that was part of his seductiveness, that and the yearning and fire he projected from the stage. If his untamed energy made him less manageable, it also upped his allure—and a woman as headstrong as Barbara must have figured she could rein him in, with time.

(Dad's energy isn't all that struck Barbara's fancy, however. Within a few months after the wedding, here is what she confided to a close mutual friend of ours: "This time, I married for money." Which might seem admirably candid, until we recall that she hadn't married Zeppo for green stamps.)

The other side of the equation—why Dad was drawn to Barbara—was more complex to me. To put it mildly, there were inconsistencies in Dad's emotional arc, in what he wanted or thought he needed. Barbara was an extreme for him, a full pendulum swing from Mia, not to mention Ava and Mom. But I believe that the swing was calculated.

Yes, my father could find refuge in denial; it was part of his survival packet. But when his future lay in the balance, he was neither oblivious nor unwitting. I've thought about this long and hard, and I think that he knew exactly what he was doing at Sunnylands that day in July. By confiding in his children before the ceremony, he was telling us that his decision was conscious, deliberate, and absolutely premeditated: marriage in the first degree.

When Sidney Korshak handed over that felt-tipped pen, something clicked for me. My father had struck a bargain. A trade-off. If he was going to try marriage one more time, he was going to get what he paid for and limit his risk. He knew that Barbara would be compliant and available. With no career distractions, she'd be content to tailor her days (and nights) to his lifestyle. She'd be committed to the marriage because she had so much riding on it; her wants and needs, though very different, were just as great as his. She would be a wife, a lover, a companion, maybe even a friend.

Not least, Barbara was a person who could withstand Dad's ups and downs. No matter how tough he might be to live with, he knew that she wouldn't run away. After all, she'd be amply rewarded: the jewelry and couture, the homes in the desert and in town, the New York apartment and two trips to Europe each year.

Dad liked a woman who liked the high life, and in Barbara he got what he wanted.

If I'm right, this union was profoundly cynical from the start, but it was also the best Dad thought he could do. He was an unsettled spirit who longed for home and hearth on the road, only to press his manager—*When do we go out again?*—by his third day back. In matters of the heart, he was much the same: restless and confused, compulsively seeking but never finding.

Could he be happy? Had he ever been truly happy? My father was a deeply feeling man who could not attain a meaningful intimate relationship. I don't know that he ever had faith in finding a soul mate, even during his pursuit of Ava. After that marriage imploded, he would hedge all emotional bets. He would keep a part of himself safe and shut off. As he once told me, "I will never hurt like that again."

Raised a Catholic, Dad figured he had it coming when he was miserable. He settled for less because he thought he deserved no more. His perpetual unease was part and parcel of his nature—and, I maintain, an integral part of his art.

Had he been a healthier, less tortured man, he might have been Perry Como.

If my father had trusted in happiness, he could have married Eva Gabor, who was good-hearted and mad about him. ("He treated me," she confided, "like a queen.") Or he might have gone back to my mother, who'd remain his loyal friend to the last years of his life. But in Dad's experience, happiness was combustible and fleeting. He wanted stability, permanence. All else was negotiable, and better to sell himself short than to come up empty. Dad wanted the protective shell of a marriage without its troublesome content—and in marched this tall blonde out of Central Casting, and at just the right time.

Looked at another way, his fourth marriage brought my father full circle. Ava was sui generis, the great passion of his life. Mom and Mia were both sweetly maternal. But with his last try, with Barbara, Frank finally got it right.

He finally married his mother.

I remember Dolly as a warm and fun-loving grand-mother—and as a self-serving, rough-and-ready woman who perpetually had her hand out. She used her son like a courtesan, and he'd give her the world; she just wanted more. She'd been forwarding her store bills to Dad since the early fifties, when he wasn't doing all that well. ("My mother's going to break me yet," he'd complain to Mom.) She thought nothing of bestowing gifts to her pals with her son's money. She would even borrow large sums from friends of Dad's, like Vic Damone, to my father's huge embarrassment.

Everyone in our family knew that Dad was so generous that you didn't have to ask for things—everyone, that is, but Dolly and Dad's newlywed bride. Like my grand-mother, Barbara would learn early on how to get what she wanted, and wouldn't hesitate to remind Dad when she hadn't. (Perhaps my grandmother bristled at Barbara because she saw her as competition—not just for her son's attention, but for his cash.)

With all this said, Dad's Faustian bargain would serve him well enough, at least as long as he stayed strong and in charge. He and Barbara would trade and negotiate and transact a life together. He wasn't so lonely anymore; she became a woman of means and social influence. For my part, I continued to give Barbara every benefit of the doubt, because I knew that this marriage would likely be his last. As Dad said more than once, "I do *not* want to do this again."

My father had no illusions about Barbara. She was exactly the right person for him—until she became exactly the wrong one.

Dad had no way of knowing that he'd pay dearly for this compromise, and that money would be the least of his losses. He couldn't have foreseen that this marriage would splinter his family and wound the people he cared most about in the world.

He'd had it all figured out . . . except for one crucial thing he'd overlooked.

My father couldn't see himself as needy or dependent or helpless.

Frank Sinatra never dreamed that he'd get *old*.

Dad wanted his mother close to him after Marty died. During his sabbatical, he moved Grandma into a house he'd bought next door, where she'd pore over the *Racing Form* with Jilly over breakfast each morning. (To help persuade Dolly to uproot herself, Dad also moved Grandpa's remains to the desert. Grandma came with Uncle Vincent, a tiny, darling man with a severe limp from World War I, where he'd earned a Purple Heart. With no family of his own, he'd lived with my grandparents since the late thirties.)

Dolly was Dad's cross to bear. They had a very particular dynamic. He adored her, indulged her, took care of her; she drove him crazy five times a day. Dolly knew all of Dad's buttons and freely pushed them. She'd exhaust him in a way that only she could get away with.

Their breach over Barbara cut deep and took months to heal. Then peace reigned for a while on Wonder Palm Drive, but soon they were at it once more. Dad would sigh and say, "She's not speaking to me again." They'd go for days without so much as a greeting—which wasn't easy, since they lived about a hundred yards apart.

In the end, it was Dolly's stubbornness that killed her.

At eighty-two, she still proudly followed her son's career and went to see him perform whenever she could. On January 6, 1977, Grandma was to join Dad and Barbara on a chartered jet to Las Vegas, where Dad was set to open at Caesars Palace. At the last minute, for some unarticulated reason, she changed her mind and opted to go later in the day.

Dad reluctantly agreed, on one condition: that Dolly leave before dark. It was a violent, stormy day, with the weather expected to worsen that evening. The chartered plane turned around and was set to take off again at three o'clock, but Dolly stalled and delayed, even after the pilots called her house to hurry her. She would leave when she was ready.

To her housekeeper's surprise, Dolly chose not to wear her best mink coat or good jewelry that day. She was in a strange, reflective, prayerful mood. As our gardener, Angel, delivered Dolly to the airport, she told him, "If anything happens to me, everything goes to my grandson."

The two pilots, meanwhile, were rushing Dolly and her friend, another older woman, to say good-bye and get on the plane. It was five o'clock, and the sky was darkening by the minute.

At five-thirty, Dorothy Uhlemann reached me at home and said, "Your father wants you to know that your grandmother's plane has gone off the radar screen. He wants you to sit tight and not go anywhere. He'll call you soon."

Dad did his first show, performing in shock and suspension, and even taped a Brazilian liquor commercial immediately afterward. But he sent apologies for the second show. There'd been no sign of Dolly's plane. When Dad called me from home, his voice was grim, his message honest: "It doesn't look good, Sweetheart." He told me to wait out the storm that night and come down as soon as I could the next morning.

Wes and I had separated shortly after Dad's wedding, and my friend Dan Melnick drove me down the next day;

I was too shaken to take the wheel. As we neared Dad's home on the freeway, under a cold, fierce rain and hail, we passed Mount San Gorgonio on my left, the natural barrier on the route between the Palm Springs Airport and Nevada. Its summit was engulfed in snow clouds. The mountain was so massive that it was hard to imagine a pilot running into it, but I knew that visibility had been awful the night before.

I arrived by lunchtime, and found Nancy and Hugh already there. Frankie had decided to stop at the Rialto checkpoint and jump into a survey helicopter, but the weather was still too inclement for flying.

Dad was stricken, but doing what he could to prop up the rest of us. We did a lot of quiet waiting together, and I couldn't help but remember the kidnapping. Only this was worse, because we all knew what the outcome would be.

The next day, when the storm broke, Dad went up in a helicopter. He came back with a face as blank as the one he'd worn after dropping the money for Frankie. He simply said, "We didn't find her."

They discovered the plane on the third day. A foot search revealed the bodies of Dolly and her friend. It was a piece of unexpected closure, as we'd been told that the search might not be completed until after the spring thaw. As Dad took the phone call, you could see a release in him, the horror a step removed. He would accept the news and comment only, "I didn't get a chance to say good-bye."

I went home, then returned for the funeral. A day or so after that, Nancy called me in a fury. She'd gone over to our grandmother's house to secure it and see what there was to be done. She found it stripped. China, silver, crystal, jewelry—gone.

It turned out that Barbara, who'd been in the family for ten minutes, had appointed herself custodian of Dolly's valuables. Wasting no time, she'd had them all moved to a locked closet in her dressing area at the Compound. Nancy harbored her resentment for weeks. I finally called Dad, who was surprised to hear what his wife had done, and said he would take care of it.

When Dad raised the issue with Barbara, she explained, "You're the sole heir, and I was protecting you." Dad handled the situation with gentle diplomacy, and thanked Barbara for her concern.

When the boxes of Dolly's valuables came back to her house, a number of things were not there: furs and jewelry, and several of Grandma's finer handbags. Had Dad told Barbara to keep these things? If he had, it wouldn't have made us feel any better. After Frankie gladly ceded the remainder of his "inheritance," we divided a few things among us for keepsakes and packed up the rest for the next generation.

I thought the brouhaha was funny at the time, much ado about a porcelain bird collection. But as I look back, it was a telling event. Barbara's first instinct had been to grab any family assets she could lay her hands on. She'd been "protecting" Dad's interests, she said. But from whom?

The answer was obvious, and disturbing. Barbara was protecting my father from the people she perceived as her stiffest remaining competition.

From his children.

❋

Dinah Shore, one of Barbara's best friends, once observed, "Her son has always been the most important thing in her life." When Barbara worked in Las Vegas, they must have been close as only a single mother and an only child can be. (Picture the Demi Moore character in *Striptease*—a fiercely maternal type making peanut butter sandwiches by day, donning her feathers and spike heels at night.)

Barbara was nothing if not ambitious for her easygoing, gangly son. Some time after she married Zeppo, the boy became Bobby Marx. We naturally assumed he'd been adopted.

But Barbara was unhappy with Zeppo's paternal instincts. With Dad, she made up for lost time. Bobby surfaced in my father's company at every turn; he was flown to Dad's concert venues here and abroad. Soon he'd be added to the road staff.

Our family expanded, and Dad expected us to embrace Barbara and her son as he had. I'd known Bobby for years prior to the marriage, and enjoyed him; he was like the kid brother I'd never had. It was all okay, until . . .

The first call came from Mickey Rudin himself in the spring of 1977, less than a year after the wedding. "Your dad needs help, and you're just the girl for the job," he told me, in that raspy voice that could make him sound conspiratorial. "Your father's inches away from adopting Bobby."

"You've got to be kidding," I said.

"I'm dead serious," Mickey said. "I'm doing all I can to stop it, but I'm not making a dent. You better step in, and quick."

I was stunned, though not panicking—there's no point to panicking when you're dropped headfirst into the Twilight Zone. *This makes no sense—who adopts a twenty-five-year-old man? . . . Only one person, my openhearted father . . . Has anyone asked Bobby? Won't he be embarrassed? Or did he get a new name each time Barbara snared a husband? . . . Was this a scenario for a John Huston movie?*

Before I could finish these flash cards of horror in my head, Nancy was on the line with Dad. She felt insulted.

Bobby Marx didn't deserve our name; he simply hadn't earned it.

"He doesn't have a father," Dad told her.

"Daddy, he has *two* fathers!" Nancy exclaimed.

"But they're really not around," Dad said weakly.

I was the next to call him, in my own inimitable style: "Are you out of your *mind*? The Sinatra name is a birthright and a bloodline and a *major* responsibility, and you can't just give it away." An adoption was out of the question, I said. I read Dad the riot act.

What was he thinking? Once I cooled down a bit, I began to see what might have led him to this pass, not that I liked it any better. Bobby Marx was an ideal companion for my father through those long weeks on tour. Relaxed and self-confident, he mixed easily with band members and minor royalty alike. Plus he could keep up with Dad's long hours after the show, no small virtue. Now that Nancy and I were busy with our domestic lives, and less available than before, Bobby filled part of the void.

Barbara would claim that the adoption was Dad's idea. While one suspects that she planted the seed, I was willing to believe her, because he'd always wanted a big family. In my father's heart, there was always room for one more. But it was also clear that he hadn't thought the implications through. He was an easy touch, and Bobby had touched him; Dad was a man who led with his heart.

You must also understand that my father's tough-guy persona was mostly a protective coating. He might have been aggressive in business and bold in his craft, but in private life, as my mother would say, he followed the path of least resistance. He never wanted to let anyone down; he hated to say no. (Which is why his children wouldn't ask him for anything compromising, because we *knew* that he could be so easily manipulated.)

Left to his own devices, Dad would do the right thing. But when pressured and pulled and forced to take sides, he would splinter. He'd tune out and shut down; he'd do anything to avoid a confrontation with someone close to him. In fighting the adoption, I realized that I was putting him in an untenable position with his wife. I was forcing him into a corner, his least favorite real estate, and I could hear the anger in his voice when we went toe to toe. It was the first time we'd ever clashed like this. (But, sadly, not the last.)

And I didn't care, because there comes a time when you cannot please everyone. My father was going to have to let *somebody* down, and I'd vowed that it wouldn't be me. Up to that point in my life, I had never let him hurt me, not in any serious way, because I knew that it would level me. Call it stubbornness, or the hypersensitivity of a girl whose father had left home before she knew what it felt like to have him there.

I also had to consider Frankie. After all that he'd been through—the divorce, the exile, the abduction and court-room slander—he'd rebounded in the early seventies. Through his music he'd found himself, and a common ground with Dad. My father admired Frankie's ambition; it must have taken him back to his own early career. Though the two of them were usually road-bound, they shared a new ease and closeness whenever they came together.

And then, just as his wounds were finally healing, Frankie found himself saddled with this gregarious step-brother for whom Dad had all the time in the world.

When we were younger, Mom recalls, Frankie was the least comfortable with sharing Dad over holidays at the Compound. While Nancy and I had great fun with our father's friends, Frankie sometimes felt crowded out to the margins. He wanted Dad's more exclusive attention, with-out the constellations of high-powered guests.

Given Frankie's history, he must have been jolted by the adoption scheme—even though, to this day, he main-tains that he was indifferent to it. He never revealed his hurt to my father, nor to me. He emotionally withdrew, instead, and took a backseat in the fray. But Mom told me what I already knew: that my brother was mortally offended by what was going on.

Before I realized it, the discord was splitting our family in two, *but the adoption would not die.* As the gossip spread, we became the brunt of unpleasant jokes from friends and foes alike. Nancy called on her therapist. My mother kept her feelings to herself, but I knew that she had to be suffering. Parenting was Mom's sacred ground with Dad, and now these near strangers were trespassing.

In the end, it took Mom to block the damn thing. She got a final storm warning from Mickey Rudin, who told her, "There's still time, but you better get involved, or it's going through."

With that, she called my father and said, "If it's not too late, I'd appreciate it if you would stop this—for my children's sake, as well as mine."

As if he'd been waiting for his cue, Dad said, "Okay, I'll see what I can do."

A few days later, Dad did a benefit for the Buckley School, where A.J. and her younger sister, Amanda, were enrolled. At concert's end, Dad brought his little granddaughters up with him, one by each hand, for their first public bow. Backstage, before rushing off to his limo to his plane to Palm Springs, he said to Frankie, "By the way, tell your sisters to relax—the adoption is off."

We never spoke with him about it again.

(Some time later, I discovered that Bobby hadn't been legally adopted by Zeppo, his name change notwithstanding. "It never happened," Robert Oliver informed me. "I wouldn't give my consent then, and I wouldn't give it now.")

On the evening of the benefit concert, I went back to the Lamberts' and put the girls to bed. Dad loved kids, drew them to him like a maypole, and I'd seen how joyful A.J. and Amanda had been with him that day. So I was surprised to see them teary eyed at bedtime, and asked what was wrong.

And Amanda said, between sniffles, "Pop-Pop was there, and then he *wasn't!*"

I felt like I'd been struck by a Buick. I saw myself in these little faces. My nieces were feeling the void I'd felt myself, that all too familiar part of the Sinatra heritage. Now I saw that I'd never stopped feeling it, really. When my father filled up the space around you, it was really *full*. This big force had swept over these little people, and then—*poof*—he was gone.

As the girls cried themselves to sleep, I turned to Nancy and said, "Boy, it's no wonder we're so screwed up!"

※

Looking back, I'm sure that Dad was seeking a way out of the adoption as soon as he realized how needless a mess it was. He wasn't brave about getting out of his jams. He needed our help, but couldn't enlist it directly, so he'd turned to the ever-ready Mickey Rudin.

I had no regrets about standing up to Dad. My siblings and I drew one big, fat, unanimous line. We didn't have the right to say no to Bobby Sinatra? The *hell* we didn't. Family and blood, first and forever—those were my father's words, his motto and cardinal principle.

The next time I saw Bobby Marx, I told him that I hoped he understood, but I didn't think an adoption was appropriate—surely he must have felt the same way.

"It's no big deal," he said. It was an awkward moment, but Bobby didn't seem hurt or angry. On the other hand, neither did he seem embarrassed by the notion of getting adopted. Bobby was his mother's loyal son.

As for Barbara? The adoption was her shot across the bow. It was the first sign that she'd go to great lengths to put herself and her son on an equal footing with Dad's family—and forty-five years of history be damned. This time her effort fell short. But as all of us would learn, Barbara was not easily discouraged.

She'd already claimed her first casualty. Frankie was a survivor from way back, but now he must have felt estranged, if not usurped. It was then that the ship really sailed on Dad and his son. As time passed, they drifted further apart. Though my nieces would call Frankie "Uncle Funny," Dad never saw that side of him. Shaking his head, he'd say, "The kid laughed once when he was ten years old, and he hasn't done it since."

֎

Having failed on the legal front, Barbara turned to the liturgical. Not long after the wedding, she'd begun the process of converting to Catholicism. (Her catechism coach, ironically enough, had been the devout Dolly Sinatra, trying to placate Dad by helping the once-scorned *whoo-er*.)

As we've noted, my father was not a religious man by nature. He had little use for a doctrine built upon that glum conception of original sin. Besides, he was never big on bowing to authority, whether congressional or holy. In his famous *Playboy* interview in 1965, he said: "I don't believe in a personal God to whom I look for comfort or for a natural on the next roll of the dice. . . . I'm for *anything* that gets you through the night, be it prayer, tranquilizers, or a bottle of Jack Daniel's."

Boy, would he change.

After Dolly's death, Nancy thinks, Dad had a full-fledged epiphany; he made a private pact with God then and there. While I'm less certain that Dad signed on the dotted line, I don't doubt that he became anxious about the hereafter.

In any case, Barbara chose the perfect time for her next step: a church wedding. To serve that end, she and Dad enlisted Father Tom Rooney, a Dublin-born priest who'd founded something called the World Mercy Fund.

Father Rooney would play Dad like a Stradivarius. My father was sixty-two years old and feeling terribly vulnerable. Like many men of his age and background, he was riddled with half-suppressed Catholic guilt. Soon he was attending Mass more often.

At Father Rooney's suggestion, Dad wrote a handsome check to the World Mercy Fund. Barbara got her church wedding.

But I am getting ahead of myself, because there was one small detail standing in their way: My father had already been married in the church. In 1939. To my mother.

Which is where Father Rooney came in. He helped engineer an annulment under the liberalized standards of the American church of the 1970s, and—*presto!*—my parents were no longer united in the eyes of God.

After Dad's annulment was granted, squaring him with the church, his marriage to Barbara was consecrated in New York in 1978. As you might have suspected, the Sinatra children were not invited. We didn't learn about the annulment until the following year, after Dad was photographed receiving Communion at St. Patrick's Cathedral and the newspapers picked up on it.

It was hard for me to grasp the implications of this latest development. Was I now illegitimate? A bastard at thirty? I didn't really care, but I couldn't resist calling Dad to ask.

"Don't be ridiculous," he said, but I could tell he was immediately uneasy about what Rooney had wrought.

My main concern was for Mom, who'd been devastated by the news. She'd been affronted when Father Rooney first approached her about the annulment, refused to sign off on his paperwork, and thought that would be the end of it. (In the old days, it would have been.) Now she felt betrayed by both the man she'd loved and the church she'd believed in. She took the annulment very personally. Except for weddings and funerals, she would never set foot in a church again.

"This has no effect on my children," Dad went on, "and please tell Mother that I never intended to say that our marriage didn't exist."

And I said, "Pop, what part of '*an-nul-ment*' don't you understand?"

My mother remained friendly and cordial with my father, and would see him whenever he dropped by. But that other door had closed when Dad married Barbara, and now Mom locked it. She surrendered the notion, once and for all, that he would ever come home to her. Nor would she have taken him.

Once again, Dad had put us in a pickle, and this time Mickey Rudin couldn't save us. My father probably figured that if the annulment was acceptable to the church, it couldn't possibly violate his ex-wife and children, and that Mom would understand. When it blew up in his face, he seemed baffled and dismayed. I don't believe he ever wittingly chose to negate us. He might have wanted to help his cause in heaven, but not at the price of hell on earth.

I couldn't laugh off the annulment, as I had Bobby Marx's adoption. I found it gratuitously hurtful, and stupid, but most of all frightening—less for what it achieved than for what it foretold. I could see an agenda gradually coming into focus. I didn't think Barbara would be content to be Dad's fourth wife; she wanted to be perceived as the only wife he'd ever had. She would control my father's future by erasing his history.

Which meant erasing Mom, and my siblings, and me.

❧

By 1979, household staff would note a distinct chill between Dad and Barbara. They were averaging one nasty fight a week and sleeping in separate bedrooms, a development that owed to more than Dad's chronic sleep disorder.

I know that my father was a handful to live with. I doubt that he could have been happy with *anyone* at that point in his life. But if he showed unkindness, I am sure that it was in kind. Barbara could extract the deep, dark anger out of Dad. She had a street fighter's résumé, and Dad was a withering counterpuncher. They hit each other below the belt and didn't stop when the bell rang.

The pattern was set early on. An argument would spark and billow through the house. Too often, it would escalate into Barbara's threatening to leave—and Dad offering to help her pack. By the next morning, however, if not sooner, he'd be contrite and ready to make up. He was always one to fight and forgive.

But Barbara was made of sterner stuff. She'd withhold her congeniality and conversation. She'd dish out the ultimate punishment, the one thing my father hated: the silent treatment. Barbara could sustain her grudge for days, until Dad was so sad and unsettled that he seemed angry with the world. He'd wear his pain on his face, and it was a piteous thing to see.

I'd call the house and ask Vine—Dad's longtime housekeeper, valet, and majordomo—how things were going. "Oh, well," she'd say, "it's very quiet around here. Why don't you come down—I know your dad would love to see you." Vine could be cryptic, but her meaning was clear.

Regardless of any domestic strife, invitations to the Compound's dinner parties remained the most sought after in town. The show would go on, and Barbara was careful to shield their friends from the turbulent truth. Dad hoped that the gatherings would distract his wife and break the ice between them, but it rarely worked that way. As soon as the last guest left, Barbara's smile quickly faded. Their détente was over.

The vitriol would only intensify through the first decade of their marriage. It couldn't have been easy on either of them, but I knew it was harder on Dad. When all else failed, he'd find Barbara's soft spot—the spot where she'd wear the latest bauble from Cartier, Dad's peace offering. And if a bauble wouldn't do, he'd buy Barbara a horse ranch, or a condo for her parents in Palm Springs, or a law school education for her son.

For Sonny, who'd watched Dad endure Dolly's endless demands, it was a disheartening case of déjà vu. "Your father was the most generous man I've ever met," he told me, "but he could never give his wife enough."

Nancy toured frequently with Dad in the early eighties. The most sensitive of his children, she took to charting his moods. When he was out on his own, Nancy found him his old self—eating and drinking after the show with Charlie Callas and whoever else dropped by, laughing his way through the night. But when Barbara was there to clamp a hand on his arm, Dad's toothy grin would shrink and fade. Her leash was short, his temper shorter.

My sister will never forget the time she took the adjoining bedroom in Dad's Waldorf Towers apartment after a night out in New York, and heard the angry voices rumble like a scene from *Who's Afraid of Virginia Woolf?* Stories like that would make my soul ache. I'd heard the folklore about Ava, and I wondered: *Was this what Dad was really like in relationships?* But I'd never seen him act this way with Mia, or with Mom.

This was not the man I'd known all my life.

The joy was draining out of Dad. It was a slow and gradual process, but progressive, like a long, wasting disease.

Nancy fretted over our father nonstop. She painted him as a victim, and Barbara as the Evil Empire, long before I came to believe she might be right. I took a cooler view back then. I hated to hear how unhealthy his marriage was already sounding, but Barbara was Dad's choice, and Dad's problem. *He'd made his bed . . .*

Then something happened that sucked me into the morass.

"How much would it cost me to get divorced?" Dad asked Mickey Rudin.

"Not as much as it will to stay married," the pragmatic Rudin replied.

In July 1983, after a trip to New York with Barbara, Dad returned alone to Palm Springs while his wife went on to Wimbledon with Bea Korshak. Late that night he placed a call to my mother. He was miserable. He was crying. He'd realized that his marriage to Barbara was a false floor, and he'd fallen through it with a thud.

"I never should have left you—I never should have left home," he told Mom. A few hours later, with sleep apparently hopeless, he called again to repeat his self-reproach, over and over. He spoke not a word about Barbara; he was looking at the whole of his life, at the road not taken.

"Frank, if you're unhappy, you can change it—you can do that," my mother said. "We're here for you."

The next morning, Mom called Vine to ask if my father had been drinking the night before.

"No, not at all," Vine said. "Not a drop."

꧁

"I don't want to be alone, but I may not have an option," Dad explained to me as he broke the news of his separation. "I said I was going to try this one more time, but I can't seem to make it work."

I tried to be sympathetic and understanding; I knew this was very hard on him. But with my close friends, I was as gleeful as a Munchkin after the house fell on Margaret Hamilton's sister. "I really think they're splitting up," I bubbled to Jacqueline Bisset. "He says it's a mistake and he wants to get out and—"

"Be careful," Jacqueline cautioned me. "Watch what you say. They may reconcile, and you don't want to be left on the outside."

She's right, I thought. But it was hard to contain myself. To this point, I hadn't thought much about how ugly and destructive Dad's marriage had become. If *he* was in denial, I was willing to join him. I'd avoided the subject—until it seemed that there might be an escape hatch, when I seized the opening. My father was vital and healthy. He had a lot of good years left, God willing, and it seemed a crime to foreclose them. It was time to show my true colors.

"You will not be alone if you leave her," I told him, in one of our heart-to-hearts. "Pop, this is better done earlier than later. If you're not happy, get out."

While my father was guarded in what he would tell me, I got a good read on his feelings through Nancy Reagan, for many years his close confidante. Dad was one of the first people she'd met in show business. When President Reagan was shot, Dad went straight to Washington to be at her side—he didn't call, he just showed up.

After Nancy became closeted in the White House, one of her outlets was to phone old friends back in California. Now she and Dad were speaking every night, at an appointed time, and my father was pouring his heart out.

Ten days into the separation, Barbara returned to Palm Springs. Dad knew that they had to talk, but had no idea where it would lead, and his heart must have lodged in his esophagus. Amid the hubbub, he missed his nightly phone to Nancy Reagan. Guessing something was up, she called him.

"I'm going to speak to Barbara," he said. "I'm just waiting for her to finish her massage."

Never a big fan of Barbara's, Nancy was flabbergasted: "You have to wait for her *massage* before you can see her? Francis, this woman is not for you. She's not going to make you happy. You've got one foot out the door—keep going!"

Rumor had it that Mickey had drawn up divorce papers. It was my father's last, best chance to get out. If he went back to Barbara this time, we all sensed, it would be for good. Even Dad had acknowledged that much.

But at the end of the day, when he stared straight into his heart and soul, the man blinked.

❋

My father went back out on tour with Nancy shortly after Barbara came home, their marriage still on the rocks. But Dad was under siege, his defenses weakening by the day.

The first offensive came from Jilly Rizzo, of all people. Jilly was the brother my father never had. He'd been around the block and then some; he knew Barbara's type from a hundred yards away, and naturally became one of her least favorite people. When he was among his pals, the mere mention of her name provoked Jilly to roll his one good eye and make a guttural sound from deep inside his barrel chest.

But now it was Jilly who tried to coax my father into patching things up. "If I would have left it alone the way it was," Jilly told a mutual friend of ours, "*I* would have ended up being Mrs. Frank Sinatra, and I wasn't ready for that." (Later on, after Barbara drove Jilly—among others—out of my father's life, he'd regret his counsel.)

The reconciliation wasn't secured, however, until Barbara showed up unannounced in Las Vegas. When Nancy walked into Dad's sitting room at Caesars Palace after a show, she found him sitting next to his wife at the bar. Barbara was teary and red-nosed, a picture of contrition and regret. At the next stool sat a stout older man with the pinkest skin and whitest hair—he reminded Nancy of

Donald Crisp in *Lassie Come Home*. He had a cocktail in his hand and a broad smile roofing his clerical collar.

"Meet Father Rooney, dear," my father said.

Since expediting the annulment, the good father had further entrenched himself with Dad. The *Los Angeles Herald Examiner* referred to him as "Frank Sinatra's personal priest," and he'd been well rewarded for his services. Dad and Barbara had raised money for the World Mercy Fund through a pro/celebrity tennis event at the Turnberry Isle Country Club in Miami. (The Father reportedly delighted his new set of patrons with his exploits on the dance floor, along with a heartfelt rendition of "Danny Boy.")

Over the next several weeks, Father Rooney made himself thoroughly at home at the Compound. He was smooth and insinuating in his soft-spoken way, a subtle sort of operator. When I saw my father take him seriously, I passed it off to Dad's playing the host, which no one did better. It didn't occur to me that Barbara had recruited Father Rooney as a marriage counselor. *What God has joined together, let no man put asunder . . .*

Well-meaning friends and dubious priests aside, my father probably would have come back to Barbara on his own. Given his track record, his age, and his loneliness, he had no place else to go. He couldn't endure the embarrassment of another public divorce, the whispers and talkshow jokes. He had to see the marriage through.

The escape hatch closed; the hook sank deeper. Barbara had weathered their marital crisis, and now she stood stronger than before. She'd be with us for the duration. I was convinced of that now, and I did what I could to make things right with Dad. "Look," I told him, "I guess you know how I really feel, but that's between you and me."

When it mattered, my father was trapped by a failure of will. By a loss of faith—by something missing inside. I think he knew how much he had to lose by staying with Barbara. On the other hand, he saw no gain in leaving her. If he couldn't love anyone again, if he just wasn't fit to be happy, a divorce would grant him nothing—nothing, that is, except his old terror of being alone.

Part Two

FROM
HELL TO
ETERNITY

7

Not a Pretty Picture

S INCE TIME IMMEMORIAL, stepparents and children have found themselves at loggerheads. Their conflicts fill the pages of myth, fairy tale, and Shakespeare. I hated to think that the Sinatras were descending to this cliché. But in the back of my mind, I couldn't stop thinking about what had happened with Gene Kelly and Fred Astaire and so many others. It sent a chill up my spinal column. I wanted desperately to believe that it couldn't happen to us.

Still, I found myself waiting for the next high heel to drop. A year or so after Dad and his wife reconciled, I heard something curious from Sonny Golden: Arthur Crowley was still being paid out of Dad's account. If the marriage was back in place, why was Barbara keeping her divorce lawyer? I asked Dad for one of our talks as soon as he came off his latest tour.

Ensconced in my small upstairs den, I gingerly told Dad that I was troubled by what I'd learned. What could this be about? Was it an omen of something to come?

It was obvious that Dad was surprised by the news, and that he wasn't pleased by it. He said he understood my qualms, and added, "I appreciate that you've tried to support this marriage—but I married her, you didn't. I'll handle this. It shouldn't be your problem."

In a fundamental way, however, it *was* my problem. My father and his children used a sort of shorthand, where not a lot had to be spoken. From the time I reached my majority, I recognized the role that Dad wished for me. I knew that I was an executor (along with Sonny Golden) of his will, but I didn't need a signed document to glean my father's intentions. Our understanding went deeper than words.

My sister and brother were focused on their careers as performers. I was the one with the time and temperament to take care of "the family business." For some reason Dad trusted that I'd be equal to the task. He saw something in me (long before I saw it in myself) that he'd rely on for the rest of his life.

The care and preservation of Dad's legacy was our long-standing family plan. But I knew that Dad and

Mickey Rudin had yet to deal with issues of succession—the long-term management of Dad's record catalogues, for example, or the guardianship of his Oscars and other awards.

Those two hours in my den would mark the beginning of a long and arduous process. We needed a master plan, and I didn't see one. I told Dad that I was looking to control what fell within the family's custodial domain: his memorabilia, the Reprise masters, the Capitol catalogue.

"They need a custodian," Dad agreed. "Tell Bob to call me—it's done." Then, with a glint in his blue eyes, he added his stock catchphrase: "This is easy. I thought you were going to ask me to do something hard."

Looking back, I believe that Dad was trying to get me out of the middle. He knew from experience that it was the last place I'd want to be.

At the same time, he was turning to someone he trusted absolutely, the man my father hoped I'd marry (as did Mom, Nancy, and Frankie, for that matter). Dad had befriended Bob Finkelstein in the mid-seventies, when Bob was a young lawyer working with Mickey Rudin. In the years that followed, Dad would repeatedly ask Bob to "take care of my children."

It would become a tougher job than either one of them had anticipated.

⚜

By the mid-eighties, Barbara was encouraging her husband to find a suitable *pied-à-terre* in town. Though the Compound had always suited Dad's needs, he obliged her—first by selling his bachelor pad on Bowmont, and then, in 1986, by purchasing a spacious, airy house on Foothill Road in Beverly Hills. (My father was so eager to please his wife that he paid more than $6 million for a property worth probably half that much. To this day, local realtors credit Dad for driving Beverly Hills home prices through the roof.)

To celebrate their new abode, Dad and Barbara invited us to a home-cooked Chinese dinner by Yvonne Shen, their housekeeper. The entire meal was wonderful, but my favorite part was the dessert from a Chinatown bakery, a white sponge cake with a fine sifting of powdered sugar. As I was leaving, I thanked Yvonne for dinner and added, "The next time you're in the neighborhood, please get an extra cake for me."

I thought nothing of it—until my mother told me what she'd heard had happened as the front door closed behind me. Barbara turned to Yvonne and told her, "You will not bother about the cake. You work for *me*, not for her."

But Yvonne said, "I work for Mr. S., and I will do anything I can for his children."

I was distressed to hear of Barbara's reaction—it seemed so void of familial feeling, and so unnecessary. It was just a cake, such a small, trivial thing.

And such a big signal.

🌿

In the fall of 1986, a most unattractive author put forth an even less attractive book about Dad that gained its fifteen minutes of notoriety. After mulling a futile suit to prevent the book's publication (prior restraint of speech and all that), my father ultimately took the high road and publicly ignored it. He issued a family gag order; we were not to respond in any way. It was particularly hard for Nancy and me to restrain ourselves—he'd been so viciously maligned—but we obeyed.

Two months after the book's publication, Dad cut short his tour and came home to the desert. It was a Sunday night and I was out to dinner, but of course Dorothy knew how to reach me. I heard the most dreaded words a child can hear: "Your dad's in the hospital." My father was in surgery at Eisenhower Medical Center for diverticulitis, a chronic condition often exacerbated by stress. The doctors were concerned about an abdominal infection and had suggested postponing surgery until a course of antibiotics could work their magic. But Dad wasn't having any of it—he was in pain, and he wanted the surgery done *now*.

Then Dorothy asked, "What's your blood type?" If I didn't feel the urgency already, that question shot me out the door and onto the freeway to Rancho Mirage. By midnight Bob and I had arrived. For reasons of security, they'd put Dad in a corner suite in the pediatric ward, where the corridors were lined with pictures of lambs and puppy dogs.

When I entered the suite, Dad was still in surgery. Barbara was in the sitting room with Dad's valet, Eddie. Barely glancing at me, she offered a curt hello and left the room.

Her reaction left me stunned. Whatever our differences, surely we were in this together—and hadn't she had Dorothy call me? I suddenly felt like an interloper.

Once alone with Eddie, I'd learn that Barbara was annoyed when she'd heard I was on my way. The revelation sickened me. I was thirty-eight years old, facing my father's mortality for the first time—and I'd crashed into Barbara's cold shoulder when I'd least expected it.

It was my first inkling of what I would come to see as an insidious pattern: the exclusion of my father's children from the central events of his life. At my next opportunity, I had a few quiet words with Barbara. I voiced my surprise that she was less than pleased to have my company and assistance.

To which Barbara replied, "You know what a private man your father is. He likes these things kept as quiet as possible."

With Dad lying in a hospital bed, it was an unassailable defense. In years to come, Barbara would repeatedly stand behind what Dad wanted, as only she could divine it—her pretext for total control. Her message came through loud and clear: *I'm in charge here.*

Dad was returned to his room hours later. I'd never seen him unconscious before, so helpless and frail. Over these past weeks he'd seemed unruffled, invulnerable to all the scuttlebutt. He was giving his children a life lesson in remaining above the fray. But even Dad had his breaking point.

I harked back to the tumultuous days of Ava, when he'd suffered his throat hemorrhage. Once again, his body had broken before his persona so much as bent.

The first days of Dad's recovery would yield precious hours of closeness for me and for Nancy, who arrived the next morning. (Barbara would be no happier to see my sister.) At times the morphine drip would knock Dad's guard down, and he'd meander into his deepest feelings:

I'm so sorry about the things I've done . . . I've hurt so many people, I've been so selfish . . .

At bottom, my father didn't think he deserved to be happy.

As always, Dad could rally better than anybody. As soon as the doctors gave the okay, he was off to Hawaii and a guest appearance on *Magnum, P.I.*, where he even did some of his own stunts. He was back on top of the heap, with the world on a string.

Upon his return from Hawaii, I told him about the incident at Eisenhower. I went on to express my wish: "When you are in jeopardy, we need to be a part of it."

Dad was perplexed by Barbara's tone and attitude with me. He offered, "I never wanted you kept out—you know better than that. I'll handle it."

Which was exactly what I needed to hear—that paternal reassurance that always made me feel better. All my life, my father had been the supreme handler of things. I could always count on him.

But my sense of security was fleeting. For the first time, I feared he might be losing the upper hand.

In the summer of 1987, while Dad struggled with a less than successful tour in Italy, Mickey Rudin was home in

California, recuperating from a heart attack. They were griping about each other like an old married couple, both stewing about making a change.

In the middle of the tour, Jeff Berkowitz, a young lawyer from Mickey's office, said he thought the two would patch things up—that they'd been together too long to separate.

But Bobby Marx, who'd accompanied Dad and Barbara to Europe, said, "I wouldn't be too sure."

The day after he got home, Dad wrote Mickey a letter asking him to step down as his manager but stay on to guide his legal affairs. Mickey blew up and sent a letter back that would irreparably sever their friendship. He resigned as Dad's manager and attorney before the end of the year.

Bobby's remark made me wonder about Barbara's involvement. While I cannot say that she instigated these events, the exit of Dad's alter ego—a man who held his power of attorney—would certainly not hurt her cause. My father had lost a most powerful and savvy protector.

༆

As my thirty-ninth birthday approached in June 1987, I told Dad that I'd like to spend it with friends in Palm

Springs while he and Barbara were vacationing in Europe. Great idea, Dad said. He always wanted us to use the Compound, whether or not he was there.

Elected as our sommelier, David Niven Jr. chose a Pouilly-Fuissé for my birthday celebration—a very nice wine, but not lavishly expensive. Bill Stapely, the butler, put out a generous spread of caviar. It was going to expire before Dad and Barbara returned home, he explained. If we didn't eat it, he'd have to throw it away.

Three weeks later, I received a heads-up from Vine, Dad's majordomo. They'd cut their trip short, and Barbara was in a rage as she hunted for the missing kilo of caviar. Knowing that I had to protect the staff, I called Barbara and told her that we'd eaten it.

She responded like Captain Queeg with the god-damned strawberries. "It was a gift," she said, "and your father and I were looking forward to enjoying it. Furthermore, how could you let that Niven boy—what's his name—into our wine closet?"

I said, "His name is David, and I didn't realize that would be a problem."

"You don't just barge in here," Barbara went on. "You know, we could have avoided this problem if you'd asked *me* about using the house."

"Dad didn't tell you?"

"But you're missing the point—this is *my* home." I

couldn't imagine her having this conversation with Bobby, but I did get her point.

For me, *l'affaire beluga* was more than just another gratuitous insult. It was a turning point, a day of reckoning. I would no longer tolerate my fifth-class citizenship at the Compound. Over the next few years, I'd do anything I could to avoid the scene of the crime. I even turned down invitations to our traditional gatherings at Thanksgiving and Easter, spending those times with Mom instead. (Nancy was doing the same.) Though I still spoke to Dad daily on the phone and saw him when he came to L.A., it seemed better for everyone if I stayed out of sight.

Besides, there were plenty of people to take our place: the Gregory Pecks, the George Schlatters, the Roger Moores, the Louis Jourdans. Bobby Marx would be there with his mother, of course, and the Pecks and Moores brought their grown children, as well.

By ceding my place in Dad's home, I would injure us both. In the process, I'd also forfeit many of my close friends, people I'd known through my father for all of my adult life. They took Dad's marriage for what it seemed on its happy-face surface. They didn't hear the cruel remarks that made the staff cringe; they didn't perceive the marital tension that was apparent to Nancy and me.

They found our distancing from Dad inexplicable, and inexcusable.

I know that my father felt our absence. He would be dressing before dinner, a safe time for phone calls, and he'd ask me: "Everybody's here with their children—why aren't mine here?"

I'd say, "The problem is, Dad, until she can treat me as well as you treat her son, I can't be with you."

Mom would anguish over our dilemma and say, "You need to see your father. It's important for him to be with his children." But I couldn't stomach Barbara's double standard, and I'd sadly come to the conclusion that my father could no longer defend me.

From here on, I was on my own.

🔱

As Dad's marriage entered its second decade, I heard a new concern from Vine, who was with him more than anyone. Dad's lifestyle was becoming quiet to a fault. My father was growing more isolated, cut off from human contact.

As his wife became busier with the Barbara Sinatra Children's Center, a facility for abused children, Dad saw less of her. His own clock remained stubbornly nocturnal; his day would begin as Barbara's wound down. It gradually seemed that they were sharing an address and little more.

Nancy and I were not Dad's only losses. Jilly Rizzo wouldn't say much—he wasn't that kind of a man—but we knew he felt unwelcome at the Compound. Thick skinned as he was, Jilly might have put up with Barbara's cold front, but he couldn't stand to watch his best friend suffer. I knew what he was going through. There is no greater strain than to see someone you love become less than whole.

After a drink or two, according to Jilly, Barbara's mean streak would surface. She'd ridicule Dad, even call him a has-been. It could get so bad that Jilly would have to leave the room. By the mid-eighties, he'd stopped coming back.

I was noticing more signs of depression in Dad. Our daily phone tradition flipped, as he initiated fewer of our calls. I'd call him instead, but I ached when I heard the sadness that resounded in three small words: "I miss you."

His emotions were easy to read; he was as transparent in conversation as in song.

But the reading did me little good, because Dad was stuck in those emotions. It was no use to bring Barbara's offenses to his notice—she wasn't going to change, and he was unable to intercede. To complain to him was like throwing rocks at a drowning man, and so I decided to stop.

I just had to let Dad go.

茶

The less I saw of my father, the more I worried about him. By 1988, his calls had become less and less frequent. He sounded listless and groggy, especially when idle at home. I was used to his melancholy, but this was something more.

At one point, Vine reached out for help to my sister. She said that she'd been told to give Dad "these pills" every day, and she was concerned about them.

Within days, Nancy paid Dad a welcome visit. Over the weekend she perused the half-dozen prescription pill bottles on his breakfast table. She found a diuretic, a sleeping pill, a barbiturate (for Dad's migraines), and a drug she'd never heard of, something called Elavil.

After doing some research, my sister grew alarmed. Though widely prescribed at the time as an antidepressant, Elavil was known for its significant side effects. The drug called for close and continual monitoring, and we feared that our father wasn't getting it.

Nancy and I were also concerned about Dad taking sedatives on top of sedatives, given the fact that he still

Dad was always the best date!
(and a very good dancer, too)
1972

42.

Jilly, Dad, and Frankie, 1965

43.

Las Vegas marquee, 1974

SINATRA THE FATHER
SINATRA THE DAUGHTER
SINATRA THE SON

PAT HENRY
WOODY HERMAN &
HIS ORCHESTRA
THE VETERANS

44.

Tina's twenty-first birthday, 1969

45.

Dad's sixtieth birthday, at my house, 1975

Frank and Tina at Chasen's, 1974 (Pardon the fur.)

48

Four generations of Sinatra women, 1974 (A.J.'s baptism)

49

Grandpop with his two best girls,
Easter Sunday, 1977, at the Compound

Thanksgiving, 1986

A.J., F.S., and Amanda, 1984

52.

53.

57.

54.

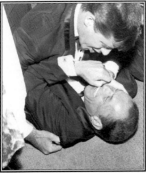

56.

55.

Dad's World

58.

59.

62.

61.

60.

A.J. dances poolside at
the Compound, Easter. 1977

Dad and Barbara, 1976

A.J. addressing those assembled at a party, December 12, 1994, Palm Springs.
That's Barbara in the foreground.

Ron and Nancy Reagan and F.S.

66.

67.

F.S., Dean, and Sammy at June 1968 birthday party for Dean, Nancy, and Tina

68.

Nancy, F.S., and Tina (at the same party)

69.

Tina and F.S. (at the same party)

Tina and Nancy, 1987

Malibu, 1994. Making an effort.

Dad, "Young at Heart." Toronto, 1994

Dad, me, and Phillip Casnoff, 1992

Amanda, Grandpop, grandson Michael, and A.J. Foothill, 1993

Bob, Tony O, Tina, and Amanda in Dad's kind of town—Chicago, 1995

The summer of 1995, Malibu

A moment between old friends, 1992

Father and son watch as the House of Representatives votes to present Dad the Congressional Gold Medal of Honor.

Note the crucifixes.

Frankie with the flag, May 20, 1998

1915—1998

enjoyed his nightcaps. It seemed dangerous to us. But nothing we did or said made any headway. Barbara felt the Elavil was working perfectly. She said the doctor agreed that it was needed to level Dad's mood swings and spare his heart.

"Your father's actually doing very well," she told my sister. "He's feeling better. I don't want you to worry about it." Dad was less argumentative, less trouble all around. Life was easier, smoother, more predictable.

Dad's children knew that he felt well when he was feisty. Over months and years to come, that side of him would seem to disappear. Dad became strangely tractable and subdued. He expressed neither joy nor sadness; he was smack in that middle plane of nowhere.

While Dad was appearing in Reno, a trip Barbara had passed on, I flew out to meet him. I looked forward to seeing him, and to see him perform—it had been a long time for me. But I was altogether unprepared for what I witnessed onstage that night. This consummate performer was *unsure*—tentative in his demeanor, unsteady of voice. I had not witnessed this before, and could barely bring myself to watch.

Concerned, I suggested that we go up to his room after the show, but Dad wanted to stop in the lounge, where a few friends awaited us. No sooner had we ordered our drinks than Dad said he thought he'd better head to his room, after all. I stayed back a few minutes to be polite—until I was summoned upstairs.

As I rushed into my father's room, I found him seated in a chair with his head down, pale and hyperventilating. Bill Stapely was having him breathe into a paper bag. After a long moment, it seemed to do the trick, but I was beyond terrified. According to Bill, Dad had forgotten that he'd already had his Elavil that day, and had taken a second dose by mistake.

I stayed with him till he slept, tuned to his every breath.

Dad's symptoms seemed to multiply by the month. Once the sharpest man I knew, with a phenomenal memory for numbers and dates, he became confused and forgetful. He'd get dizzy after standing up. At other times he'd lose his coordination and stumble. One day while driving, Dad found himself disoriented within blocks of the Compound. It happened only that once—he voluntarily surrendered his keys, never drove again.

These were all textbook side effects of Elavil, and we had to wonder why Dad wasn't switched to a less sedating antidepressant. While Barbara continued to be satisfied that Dad was getting the care he needed, his decline was a painful thing to watch.

For the better part of his life, my father was a reluctant pill taker, one who'd treat a splitting headache with baby aspirin. He would never have accepted this smorgasbord of medications had he not been so depressed, so out of touch with himself.

Dad's prenuptial agreement was pretty much standard for a high-profile individual marrying later in life. Beyond preserving all of Dad's premarriage assets as separate property, it also defined his future earnings as separate. Barbara would receive a generous monthly allowance. (After the agreement was signed, Dad would say to Sonny Golden, "We just added to our overhead.")

The prenup was fair and logical, since Dad had become *Frank Sinatra* long before Barbara Marx became Barbara Sinatra. Though my father was not one for legalisms, he and his wife had entered their marriage as a mutually beneficial exchange. Each understood the other's requirements.

It's safe to say that Barbara would not want for anything after marrying Dad. But Barbara kept asking for more, until Dad grew weary of the refrain. He told Sonny, "Just make sure she has enough, so I don't have to hear about it." Barbara's annual allowance quintupled into the high six figures.

After Mickey Rudin's resignation, Bob Finkelstein developed a closer working relationship with my father. Bob's first task was to settle the professional divorce between Dad and Mickey—a delicate, painful, intricate job. He went on to negotiate the rerelease of *The Manchurian Candidate* (on the shelf since JFK's assassination) and a number of performance contracts.

Bob also helped Dad flesh out the plans from the meeting in my den, years before. Dad made a gift of his Capitol royalties to his children. He sold us his interest in Bristol Inc., a corporation that controlled the masters of his Reprise recordings. (Dad would still receive his artist's royalty from Bristol.) He established a family business called Sheffield to govern the rights to his image and likeness, and created a three-member board to run it: Sonny, Bob, and me.

Within the same window, Dad placed a beer distributorship and some cash assets into the Somerset Trust. He was the sole beneficiary, with his three children succeeding him.

None of these moves were extraordinary for a man of my father's means and stature. There was just one unusual element: my father made Somerset an *irrevocable* trust. It could not be altered.

❈

Barbara was apparently not happy when Dad restructured his affairs. Since a number of assets had been taken off the board, she turned to his remaining separate property: his future fees as a performer and recording artist, and his real estate.

But Barbara had one small hurdle in her path, the contract she'd agreed to reluctantly a dozen years before—the document that Dad, a three-time divorcé, had required that she autograph before their wedding went forward.

A month after Sheffield was established, less than three months after Mickey's resignation, Dad and his wife signed an "Agreement to Rescind Pre-Marital Agreement." While it was common enough to modify a prenup after a marriage was well established, the contract prepared by Arthur Crowley's firm essentially tore it up in three perfunctory lines of type.

Under the agreement's terms, all that Dad had earned during the marriage—along with any future income—would fall into a community pool. Barbara would be entitled to 50 percent of everything. It would be as though the prenup had never existed—as though Sidney Korshak's Flair pen had vanished into a parallel universe.

(In fact, Barbara would take *more* than half of Dad's

income for the balance of his working life. Even after the prenup was rescinded, she would continue to get her six-figure allowance, along with anything else she asked for.)

I was especially troubled by the fact that Dad had signed the document without having a lawyer review it. My father had learned this lesson the hard way. (Back in 1939, in his contract with Tommy Dorsey, he'd signed away one-third of his income for life, a deal he'd later buy his way out of.) With assets as substantial and complex as Dad's, it seemed crazy for him to proceed without the full benefit of counsel. I couldn't help wondering what was going on behind closed doors in the desert.

My father always had the capacity to duck and cover when the emotional going got too tough. (As Mom would sagely say, "The unknowing person has a lot of freedom from pressure.") His passivity had cost him in the past, but now—given the woman he'd married—it was positively self-destructive.

The people who loved him tried to help, to no avail. Bob Finkelstein, in friendlier times Barbara's gin rummy chum and backgammon pal, was now persona non grata. Though Bob and I were no longer going together, we would remain the closest of friends—too close for Barbara's comfort. She was displeased with our control of Bristol, Sheffield, and the Somerset Trust. She made sure that he would no longer represent her husband.

After the rescission was signed, Sonny Golden recruited the prominent attorney Frank Rothman, an old friend of Dad's, to look after his interests. Frank sized up the situation and realized that Dad wasn't prepared to listen to him. He ultimately did the ethical thing: he quit. The vacuum remained.

According to paragraph F of the agreement to rescind, "Husband and Wife acknowledge that each of them has been represented by independent counsel . . . and that they fully understand and agree with the terms and conditions of this Agreement."

As far as I could see, that provision failed to square with the facts.

Arthur Crowley would later argue that Dad's counsel was aware of the terms of the rescission. But what counsel? Bob was out; Frank Rothman had not yet been retained. And it didn't clarify the situation when Crowley contended that the prenup was void from the start, because it was handed to Barbara shortly before the wedding ceremony—and that she signed it without reading it or consulting an attorney.

A look at the paper trail belied Crowley's contention. In a letter to Sidney Korshak dated July 7, 1976 (three days before the marriage), Mickey Rudin noted that he'd advised Barbara to seek independent counsel regarding the prenup—and that she'd received such counsel from

Sidney, even though he wasn't licensed to practice in California. Both Sidney and Barbara signed the letter in acknowledgment.

As far as I could tell, only one person was signing a document without a lawyer, and that was Dad.

The rescission was witnessed by Bill Stapely and Yvonne Shen, the butler and housekeeper. It was dated March 8, 1988, but I'm told that Barbara actually gave it to Dad two days later, on her birthday.

She knew that he was thoughtful that way.

※

In the spring of 1987, Dean Paul Martin—our beloved Dino—flew his Air National Guard Phantom jet into the same massive mountain that had claimed Dolly. He left behind a teenaged son—and a rich vein of memories of this warm, kind, and funny man. We loved Dino like one of our own; our whole family was grief-stricken.

Dad would say, "Fathers are not supposed to bury their children." He was torn up for Dean, worried constantly about him. A year after Dino's death, he coaxed his old friend into a twenty-stop Reunion Tour. Frank, Dean, and Sammy: the Summit revisited for one last uproarious hurrah.

For my father, the tour was a chance to recapture what

he'd lost for at least a few hours a night. He'd have two of his best friends to play with—what could be finer? As the kickoff approached, in March 1988, I heard Dad's old lilt again.

The reunion was a grand idea, and everyone's hopes were high, mine included. But when I saw the publicity photo, the age and fatigue written on those three famous faces, my heart sank. I wanted them to forget the whole thing and just stay home. I most worried about Dean. No one was surprised when he dropped out on the first leg. Fortunately, Liza Minnelli—who was like Dad's third daughter—stood ready to step in.

While his old friend hankered to sit back and relax, Dad held to the other road. Yes, he might have lost a step or two. But my father was still running for all he was worth.

❋

By the fall of 1988, Frank Rothman had come and gone as Dad's adviser, but not before leaving us with some fresh anxiety about the unknown. He told Sonny to keep an eye on Dad's affairs, and that he feared that trouble was afoot.

Alienated from family, oblivious to advice, Dad was

vulnerable. Nancy kept urging him, "Just don't sign any-thing, Daddy," and he'd promise her he wouldn't.

My father was his own best manager, in many ways ahead of his time. He was one of the first entertainers to own his own record label and produce his own movies. He understood his business as well as anyone, but he'd be the first to say he wasn't a businessman. Even at the height of his powers, he'd skirt the ramifications of his dealings. That's why he hired people he trusted, like Mickey and Sonny, to look out for him.

My father's passivity was most apparent on the home front, where Dolly had left a lasting imprint. She'd ham-mered it home that he could never do enough for some-one he loved, and Dad's wife picked up where his mother had left off. Dad would do almost anything to keep Bar-bara happy, if only to fend off the deep freeze—and her periodic threats to leave him. We suspected that the worse he was treated, the more dependent and malleable he became.

With this in mind, we put Vine on the alert. It wasn't long before she called Nancy and said that Dad was being pushed to sign some paper.

Vine added that Dad was resisting—for now.

My intuition told me that something precious was at stake. I wasn't so worried about the memorabilia dating from before 1976, as they remained his separate property. Dad knew better than anyone their historic and sentimental value. I assumed that he'd properly provided for them in the will he'd signed in the early eighties, when he was still very much in control of things.

But once the prenup was rescinded, the hundreds of honors and awards Dad received *after* 1976 could be deemed community property. If Barbara went after them, we might never see them again.

※

The legal vehicle they settled on was simple and conclusive. What Dad ultimately signed was a postmarital contract that made him and Barbara "joint tenants with the right of survivorship" for three parcels of real estate (along with their contents): the desert Compound, the nearby horse ranch, and the Foothill Road house in Beverly Hills.

Known as a "poor man's will," joint tenancy is rarely used in California within a marriage. For one thing, there are often steep tax disadvantages for the surviving spouse. In this case, the arrangement was a binding contract that—in contrast to a will—could not be freely changed.

There was, however, a method to the madness, a logical progression. By rescinding the prenup, Barbara and Dad had already converted a substantial portion of my father's separate property into community property. Barbara would now claim 50 percent of what Dad had made or acquired since 1976, *plus* her generous annual allowance.

Her job was incomplete, however, as Dad retained *his* half of their community property—along with the Compound, which remained separate. To this point, Dad could have willed any of this real estate to Barbara or to family or to charity, however he saw fit.

The joint tenancy contract erased that freedom. It tied up a sizable portion of Dad's assets—and, assuming that Barbara survived him, disenfranchised my father from his own real estate.

But Barbara was taking one big risk. If she failed to outlive my father, her heir could be disadvantaged; Bobby would lose the real estate unless Dad willed it to him.

On the other hand, the odds were stacked in Barbara's favor. She was twelve years Dad's junior, and descended from hearty Midwestern stock.

She was a survivor, born and bred.

By the time we found out about joint tenancy, in the summer of 1989, we had no recourse. I was distressed to hear that Dad had somehow agreed to sign another critical document without his own lawyer looking at it.

The property was not the issue. I'd assumed that the Compound and the rest of Dad's real estate was going to Barbara anyway. He would provide for his wife, and I wouldn't have had it any other way.

But I did have a concern for the irreplaceable personal items that predated his marriage and symbolized his life—items that I'd thought were his separate property, to do with however he chose. (Over the years to come, and culminating in an auction at Christie's in 1995, Barbara would liquidate many of these precious keepsakes and transfer the proceeds to a joint tenancy bank account. Once they were sold, of course, the issue of whom they should go to was moot.)

Barbara was welcome to Dad's Hoppers and French Impressionists, but I was desolate to think we'd be losing three portraits of our father that long preceded his fourth wife. There was one by Norman Rockwell; a second, more contemporary rendering; and a third—a gift from Ava in the 1960s—by Paul Clemens, the artist who'd captured Dad's spirit best. (Clemens's work graces the album cover for *Everything Happens to Me*.) My father expressly intended that each of his children might have one of the three portraits. Years earlier he'd wanted to dole them out to us, but I did the foolish, responsible thing: I declined.

Under joint tenancy, those paintings would be lost to us forever if Dad died before Barbara. They would go to Barbara's son upon her death, and then to succeeding Marxes for all time—unless, God forbid, somebody cashed them in.

※

That summer I asked Dad for another talk—this time with Barbara's representatives. I didn't particularly care whether she herself showed up or not.

We gathered at Sonny's office, around a table, in the following order: Arthur Crowley, Nick Cuneo (Arthur's associate), Barbara, Dad, Sonny, Bob, me. It marked the first time I'd come face-to-face with Arthur, who seemed perfectly typecast: short, thin, tanned, and very groomed, with a silvery hairpiece that perched on his head as though it had a life of its own.

It was my meeting, my agenda, so I jumped right in. I began by summarizing joint tenancy as I understood it, in lay terms. I explained how it differed from a life estate, where Dad's property would remain with Barbara for the rest of her days—her lifestyle wouldn't change one iota. Upon her death, Bobby Marx could receive whatever

Dad and Barbara had decided—as would Nancy, Frankie, and myself.

I directed my focus to Dad, careful not to confuse him. And then I asked him two simple questions.

First, did he understand what he'd signed?

"I'm not sure," Dad said.

Second, had he been represented by an attorney?

With all eyes on him, looking truly pathetic, Dad said, "No, I wasn't."

The expression on Barbara's face was priceless, suitable for framing. Turning to Arthur, I expressed my outrage and added, "That's the dumbest toupee I've ever seen!"

As soon as Dad answered my questions, we all knew the meeting was over. I kissed my father good-bye; he left with his wife and her minions.

To this day I'm shocked that Barbara took that meeting with me.

She would never take another one, that's for sure.

I was a child raised on a bedrock of security and trust. While our home might be "broken," it was never divided against itself. The Sinatras were inviolate, impenetrable. Family and blood, first and forever—those were my father's words, his motto and cardinal principle.

I adopted that principle as my own. As long as our family stayed united, all else was negotiable. Following my mother's lead, I compromised for Dad. I forgave him his omissions and weaknesses. With my siblings, I stood by him and loved him. We were *his*. Our loyalty was as natural as breathing.

But there was one thing I could not abide: to be denied as his daughter. Nor could I stand by and let anyone diminish Dad, or rob him of his dignity. He was a symbol of strength and fairness to the world, as well as to his family.

I was virtually born into a family of divorce; I came in after the fact and made the best of it. I didn't really *feel* my loss, full force, until Dad entered a marriage that had no room for us. My delayed reaction led me to a solemn promise: that I would not allow any further breach between us. I could not bear to be reduced or rejected. I would be the family's Jack Russell terrier; I'd get hold of Dad's leg and would not let go.

I wasn't diplomatic like Mom, or conciliatory like Nancy, or self-protectively contained as Frankie was. I wasn't a passive, dutiful daughter who would do as I was told. I was the monster child, the outspoken one, just as immovable as Dad.

If my obstinacy vexed him at times, it also saved us. Had I rolled over and allowed him to negate us, it would have been catastrophic on every level. I believe that it would have broken Dad's heart, and mine. We would have lost all relationship, the one loss that my father could not have survived.

❀

With the disclosure of joint tenancy, I thought we'd seen and heard it all. So imagine my surprise when Dad called me a few weeks later, angry and emphatic, and said, "You kids get yourself a good lawyer—a *court* lawyer."

I wasn't sure whether I'd received a declaration of war or a cry for help. Was my father telling us to protect ourselves—or to save him from himself? I was so taken aback that I called Vine for a weather report. It was bad between Barbara and Dad, she told me. "She's locked away in her room, and he's really suffering."

Within a week I'd be sitting with Bert Fields, one of the top entertainment lawyers in Hollywood. Bert understood the situation immediately, and seemed just as disgusted as we were by the rescission and joint tenancy.

A flurry of lawyer letters went back and forth. Crowley argued that Dad had been represented by Frank Rothman throughout the negotiations over joint tenancy and that my father had agreed to the terms. But Bert confirmed that Rothman had not seen the joint tenancy agreement before it was executed. Crowley's explanation—that he'd been asked to send the document directly to Sonny Golden, Dad's accountant—seemed less than persuasive to me.

But there was nothing we could do about Dad's predicament, short of challenging his competency in court. For me and my siblings, that was unthinkable. Dad was still *Frank Sinatra*, public icon. A competency battle would likely end his career.

Not to mention what it would do to his tender heart.

❋

In December 1989, still shell-shocked by what we'd learned that summer, I was summoned to Bob Finkelstein's office to meet with Eliot Weisman. With Mickey gone, Eliot had become the point man for Dad's management team, at the center of his business affairs—which worried me, since I knew how close he was to Barbara.

When Eliot asked what was on my mind, I didn't hold back. I began by telling him that it would be hard for me to trust him. Then I voiced my concern over Barbara's recent hiring of her own business manager, Marshall Gelfand—was Sonny about to follow Mickey down the gangplank?

"Sonny isn't going anywhere," Eliot said emphatically.

(He added that when Dad heard about Marshall, he'd made light of it: *What's the big deal? She already has her own divorce lawyer.*)

But what about Bobby Marx, then recently out of law school—was it true that he might be installed as Dad's full-time attorney?

"That will *never* happen," Eliot said. He promised that he'd find Dad an experienced lawyer.

"Look," Eliot continued, "I need this job like I need another ex-wife. But I really want to help your father out." From what Eliot was saying it was clear to me that Dad was being pulled in different directions, and that the pressure was taking its toll. "He feels terrible about you kids," Eliot added, "but he's got nowhere to turn. We've got to get him out of the middle."

Eliot must have sensed that I wasn't sold, because he caught up to me on the sidewalk after our meeting. "You've got to give me a chance," he said. "You have to believe that I have the best intentions for the family— the *whole* family.

"I can make this come out right for all of you."

❋

For Barbara, there was always a new frontier. Some months down the road, I'd discover that Dad's telephone warning had been triggered by her most ambitious maneuver to date. According to the grapevine, she was pressing Dad to restructure Somerset, Bristol, and Sheffield. If that was true, she apparently hoped to get my father to reclaim these entities and start over—leaving his separate property up for grabs.

Though that campaign was aborted, Dad's wife would persevere. When Sonny negotiated better royalty deals with Columbia and RCA, Barbara pushed unsuccessfully to get a cut. Her behavior provoked Dad and Sonny to the point of laughter.

Next, Barbara's attorney insisted that Dad stop using community funds for his alimony to my mother, and reimburse the community for past payments. Dad took the money out of his separate property, but nothing else changed. He and Mom had pledged to care for each other all their lives. Their love had nothing to do with contractual obligations.

It was the kind of relationship, it seemed to me, that Barbara could never understand.

⚜

I've thought a lot about those years of legal mayhem, and how they tore my father apart. With one hand he tried to protect his children; with the other, to satisfy his wife.

Dad was conscious enough to warn me to get a lawyer, yet incapable of protecting himself. He always did the best he could, but never felt that he was doing enough.

He could not win.

Barbara still had one more piece of paper up her sleeve—a new will that would remove me as executor and consolidate her gains. But this document needed a credible lawyer attached to it, to make it challenge-proof.

By 1991, Eliot thought he had found just the right man: the powerful and vastly wealthy Harvey Silbert, of the prestigious firm Loeb & Loeb. As it turned out, however, Harvey would prove no match for Barbara. His stewardship would culminate in Dad's new will—a document, as we shall see, that gave Dad's wife exactly what she wanted.

In the final analysis, I realized, it didn't matter who was advising Dad, or whether he had legal representation at all. Once a figure of legendary command, he would now defer to his wife.

To the bitter end.

8

Without a Trace

WHEN HUMPHREY BOGART died, rocking my third grader's psyche with the revelation that parents were mortal, Dad was quickly on the phone to me. "Don't worry about me, Sweetheart," he'd assure (and reassure) me. "I will never grow old. I'm going to be around for a long, long time." He meant it, and I believed him.

My father seemed impervious to mortality. But if the decade of the eighties robbed our family of its stability, it also stole a number of Dad's closest contemporaries. In numbing succession, I watched him bid farewell to Gordon Jenkins, Count Basie, Nelson Riddle, Orson Welles, Ruth Berle . . .

And then Ava got sick.

Though so many years had passed since their divorce, not a week went by without contact between Ava and Dad. Their tender affection was conveyed through funny notes and gifts, and routine phone calls. Dad advised Ava in her business affairs and provided whatever she needed that she could not afford.

I'd visit with Ava over the years, occasionally rooming with her at Dad's apartment in New York. The last time I saw her, at her London flat, she seemed frail and weary. Her beauty had faded, but not her feelings for my father, which spilled over in my presence. I could tell that she still loved him—that his adoration was thoroughly mutual.

Ava was always reclusive. When I left her, I sensed that I'd never see her again.

Sadly, her condition would only worsen. After Ava began failing, in 1989, Dad quietly monitored her progress until she became too ill to speak. He flew her in a private plane to see a specialist in Los Angeles. He did everything he could, until there was nothing more to be done.

When Ava died of pneumonia, on January 25, 1990, I awoke to the news and called Vine. Dad hadn't stirred from his room since receiving word the night before. I phoned again around dinnertime and Barbara answered. I wasn't surprised to hear that Dad was still holed up.

When he finally picked up on the extension in his room, he was distraught, barely audible. My heart broke for him. I wondered how long he'd stay in his room—and how he'd be received when he emerged.

Four months later, it was Sammy's turn. After they found a malignant tumor in his throat, he decided against surgery because it would have cost him his voice. He said, "If I can't sing, I'd rather die." At the end he lost his voice anyway, and communicated with chalk on a small blackboard.

Nancy and I sat vigil with Altovise, Sammy's wife, for the last few days of his life. I think Dad took comfort that we could stand in for him.

Sammy was the eternal little brother of Dad's troupe. As with Dino and Natalie Wood, my father felt that death had come out of order. Each time he'd search for acceptance but never found it. It took all he had to gather himself to go to Sammy's funeral, the last one that I would see him attend.

I didn't know how many more he could take.

When Dad established Sheffield in 1988, he cared relatively little about marketing revenue, though some added cash flow wouldn't have hurt. In the tradition of the John Wayne and Elvis Presley estates, the pioneers in celebrity licensing, he most wanted Sheffield to exert quality control over the use of his image and likeness.

As he'd say to me more than once, "Please don't let me wind up on a coffee mug."

Since then we'd pursued a handful of licensing deals: a gourmet pasta sauce line (Mom and Dad's idea), a series of musical collectibles with the Franklin Mint. My favorite was the Frank Sinatra Neckwear Collection, a set of silk print ties that borrowed its designs from Dad's abstract paintings. (My father enjoyed that project so much that we'd put out a coffee table book with Random House—*A Man and His Art*—and then a series of signed lithographs.)

Dad and I worked together informally. When I needed his input on a project, I asked him for it. Otherwise, he trusted my judgment.

After two years of operation, I was informed that Dad wanted to expand Sheffield's three-member board to six. Joining Sonny, Bob, and me would be Eliot Weisman, Harvey Silbert, and Bobby Marx.

I blew my stack. The proposal had Barbara's fingerprints all over it, and I took it personally—the obvious implication was that I wasn't doing well enough by Dad. You'd think I would have learned when to pick my battles by that point. But though I knew better, I felt betrayed. I balked—I refused to broaden the board. Finally Dad called me directly. "You don't understand," he said. "I *need* you to do this for me."

"The hell I will," I said, and hung up.

The next day Eliot called and told me that Dad was under a lot of pressure. "You've got to do this for him," he said.

But the only one who moved me was Mom, when she said, "You need to help your father here. He's cornered, and it's wrong of you to add to his problems."

With that I gave in—and realized it was much ado about nothing. Our board meetings got bigger and created the occasional annoyance. But I proceeded just as before, doing what I thought was right for Dad.

Why had I reacted so emotionally? Aside from the personal affront, Sheffield marked a line of demarcation for me. We were in the *legacy* business. Whatever else Barbara might grab for, she had no business butting in here.

✳

The brass plate by Dad's gate read, *If you ring this bell, you better have a damn good reason.* His sisal doormat was more succinct: GO AWAY. But if you knew my father, you knew that he was joking; he was the most accessible of celebrities. If you used Dad's private home number, in fact, you knew you were going to get the man himself.

But as depression became my father's constant companion, he withdrew from the telephone as well. It reached the point where Vine was doing all the calling: "Hi, Tina, it's your pop."

Before bowing out, Jilly had warned me, *Be careful on the phones.* Dad seemed oblivious to the caution, but he was repeatedly exasperated by Barbara when she'd "mistakenly" come on the line—"Hello, hel-*lo*." Aside from disrupting his conversation, she'd manage to find out who was on the other end. (It got so bad that Mom would furnish a cell phone to call her on for privacy.) Since the blowup at Sonny Golden's office, Barbara guarded access to Dad more zealously than ever. She trusted no one beyond her closest confidants and paid advisers.

I lost count of the times that people would tell me they'd tried to reach my dad, only to have Barbara intercept their calls and take messages that were never answered. I'd tell them to go through Dorothy "the Indispensable" Uhlemann, who could patch Dad in via her private tie-line at Sinatra Enterprises. Dorothy always got through because Barbara had to respect her business calls.

Sadly, all of that would change in January 1991, when Sinatra Enterprises was downsized, trading its proud studio address for a small office in Sonny Golden's annex. Only Eliot's intercession stopped Barbara from discharging Dorothy and closing the office altogether.

Meanwhile, Dad's home office in Palm Springs, which housed all his many awards and a twelve-car model train that circled overhead, was taken over by Barbara and her personal secretaries.

Friends, mobility, office, phone privacy—all lost relics of a man whose life was falling away.

I had always thought marriage should *embrace* and *liberate*. But I saw no tenderness embracing my father, and little liberty for his body or soul.

I just saw a life getting smaller and sadder—and more easily patrolled.

※

I knew we were in trouble when our pictures started vanishing. The grand piano's lowered lid was packed with silver gilt-framed photographs of everyone from Ronald Reagan to Don Rickles. There were pictures of friends and their children and godchildren. Bobby Marx was well represented, and A.J. and Amanda could be spotted here and there, but there was not a single picture of Nancy or Frankie or me. It was as though Dad had no children.

Out of sight . . .

Within the family, Barbara no longer bothered with appearances. Our visits, though less frequent, were no better received. In contrast to her patience and solicitude with Dad around outsiders, Barbara might be openly dismissive toward him, or even flip off the lights when we stayed up with him talking: time for bed.

When I noticed that Dad was coming out of his room later and later in the day, Barbara observed, "You know, he's not like this when you kids aren't here."

Ouch. I knew this wasn't true, because Jilly had complained of Dad's lethargy for months prior to his exile. But I mentioned it to Dad anyway. He knew exactly what I was talking about and angrily rejected the idea.

For quite some time now, my father had lived snugly in denial. To the extent that his flagging memory and Barbara's mood allowed, he could convince himself that he'd found the happiness he'd hankered for. But the presence of his children would jar him awake. By evoking his past, we placed his present circumstances in sharp relief. Whenever I left him—I would call a couple of times from the road, shortly after my departure, to soften our separation—I believed that it *did* make him sad.

For the first time in my life, I wondered if we perhaps were not making his situation worse. I thought back to the pain he'd felt in saying good-bye to us as children. *The very sight of your three little faces would nearly kill me.* Now we were saying good-bye to *his* sweet face. Now he was receding in our rearview mirror.

❋

Back in the 1970s, a feature film project on Dad's life had stalled in development. When he told me about the problems he was encountering, I suggested an alternative: a TV miniseries, which seemed more practical for a saga of this scale. I was simply offering my meager expertise, not looking for a job.

"That sounds good to me," Dad said. "You do it."

The next sound he heard was his daughter hyperventilating. I didn't feel competent or experienced enough to take on a project of this scale—and what if I were to fail him? I thought long and hard about it, sought counsel wherever I could. I'd be told by the likes of Burt Lancaster, my mentor, "Don't do it. You're just beginning to get your *own* identity in the business."

Burt's advice gave me pause, and I would take it to

Dad, but he thought Burt was wrong. And I couldn't disagree that his life story would be a fantastic challenge, an invaluable education in production. On a personal note, I thought of all the times that Nancy and Frankie had worked with Dad, an experience I'd never had. This would be *my* chance to bond with him on a professional level. It was such a grand opportunity, on so many levels, that I'd be a fool to turn it down.

It didn't take long for Warner Bros. and CBS to commit to the project. We started off with a press reception at Chasen's in December 1984. For Dad and me, it was a day of armed determination as we banded together to meet the media. Dad was warm and engaging with the reporters, not ordinarily his favorite cocktail buddies. He expressed his commitment and full support to the telling of his story, warts and all. We were off to the races.

The finish line was further off than we'd thought. Seven years and three writers later, in June of 1991, we'd be arm in arm again to celebrate the launch of production. Dad kept himself up to date through our evening phone calls; he was especially interested in casting.

I hadn't foreseen how difficult it would be to find the right man to play the title role. We had our pick of some very fine actors, but I was surprised at how one-dimensionally my father was perceived. Frustrated, I said to Dad, "I can't find anyone with a street edge who can come close to matching your polish."

And he said, "Then get a polished one, and rough him down."

Phillip Casnoff was polished and then some. When he walked into my office in his dark suit and open white shirt, I held my breath. Phillip was confident, subtly seductive. He had a background in musical theater, where he was best known for his roles in the Broadway productions of *Chess* and *Shogun*. He also had a wonderful chameleon quality; I'd seen him do a convincing job as a transsexual serial killer in a TV movie of the week.

Phillip captured my father's *edge*, his essence. As secure as I felt about him, I wanted fresh eyes to see his audition tape. I chose Sidney Poitier, who was blown away. Dad would have a similar reaction.

Preproduction took us through Christmas. We started shooting in February 1992, and the word of mouth was exceptional. We had a vivid script and a sterling cast, and were making the most expensive miniseries (at $18.5 million) to date. No one could tell Dad's complete story in five hours. But I believed that we'd arrived at a compelling psychological portrait of an exceedingly complex man. I was pleased for myself, and for Dad.

It was Dad's choice to wait to visit the set until everyone had settled in. Together we picked a date in

April, when we'd be on the studio lot, a must for security reasons. Dad would say a few words and meet everyone who'd worked so hard. Unbeknownst to me, the crew had planned a little presentation: a director's chair—his favorite orange, of course—with THE VOICE stenciled on the back.

The day before Dad was due, Dorothy Uhlemann told me that she was worried about the event. "He doesn't seem quite right," she said. "There's something going on." But I filed her warning away, never took it up with Dad—whatever else might be happening in his life, I knew that he'd do the right thing by me.

Come the great day, we had 150 of our people gathered at our set, and another hundred who'd collected around us after word got out. I greeted a number of actors who weren't even shooting that day, but had made a special trip just to lay eyes on Dad.

Zero hour was set for 3 P.M. At two-thirty, I got a call from Dorothy: Dad was sick. I called the Compound. He said, "I don't feel well—I'm so sorry."

I don't remember all of what I said before I hung up. I was simply flabbergasted.

When my father was under pressure, or faced with conflicting obligations, he had the capacity to wriggle out of his commitments. It was one of his well-honed survival skills. Back in the 1970s, when Dad asked out of his French holiday vacation with Mom and Nancy at the very last minute, I remember thinking that I wouldn't be able to bear it if Dad ever disappointed me that way. But now he'd done exactly that—and, to make it worse, it was being played out in public, on my professional turf.

This was my one opportunity to present my father to the people I'd been working with, and to show off my work to him. Given Dad's other commitments and our shooting schedule, I knew that there would be no second chance.

We'd missed our moment together.

After breaking the news to everybody, I walked over to my office for a good long cry.

When you live and work and collaborate with people, you become family. I returned to the set to much embracing. The cast and crew surprised me with flowers, and gifts for forwarding to Dad.

Lost as I was in my hurt and anger, I wasn't focused on my father's recent deterioration or what might be going on in *his* life. When I took the time to mull it over that weekend with Mom and Nancy and Vine, my perspective shifted. It was so unlike him to let me down so miserably. He should have been thrilled to be with us that afternoon—what was *happening* to him? Had he lost touch with all the pleasure in life?

I had many questions but few answers—just the

unsettling suspicion that something had gone horribly wrong for us all.

❊

In the midst of all of this muddle and resentment, my father lost his best friend.

With the banishment of Jilly Rizzo, Barbara had gone too far. Dad was now isolated to the point where he'd gotten too dependent on her. A few years after pushing Jilly out, she ushered him back into Dad's life.

For Dad it was a godsend, a breath of freedom regained. Jilly would pick Dad up for a dinner out with friends, or to watch Monday Night Football at a nearby restaurant. These boys' nights out were Barbara's idea, and she screened each evening's guest list. She favored local doctors, the respectable types.

Dad would have a great time: a few drinks and a lot of laughs, a chance for some unfettered phone time. When he called us at halftime, I heard joy in his voice for the first time in ages.

On May 5, 1992, the night before his seventy-fifth birthday, Jilly was at home with Tony Oppedisano (known to us as Tony O), a young musician friend who was cooking for the next day's festivities. Dad was really looking forward to it.

Because his master suite was under renovation, Jilly left for his girlfriend's shortly after midnight. It was a short drive, but Jilly never made it. A drunk driver broadsided his borrowed Jaguar, which exploded. The coroner would say that Jilly passed out from the smoke before the flames got to him.

When Tony and Barbara finally entered Dad's bedroom and told him, with a doctor friend there just in case, my father literally fell to his knees.

Jilly's death was a wound that would never heal. You don't replace friends when you're seventy-six years old. You just feel your world shrinking a little more around you, until there is scarcely room to breathe.

❧

Through months of postproduction on *Sinatra* that summer, I was still smarting over Dad's no-show. As we approached a September *TV Guide* photo shoot, I felt anxious, though I wasn't sure why. I drove to Foothill to clear the air. Once we were alone, I asked Dad if everything was all right with the miniseries.

He was vague, struggling to find the words. Then he said, "I really didn't feel well that day, but it wasn't a very good time, either."

When I asked him what he meant, Dad could only

repeat himself, and I didn't push it. And I said, as though words could inoculate, "Please do not *ever* let me down like that again, because I will die."

On my way home, I thought about the Douglases, the Reiners, the Thomases, the Fondas, the Bridgeses, the Redgraves—all the families who'd successfully collaborated in our business. God, I wanted that so desperately. I couldn't understand why it wasn't happening naturally, normally.

On the morning of the photo shoot, I awoke to a broken water pipe—and that would be the best part of my day. When my father arrived at Harry Langdon's studio in Beverly Hills, he seemed agitated and impatient, as though he were reluctantly doing someone a favor. Harry had shot Dad before, recognized the signs, and worked quickly.

That night I told Nancy about Dad's demeanor and she said, "He is *depressed*."

As we neared our November airdate, Warners and CBS spared no expense in promoting the miniseries. The New York reception was set at the Rainbow Room, where I'd introduce Phillip, Gina Gershon (who played Mom), and James Sadwith, our director. Then everyone would head over to Radio City, where Dad was performing with Shirley MacLaine. A hundred and fifty tickets had been acquired for the press.

I awoke at the crack of dawn, had breakfast with the *New York Times*, did two segments for *CBS Good Morning*, and taped radio interviews till midafternoon.

I got back to the Regency at three o'clock and—*wham*. Messages from Dorothy and Eliot: *Phone your father at the Waldorf—it's urgent.* This could not be good news. I didn't call; I walked. I wanted Dad to have to deal with me in front of him, and I knew I needed time to count to ten.

By the time I reached the Waldorf, I felt sure what lay in store for me: I was dead.

On autopilot, I stepped through the Towers entrance and into an open elevator. Dad's apartment door was open. I walked into the foyer, turned right into his room, found Dad peering out from under his covers. I sat down on the floor by his bed, my back to him, and took off my high heels.

"Hi, Sweetheart," Dad said tentatively.

"What's going on?" I said to Vine.

"Well, he's got a little fever," she said.

I looked at my father and said, "You're not going to perform tonight, right?"

He said, "I don't know if I can."

I'd passed into numb resignation. All I could keep thinking was, *This has been eight years of my life, and I'm fucking tired.*

Then Barbara entered the room with a small box from Cartier and said, "This is from your father to thank you for doing the miniseries." I opened it to find an inscribed gold cigarette lighter, something you might present to a contractor for completing the kitchen renovation on time. I looked at the lighter, and back at my dad. I kissed him and thanked him, and I left.

Now I would be mortified in front of the network and studio executives, plus the eastern seaboard press corps. I walked back to my hotel to make my round of depressing calls. I attended the Rainbow Room reception, gave my speech of apology and introduction. While the press went on to see Shirley MacLaine, I retreated to Patsy's with our little group from Los Angeles and threw back a fair amount of red wine, for lack of a bottle of Phenobarbitol.

And that lighter? I gave it to the first smoker friend I came across. I've never seen it since.

※

Sinatra was mostly well reviewed, silencing the skeptics who'd forecast a whitewash. It went on to win the Golden Globe for best miniseries. We received nine Emmy nominations, and won for best director and costume design.

I was gratified, but the review I cared most about was Dad's. The miniseries was a daughter's homage to her father and by far my greatest professional achievement, rolled into one. With hindsight, it could have been better. But I couldn't have made it more truthful, and we'd always been a family that respected the truth.

I needed my father to be proud of what I'd put together. To be proud of *me*.

For Dad's comfort and convenience, I sent the show down to the Compound. After several days, I called. And got Barbara's review, which was less than favorable. When I spoke to my father, he seemed sad and withdrawn; he said he hadn't been able to absorb it yet.

With hindsight, I realized that I had blundered by sending the tapes into enemy territory. Dad should have watched *Sinatra* in a safe, supportive environment. Had he viewed it with my mother, I believe that he would have enjoyed every frame.

To this day I don't know if he ever saw it all.

※

A week after *Sinatra* aired, I was puzzled. I'd heard from friends I had lost touch with. I'd received hundreds of letters from strangers. But I'd yet to get word one from Dad and Barbara's inner circle—from people who'd been close to our family since my childhood. Had they all hated it?

The mystery was solved at the Korshaks' Thanksgiving fest, where Tommy and Suzanne Pleshette Gallagher were annual participants. Suzanne made some casual comment about the miniseries, to which Katie Korshak, Bea and Sidney's teenaged granddaughter, replied, "Oh, we didn't watch it. Auntie Barbara didn't want us to see it."

And Suzanne, taking the opportunity to teach a life lesson, said, "That's okay, Sweetheart, but you shouldn't allow anyone to decide what you should read or see. Don't let anyone censor you that way."

I was genuinely appreciative when Suzanne relayed this conversation. Everything fell into place.

I would never mention the miniseries to my father or his wife again.

I'd envisioned *Sinatra* as a project for Dad and me to share on the deepest level. It should have been the most fulfilling experience of my life.

It wound up a knife through my heart.

❋

In the period that followed, I noticed that Dad's TV was starting to get louder. By the mid-nineties, you'd leave the den with your ears ringing, as though you'd been to a rock concert.

Dad's eyesight was fading as well. He had cataracts removed in 1993, but showed only slight improvement. His eye problems disrupted the rituals of a lifetime. Saying he was "out of ideas," he stopped painting, his avid hobby of fifty-some years. For a time he did his crossword puzzles by proxy, with Barbara reading the clues, but then called it quits. Reading became a physical chore, even with magnifier glasses. The daily newspapers he once consumed, front to back, now piled up untouched.

As long as I could remember, my father carried nothing smaller than a hundred-dollar bill. He was a grandiose tipper: $100 for a round of drinks, $200 for valet parking. But Eliot Weisman, reining Dad in where he could, replaced the hundreds with twenties. One day Dad complained to Tony O, "My eyesight is getting so bad, I can't seem to find any hundreds in here." He couldn't see any, Tony said, because there weren't any.

There was no getting around it. My father was showing his age—a fact that had made me uncomfortable when Eliot laid out his game plan for Dad back in 1989: "I can keep him on the road four or five years if we're lucky, two or three if we're not."

I thought they were pushing the envelope, but I

agreed with Eliot that Dad wasn't ready to call it quits. As his friends began to pass away around him, he had a standard line: "If I stop working, I know I'll be next." Music was his life force, what was left of his identity. The audience was where he lived.

His performances, sad to say, were becoming more and more uneven. Uncertain of his memory, he became dependent on TelePrompTers. Unfortunately, he couldn't see the words unless they were so large that only four or five would fit on the screen. On a bad night, Dad's once peerless phrasing would sound choppy, mechanical.

When I saw him at the Desert Inn, he struggled his way through the show, and felt so sickly at the end of it that he needed oxygen from the tank he kept on hand. In an appearance at the Riviera, he forgot the lyrics to "The Second Time Around," a ballad he'd sung a thousand times, and his adoring audience finished it for him.

At times like these, I would die a little. I couldn't bear to see Dad struggle in imperfection. I remembered all the times he'd cited one of Marty's old boxing maxims: "You gotta get out before you hit the mat." He wanted to go out at the top of his game, and I always thought he'd know when the time came.

But the same factors that hurt his performance also clouded Dad's judgment. He'd lost track of when to quit.

After seeing one too many of these fiascos, I went to

him and said, "Pop, you can stop now. You don't have to stay out on the road. You can ease up and relax."

A stricken expression passed over Dad's face, and he said, "No, I can't stop. I've got to earn more money, got to earn more money. I have to make sure that everyone's taken care of." He looked genuinely terrified.

Nancy and I would repeat this exchange with him countless times, and the dialogue never varied. We knew that Dad had more than enough money to live comfortably for several lifetimes—especially if he cut some unnecessary expenses. He was now supporting three houses: the Compound, Foothill, and a Malibu beach house he'd bought for Barbara in 1990. It seemed like a bloated overhead for a man pushing eighty, an artificially swollen lifestyle.

And Dad kept doing more: sixty-five dates in 1990, seventy-three in 1991, eighty-four in 1992. They weren't just commuter hops to Las Vegas, either. In 1991 he performed in seventeen different countries, from Ireland and Sweden to Australia and Japan.

Eliot told me that he needed "to keep your dad's income stream going, so that Barbara thinks she's getting an equal slice of the pie." His theory was that if Dad stopped working and had to tap into their community property, Barbara would make up the slack by taking it from his children. Eliot would say, "We don't want her invading your trust, now, do we?"

I believed that Eliot had real compassion for my father, but it's hard to gauge what's best for a client who is so unknowing himself.

In any case, Eliot's pie graph made no sense. There was nothing more to slice. Barbara had already corralled her share of Dad's postmarital income. Even so, Nancy and I suggested that he dip into the Somerset Trust if it would ease his way into retirement.

Whatever else Dad was losing, his guilt was still going strong. When Barbara harped that she and Bobby were being shortchanged, she struck Dad's deepest chord. If she intimidated or inflamed him, she also elicited his protectiveness. During one battle royal at Foothill, Barbara criticized a fee that Eliot had negotiated. She said, "You won't be earning much longer, so you need to make better deals—and you shouldn't be so worried about your children!"

She stormed upstairs, and Dad and Tony finished a drink in silence. And then Dad shook his head and said, "You know, deep down, she's really just a scared little girl."

Each morning toward dawn, as Dad finally looked to the refuge of sleep, Tony would overhear his nightly prayer: "God, give me my health. Let me provide for

Barbara and Nancy and Frankie and Tina, and for A.J. and Amanda."

Dad could never do enough for the people he cared about. Still, he was getting a little tired in the doing, and as he shut his eyes he'd amend his request: "But God, I don't want to make a ton of money. Just let me make a dollar more than I need."

＊

Whenever I heard my dad sing, we were on a special wavelength. I thought I could feel what he was feeling—which wasn't so far-fetched, since no singer's songs came more organically out of his life. He'd never failed to lift me in performance, ever since I was six years old and we traded our first showroom winks.

Until now, when I saw a man wrung dry, offstage and on.

The people who traveled with Dad always knew when Barbara was going to be in the audience that night—she'd be especially nice to him in the hours leading up to his performance. Tony and Vine could only wince when my father sang "Barbara" (a treacly ballad, soon mercifully interred), or roll their eyes when he'd pick out his "beautiful wife" in the audience, and Barbara would beam back at him like the most doting helpmate in the Western world.

The beating pulse of Dad's art, and his life, was his emotional conviction. He'd never been capable of sounding a false note. But now he sounded programmed, disconnected, at odds with himself.

For Dad's fans, it was enough just to see him; the music making hardly mattered anymore. But the press could be less reverential. After a disaster at the Westbury Music Fair on Long Island in June 1993, a *Newsday* critic wrote, "It was agony to watch the greatest entertainer of our lifetimes stumble around the stage, unable to read the seven oversized video screens that coached him with the lyrics. . . ."

For that entertainer's youngest child, the agony was exponential. It was like watching a puppy suffer. I couldn't take it, and so I stopped going, cold turkey—a radical, heartbreaking thing to do.

I never discussed my decision with Dad, nor did he question me about it. I think—I hope—he might have understood. But I knew he was missing me on the road, as I missed watching him. It would tug at me when Eliot called and said, "Would you *please* get your ass up to Vegas? Last night was a gem, he's sounding really good."

And I'd say, "That's great, but I can't." The reward wasn't worth the risk to me.

Like my father, I could really dig in.

Dad put up a good front with the best of them. But behind the bustle and deadlines and indiscriminate applause, a spirit was dying. I couldn't stop the grotesque merry-go-round, but I could sure as hell get off.

❋

In the early nineties, Eliot brought a duets album concept to Mo Ostin at Reprise, now a Warner subsidiary but still the distributor of Bristol's Sinatra catalogue. I told Mo that I didn't think Dad would ever return to the recording studio. He hadn't put out a new album since 1984, and I doubted he was up to the task.

We would not get a chance to reconsider. After his one call to Mo, Eliot jettisoned a thirty-year relationship with Reprise and took the duets project to Charles Koppelman at EMI/Capitol.

There was just one catch: the deal with Capitol infringed upon our Bristol contract regarding some of Dad's classic numbers. Under his agreement with Bristol, Dad could not rerecord any song in the Reprise catalogue as long as we were distributed by Warner/Reprise.

In addition, the deal violated Dad's cardinal business tenet, the first advice he'd given Nancy when she set out on her recording career: *Own your own masters.* The *Duets* masters would be owned by Capitol. As in so many aspects of his life, my dad had been spun around 180 degrees. The people directing his business affairs were focused on the short term.

I don't believe that Dad fathomed the agreement with Capitol any better than he'd grasped joint tenancy. But Barbara undoubtedly understood that any money made would be community property, with half going to her.

When I questioned the propriety of what was going on, Eliot fell back on his standard rationale: "This will keep Barbara off our back and out of the trust." The issue was moot, in any case. By the time we found out about Capitol's *Duets*, it was too late to do anything about it. Besides, it was the first time Dad had been excited about recording in years, and who was going to take that away from him?

One evening, against my better judgment, I surprised Dad by attending one of his sessions. He liked to have an audience when he recorded, and he'd always been a special treat to watch. The studio was his dominion, where he would soar. But I knew something was off that night as soon as I stepped into the engineer's booth. For the only time I can remember, my father wasn't happy to see me. He wore that put-upon look that reminded me of the *TV Guide* shoot.

It didn't get better once Dad started singing. From his

first cue, he was strained, uncomfortable, and frustrated—mostly with himself. I left as quickly as I could.

But when *Duets* was released that October, whatever its flaws, I thought it was a triumph. It would ultimately top *Billboard*'s chart and sell three million copies, the most commercially successful Sinatra album ever.

I was the one who got to call and congratulate him first when the album topped the million mark. "That's marvelous," he said, audibly preening. "That's wonderful."

And it was.

❋

In June 1993, I picked Dad up on the way to Amanda's high school graduation. I found him foggy and running late. Barbara was out, and for the first time I could remember, Vine seemed a little helpless. I wound up having to step in and help Dad get organized; I was shocked at how unfocused he was. I knew that mornings were tough for him, but he'd always been such a regimented man, never tardy.

By the time we made it to the Beverly High athletic field, Amanda had already received her diploma.

Once back in the land of the living, Dad was fine. His mood visibly improved at lunch at the Bistro Garden. He came alive, got his glint back—it was something that I'd see whenever he was with us, but that day he was especially vibrant. He happily signed autographs for tourists, posed for pictures with strangers at other tables. He was having the time of his life.

And I remember that Dad couldn't stop holding Mom's hand. When he left us that afternoon, he hugged her tight, like someone who hated letting go.

A week or so later, he flew back to L.A. for my forty-fifth birthday. Knowing how costly these trips could be for him, I was touched that he'd come. (Vine told us that whenever he saw his family, Barbara would withdraw from him back home for days afterward.)

Dad was in great spirits through the evening. But in the car, on the way to the airport, he started to cry. When he was with us, he explained to Tony, it gave him a glimpse of the life he might have had. He knew it would take him a few days to recover, he said, but it was worth it.

Though my father's family outings became rarer with time, he and Mom kept up over the phone. She lived on inside him. The qualities she represented—honesty, loyalty, kindness—had only grown in value. He still relied on Mom to tell him the truth. He'd remember the little things, like how she was the only woman who could reliably select the right tie for him. (When he made that observation in front of Barbara one day, you could feel the fur rising.)

Mom and Dad had discovered Palm Springs together, way back when. My mother sustained many friendships there over the years, and in 1994 she bought a condo just down the road from the Compound.

When my father was alone with Tony, he often spoke about patching things up with his first wife. One afternoon he took it a step further and asked to be taken to see her. But by the time Tony pulled into Mom's driveway, Dad had become cautious and confused. He could not get out of the car.

He could not go home again.

"He'd never stopped caring deeply for you," Tony wrote Mom sometime later. "He just never had the nerve to do anything about it."

As Mom would say, "I don't think you ever forget a first love. That was true for him, and true for me."

9

Down and Out
in Beverly Hills

I WOULD NEARLY be thrown from my bed in
the predawn hours of January 17, 1994. I awoke in total
darkness to a violent shaking and a noise so thunderous
that I covered my ears. My first thoughts went to Mom
and Nancy—if the quake was this bad up in the hills,
where Frankie and I lived, it was likely worse in the flats
below. I wondered about the epicenter—what if it was
near Dad in the desert?

My phones were dead; my emergency backup system
failed. I had no flashlight or working radio. My cell phone
was in the car. (I wasn't exactly the poster child for earth-

quake preparedness.) There was no light anywhere, except for flashes of spark and flame in the city below.

Cut off from the world, my house still heaving in the aftershocks, I sat paralyzed on my bed—until I heard a man calling my name from outside.

Frankie had driven out from two canyons away, swerving around downed trees and lampposts to make the rounds. He had already seen to Nancy and Mom, and now he'd make sure that I was safe. He gave me the confidence to come downstairs to the front door. Armed with his flashlight, we inspected my house—the damage was minimal. By the time Frankie suggested that he take me to Mom's, I felt secure enough to stay.

As he drove off, I felt like the tiny girl who'd locked herself in the bathroom until her brave big brother clambered onto the balcony to set her free. Frankie was still my protector, the guy I could count on in a pinch.

Like his father, Frankie was happiest when working. In a natural progression, he'd become Dad's musical director. Though it wasn't always an easy job, he was supremely competent, and Dad knew it. Without Frankie's support on the road, Dad couldn't have lasted as long as he did.

But if it was tough on Dad to see Nancy and me on our occasional visits, it had to unnerve him to work for weeks at a stretch with my brother. I know that Dad was proud of Frankie. They were mutually devoted and shared a great camaraderie, especially around the music they loved. But my father was not growing old gracefully. Angry and frustrated with himself, he lashed out at the person with whom he had most in common, and to whom he felt most exposed: his son. Dad had to pick on somebody, and Frankie was the safest target.

Frankie seemed to take these occasional caustic remarks in stride, and even made them a weird part of their act. But when Mom and Nancy and I heard about what they were going through, it broke our hearts. Dad's mistreatment of his son spoke to the depth of his problems—even to the loss of the man we'd always known.

҉

My father was seventy-eight years old. His antidepressant might not be working too well, but his public lifted his spirits each time he took his bows. Dad was fighting not to lose himself. The stage was his last bastion, the place where he was most comfortable and in control. As his powers diminished, he held tight to the edge of the precipice.

Tony found Dad at his clearest when he awoke in midafternoon, before he took his pill. The medication kicked in at the worst possible time—just as he was about to perform. In the wings, waiting to go on, Dad would feel light-headed and hazy, shaking his head in a vain effort to clear it. He'd tell Tony, "I need a dizzy pill." (On top of all his other medications, a prescription drug called Antivert had been added to Dad's regimen, to counter the Elavil's side effect.)

It was a testament to my father's willpower that he could stand out there under the lights for seventy minutes at a stretch, much less deliver a performance. His audience was thrilled to be in the same room. Even the critics had softened. It still took five hundred dollars and a handsome tip to the captain to get a decent seat at one of Dad's Las Vegas shows. But for those who cared most about the man and the standard he'd set, it could be a hard thing to watch.

Just before New Year's in 1994, while appearing at the MGM Grand, Dad kept dropping the lyrics to his signature songs. As he moved off the stage, he was shouting at Eliot Weisman to find everyone in the audience and give them their money back. Eliot scurried for cover, because he knew Dad was serious.

I began to despair that my father would ever make a graceful exit and take his deserved rest—or that he'd ever find the peace of mind to make that rest possible. I asked Eliot to do something about Dad's medical situation. But Eliot received the same response we did; Barbara remained satisfied with my father's care.

On March 2, 1994, Dad was set to receive a Legend Award at the Grammys. This wasn't just another roomful of fans—my father would be appearing before a worldwide broadcast audience, and I didn't know how he'd manage to pull it off. As I tuned in at home, I held my breath. Dad came out to a loving bedlam of applause and was overwhelmed. As he rambled through his acceptance speech, I could tell he was in one of his fogs. There was no one in the wings to save him; they finally cued the orchestra to cut him off. It was awful.

Four days later, Dad appeared in Richmond, Virginia. Though the weather was unseasonably mild, they had heaters running full blast, compounding the warmth of the stage lights. Dad performed sitting on a stool. Two songs from his closing number, in the middle of "My Way," he muttered to Frankie to get him a real chair. Before my brother could furnish one, Dad started to stand up, reached back for his stool, and slowly collapsed, striking his head on a speaker.

When Tony reached him, he found Dad soaked through with sweat to the outer shell of his jacket. As Tony loosened his tie and opened his shirt, Dad said, "What happened? Can the audience still see me?" Even then he was the consummate, prideful performer.

Everyone would tell me that Dad's problem was dehydration. But since he refused to stay in the hospital for tests, we wouldn't know for sure.

Five months later, on a hot August night in Atlantic City, Dad collapsed again. This time he made it off the stage, out of his fans' view. As before, Dad walked out of the hospital, but Eliot insisted that a doctor fly home with him.

Feeling frightened and angry, I called my father's manager and said, "How can you let this keep happening?" Eliot was shaken. He said that Dad would complete his obligations for the year, and that would be the end.

※

After Dad's second spell, Dr. Pat Picchione, a good friend, joined the road company. When Dad's memory problems flared in Baltimore, Tony and Eliot were determined to help him. After Pat assured them that they'd be running no medical risks, they shifted Dad's dose of Elavil to bedtime, so that he might sleep through the heaviest side effects.

According to Nancy, an eyewitness, the results were dramatic. Dad did a great show in St. Louis, then boarded his jet in high spirits. In Chicago he didn't need the TelePrompTer. Every word to every song fell in place. His performance was phenomenal, the audience wildly appreciative—Nancy thought the building would come down.

Still riding his momentum from Chicago, Dad embarked on a side trip that was important to us both. I was producing a TV movie called *Young at Heart*, shooting in Toronto. It was written with a cameo for Dad to play himself, but I toyed with the idea of using digital manipulation—a virtual Frank—instead. I was gun-shy after the miniseries, fearful of another letdown. And I was reluctant to add to Dad's workload—he was already under more than his fair share of pressure.

In the end I damned the torpedoes and asked him to do it, and of course he said he would. I hired him for scale but sent a private jet to pick him up in New York; Nancy had stayed with him to make certain he got on. Dad was a good sport about boarding a hired minibus from the airport to our set. (Others in the troupe teased him that he hadn't been provided a limo, but Dad said, "I started my career on the bus, and I guess I'm ending it the same way.") I was a nervous wreck while they were en route—I had the Teamster captain on the cell phone for ETA updates through the Toronto rush hour.

As the bus pulled up and Dad saw the sea of lights and people at our location, he started slapping on the window with both hands, shouting my name—he couldn't wait to get to me. If he'd felt anxiety about what lay ahead, it was quickly gone. We embraced in tears.

Rarely have two people been so happy to see each other.

As he stepped onto our set, Dad seemed a foot taller than I'd seen him in years. He was a man at home in this environment; he took command. Though he hadn't read the script, he got the setup from the director and met the actors. He rehearsed his scene with Olympia Dukakis, who'd played his mother in the miniseries. Then we repaired to Dad's Winnebago, stocked with all of his favorite foods, from Italian deli to Tootsie Rolls. Dad was in gracious form, obviously enjoying himself. His fatherly pride was unmistakable, and I basked in it.

Back on the set, we were so well prepared that the whole thing was over in forty minutes—it went by almost too fast. All too soon, he was hugging me good-bye. It would be the most memorable visit—and the most emotional farewell—that we'd ever have.

(Later that night, the director of photography told me that when he took his mark, Dad could tell that he wasn't quite in the right spot. Before the camera operator could make the adjustment, Dad inched into his key light. He knew precisely where he was supposed to be; his instincts were still intact.)

It was Dad's last screen appearance, and his briefest. But we did it. We had our moment.

Chicago would have been the perfect swan song for a

remarkable, unparalleled career. But Dad had one more booking, one last big payday to fulfill: at the Fukuoka Dome in Japan. It was too far for him to travel and work without having a day or two of rest upon arriving. But as usual, he was in a hurry. His performances were reportedly disastrous.

I didn't care. All that mattered was that Dad was finally coming home, to stay.

※

I was for the move as much as anyone. When Barbara sounded me out about selling the Compound, I was thrilled at the prospect of Dad living closer to us—and to Rex Kennamer, our family doctor in Los Angeles. Nancy worried about the trauma to Dad of leaving his beloved desert, but I was the practical one. I considered it a sacrifice worth making.

As it turned out, Nancy was right.

The Compound was sold in March 1995 for close to $5 million. To that point, Dad had seemed amenable to moving. But as the closing approached, he began stalling for time. He was grieving as though someone had died.

Fortunately, the new owner kindly allowed Dad and Barbara to stay on as guests for two months. It was an afternoon in late May when my father faced the music.

He didn't say much that day, I'm told, and he wasn't hungry, either. When he left the Compound for the last time, I hoped that somebody remembered my mosaic snowman, and the brass plaque on the door of the room where JFK had slept thirty-five years before.

❋

His last performance behind him, uprooted from his home of fifty years, Dad was ill at ease in his new surroundings. As bad as the road had been for him, it was also an outlet, an escape from his discontent. Though Barbara would skirt the issue, Dad's depression was deepening—not in the eyes of their L.A. friends or the headwaiters at their favorite restaurants, perhaps, but it was obvious to his children and to the people who took care of him.

The surest way to drive Barbara to distraction was for Dad to pose his favorite question: *When are we going home?* There were moments when he'd be literally disoriented; he couldn't understand why they weren't back in the desert. But there were also times when his query was more knowing and playful. On one occasion they'd passed an unusually pleasant evening together: cocktails in the den, a battle-free dinner, then back to the den for a little television.

"Sweetheart?" Dad said, with a wink at Tony.

"Yes, dear?"

"Can I ask you something?"

"Of course, Sweetheart."

"When are we going home?"

Barbara began to stiffen. "We *are* home, darling."

"No," Dad said, "this is *your* home. When are we going to *my* home?"

"We have discussed this before, and I don't want to discuss it again! Good *night!*" And Barbara was gone.

An hour or so later, Dad looked at Tony and said, in all innocence, "Is my wife steamed about something?"

Foothill would never feel like home to Dad. The house had been purchased furnished, down to its oversized sofas and contemporary artwork. It contained none of my father's history or personality. There were times when he'd get confused by Foothill's open floor scheme, which reminded him of a hotel lobby. Sitting at the bar one day, he said to Tony, "I never see any people here—they must be doing lousy business in this joint."

If he wasn't already suffering enough, Dad was riddled with neck and shoulder pain for weeks that summer, much of which he spent in Malibu. Surgery was out of the question; he couldn't have endured the claustrophobia and confinement of a neck brace. His orthopedists could only keep him comfortable, with pills and two epidurals.

On a July visit to the beach house with my niece Amanda, I asked about plans for Dad's eightieth birthday, coming up that December. "Your father's preference is to play it down," Barbara said. "He wants just the family. If we invite one more person, we'll slight twenty others." We agreed that we'd get together at Foothill or Nancy's or a restaurant; we'd confirm the details down the road.

Once this plan was established, what Eliot told me several weeks later made no sense. With Barbara's active endorsement, George Schlatter was producing an octogenarian tribute to Dad—as an ABC special.

We'd finally gotten Dad out of the public eye. The last thing that he needed—especially after the Grammys debacle—was to be pushed out into another network broadcast. I heard from Eliot and Sonny how much Dad was dreading it. When I called Dad myself, he begged me to "kill it, *please*."

My father would willingly sit down and be sung to by very few people in this world, and a fair number of them were dead.

I had that sinking feeling that I'd been placed in an untenable position. But I couldn't let my father twist slowly on his own; he'd put me on a mission. I called George and told him that Dad wanted out.

"That's not what he and Barbara are telling me," George said. "He's excited about it, and it's going to be great fun." To know George is to love him—and to appreciate his tenacity. Like any good producer, he was going to get this done.

I spoke to Barbara, and she echoed George's opinion— and *now* what the hell was I supposed to do?

I called the network executive to file my protest. The only weapon I had was Sheffield, which could withhold the authorized use of Dad's image and likeness. But the executive pointed out, quite reasonably, that my father had agreed to do the show—it was locked into their fall schedule. "And by the way," he added, "we're making a significant contribution to the Barbara Sinatra Children's Center."

That was the carrot no one had told me about—and had I known, I wouldn't have made the call. I knew that Dad would have been happier simply writing a check to Barbara's charity, but that wasn't an option. My mission was a no-win from the start. It was like pushing a car uphill with a rope.

At a Labor Day barbecue, I found myself face-to-face with George. When I asked him why he'd pressed on the special, he repeated how good it would be for Dad. I wanted to believe him, but I knew better.

The taping that November lasted an uncomfortable

two and a half hours. For all the talent on display (from Dylan and Springsteen to Hootie and the Blowfish and Salt-n-Pepa), the show was hung on Dad like a poorly fitted tux. It was all that Barbara and Tony could do to keep him from getting up and leaving.

From where I sat, within earshot of his table, I could tell that he hated almost every minute of it.

಼

The sale of the Compound triggered the spring cleaning to end all spring cleanings: the auction at Christie's. On December 1, 1995, more than two hundred of Dad's treasures were sold to the highest bidder: jeweled and enameled Fabergé boxes, gold and silver cigarette boxes, paintings by Grandma Moses, Andrew Wyeth, Rouault, and Bonnard. Also on the block that day were Dad's Bösendorfer grand piano and his 1976 green Jaguar coupe.

The net proceeds of the liquidation totaled $1.9 million, which went into Dad and Barbara's joint tenancy account—except for the $70,000 netted from the Jaguar, which was forwarded to its rightful owner: Bobby Marx.

Originally a wedding gift from Barbara, the Jaguar had been given to Bobby years earlier, after Dad stopped driving. In the Christie's catalogue, however, there was no mention made of Bobby's ownership. The Jaguar was listed along with everything else, as "Property from the Collection of Mr. and Mrs. Frank Sinatra"—which no doubt enhanced its value to bidders.

After the auction, Barbara returned to their Waldorf apartment all atwitter, reeling off the prices that various objects had fetched. But I'm told that my father, who hadn't attended the sale, was silent and glum.

They were dismantling his past, piece by piece, and he saw nothing to celebrate.

※

A week or so after the auction, a few days before Dad's eightieth, I arrived at Eliot's suite at the Peninsula Hotel in Beverly Hills for a Sheffield board meeting. Eliot told me that Dorothy was looking for me, so I rang her back, expecting to hear the time and place for Dad's birthday dinner.

Dorothy said, "I was asked to tell you kids that you'll be celebrating your father's birthday on the thirteenth."

I said, "Excuse me? What is he doing on the twelfth?"

The Schlatters are giving him a party, she said. Before I had time to react, she went on, "Mrs. S. said that she hadn't heard from you, so she went ahead and made these plans, and they'll see you the next night."

I said, "What is she talking about? We've had a plan since July."

Rather than shoot the messenger, I hung up and headed to the bedroom for privacy, with Eliot at my heels. "Wait till you calm down," he pleaded.

"You *knew* about this, didn't you?" I said.

"Well," he said, "Maria and I are invited."

"Thank you, Eliot, I feel so much better now." I understood by now that Dad's life was completely out of his control. But that didn't make me feel any better. I picked up the phone and called Foothill. Vine answered and handed me over.

I don't remember exactly what I said, but it went something like the following: "This doesn't please me, but I have to tell you what I'm feeling—I've tried for a very long time—I don't know if you understand what's happening, but George and Jolene are giving you a birthday party and your children are not included." It all came out in a rush; I didn't pause to let Dad speak until my voice began to crack.

"That's not right," my father said, his own voice quavering. "I don't want to spend my birthday without you." After forty-seven years, he didn't have to tell me that— birthdays were a hallowed tradition in the Sinatra family.

"Well, you're going to," I said. By now I was choosing

my words carefully, and hanging on his. Dad's sadness slowed me down a little, but I couldn't let it stop me.

"I'm going to do something about that," he said.

"You can't—it's too late. I have tried to keep my place in your life, but I can't do it anymore—I *won't* do it anymore. I love you, but I'm done."

At that moment, I must tell you that I was filled with . . . *release*, as though I'd broken through the waterline for a saving breath. I'd held my feelings inside for such a long time, and now they were finally out.

I thought that Dad would be all right with my absence, as he was retaining less and less of what was going on around him. I wasn't so sure about myself. But it was a decision I had made, however drastic; I would learn to live with it, because I had no choice. I understood how Jilly must have felt in his exile. I just could not do this another day.

Nancy and Frankie would call Dad on his birthday; I did not. When Nancy told him she was sorry that she couldn't be with him, it prompted tears on both ends of the line—and a showdown at Foothill.

According to Tony, my call had led Dad to confront Barbara about the party, to no effect. When Nancy reminded him what was happening, he was furious. But Barbara held her ground. She told him that we'd never organized anything and that we could have been with him the next night, but opted not to.

Dad said, "I don't want a birthday party if my kids aren't there."

And Barbara said, "It's not a birthday party, it's just a *dinner* party—and I'm not the hostess. I can't dictate who's invited."

"I don't think I'm getting the whole story here!" Dad barked. By then Barbara was leaving the room, and he yelled after her, "I'm not going, either!"

Of course, Dad went to the party. To the outside world, once again, he and Barbara were in perfect harmony; Barbara was perceived as the loving and devoted wife. There was a public marriage and a private marriage, and only a few of us knew how very different they were.

I believe that my father was deeply troubled by these conflicts, even if his perception of reality was less than twenty-twenty. But at the end of the day, he would do what he had to do to survive—and, as of now, so would I.

I would not see or speak to him for the next eleven months.

As weeks passed, I was adjusting to life without Dad, but it would take all of my strength and resolve. The people closest to us were alarmed by our separation. Nancy warned that I'd be sorry. Mom—who may have been hurt the most—would tell me I was being selfish: "Your father depends on you children. He may not be exactly what you want him to be, but he needs you, and you need him."

Bob said, "You've got to remember, he's just a man. You're seeing all that he is now—you've got to learn to live with that and protect it, because he needs protecting."

I could not argue with any of them. Most parents reside on pedestals, and if Dad's had been a little higher than the norm, he had that much farther to fall. I'd seen him topple of his own accord, years before—and yes, I could accept him as just a man. But he'd stood so large in my eyes that I couldn't bear to see him *smaller* than life. I couldn't stay involved and be silent, nor could I help by speaking my heart.

My father would never be out of my thoughts; I could only hope and pray that he knew that.

My strength would be tested just two weeks later, when Dean passed away on Christmas morning. He and Dad had long before come to terms with the ill-fated reunion tour, and had seen each other for the occasional dinner. Now Dad had lost his last close comrade. I would get as close to him as my sister's end of their phone conversation that day. I was sick for him, but I shook my head, in tears, when Nancy offered me the phone.

Seven silent months later, in July 1996, I was invited to a church ceremony to witness Dad and Barbara's twentieth anniversary, and respectfully declined. (Nancy also passed; Frankie attended.) They renewed their vows, then hosted a dinner party at the beach house. I'm told that Dad enjoyed seeing some old faces. After the guests left, he chose to stay dressed downstairs till dawn, drinking and talking with Tony.

The next day, there was no sign of the groom well into the afternoon. Sometime after 4 P.M., Barbara insisted that Tony go check on Dad in his small room that overlooked the pool. He found my father awake with his robe on, lying with his arms folded, staring at the ceiling.

Deeply pensive, Dad said, "What the hell have I *done?*"

Tony couldn't be sure if my father was referring to the ceremony or to the twenty years preceding it. But there could be no mistaking that this was a most unhappy, disconsolate man—and one who believed he deserved no better.

💮

As summer dwindled, Nancy and Mom stopped nagging me to reach out to Dad. My sister told me that he wasn't calling her, either. (What I didn't know was that whenever he wanted to call either of us, Vine and Tony were asked to distract him.)

For me, the toughest moments came in public, when my friends or business associates asked me how Dad was doing. As much as I cherished my privacy, I didn't want to lie. So I'd tell them, "I hear he's doing fine"—my response was all too clear by what I'd left unspoken. Depending on what they'd already heard, their faces would register surprise or concern; my words were so at odds with the close-knit family they knew us to be.

I didn't know how long our breach would last. I didn't want to believe it would last forever, but I feared that it would take some cataclysm to reunite us. I prayed each night that whenever it came, I'd have the time and opportunity to be with him again.

When my private line rang very early on the morning of November 2, I knew it had to be bad news. My first thoughts went to Mom—until I heard Barbara's voice.

"He's going to be okay, but we're here at Cedars," she said.

"What is it?"

"It's his heart."

I rushed through the dark to Cedars-Sinai. When I arrived at Dad's room, he was sleeping. Barbara was sitting on a sofa, reading a magazine, with a towel draped over the lamp to dim its light. We greeted each other, and she introduced me to Rosie—the registered nurse, I was told, who'd looked after Dad the previous summer, when he was felled by a flare-up of his neck and back pain.

That was my first stab of guilt for stepping out of Dad's life—when I learned that he'd felt so poorly that he'd needed constant nursing care, and I wasn't there for him.

I looked at Dad and started to weep. I bent to kiss his forehead. I glanced back to Barbara, who motioned me over to explain what was going on. I heard the term "infarction" and dully registered what it meant.

My father had suffered a serious heart attack—with complications I'd yet to fully understand.

When Dad awoke a few minutes later, I was sitting next to him. I wondered if my presence would frighten him, make him think that he was dying. "Hi, Poppa, it's Pigeon," I said. I was so relieved that he knew me—and that he seemed glad to have me there.

And he said, "Hi, Baby." They were our first words in nearly a year. I kissed his hand and sat back down next to him, and he drifted back to sleep.

As morning broke, the doctors began their rounds. I felt heartened to see Rex Kennamer, our family friend and one of the top heart specialists around. A slight man in his seventies, Rex was unassuming and understated, an authentic Southern gentleman. I wasn't accustomed to seeing him so serious, almost grave.

"We're all lucky that he survived the heart attack," he said, and proceeded to give Nancy and me an overview. Dad's heart had been stabilized, but he'd developed a critical case of pneumonia, with fluids backed up into his lungs and heart cavity.

I strained to take in each frightening word. But at the same time, another word kept echoing through my brain. My father was *alive*.

(Later I would learn that Dad had been diagnosed with cancer of the ureter. It was a localized case—his bladder and kidneys were clear—and not life-threatening. A few days before Dad's heart attack, his urologist had cauterized the lining of the ureter, then inserted a stent to keep the canal open. After he got home, Dad pulled out the stent. Without it, his body retained excess fluid. His lungs began filling up, which in turn stressed his heart.)

Dad stayed at Cedars-Sinai for eight days. Barbara and Vine took the day shifts, Nancy and I the nights. As Dad gained more strength, I'd look for little windows to say things I needed to say—that I'd missed him, first of all, and never wished him anything but happiness.

There were no house rules on the eighth floor at

Cedars. Elizabeth Taylor was permitted her tiny white dog, Dad his occasional Camel. As my father tended to get thin and anemic, the doctors told us to feed him whatever he wanted: rice pudding, Eskimo Pies, Mom's eggplant parmesan. Nothing cheered us so much as the sight of Dad munching on a rare minute steak.

On the eighth day, we smuggled our patient out of the hospital and past the media camped outside Foothill. For Dad it felt like Christmas morning. Barbara offered an open invitation to Nancy, Frankie, and me: "Whenever you guys want to see your father, day or night, you just come by. The door is always open." We were most grateful.

Something cataclysmic *had* happened, and it remained to be seen whether I'd be granted the opportunity I'd prayed for. My relationship with my father was heading toward its worldly end. We were together again for now. But I felt overwhelmed by the separation that lay ahead, too final to comprehend.

10

End of an Era

I TOOK FULL advantage of Barbara's invitation. For the next six months, I'd split all my time between Dad's home and my office, until my friends thought I'd thrown out my address book. By day I'd be on the phone to Foothill, peppering Vine and the nurses with questions: How was he eating today? Did he get any exercise? What about his oxygen therapy?

As my mother always said, it's the small things that matter.

After work, I'd go straight to Foothill and join Barbara and Nancy in the quest to keep Dad comfortable and happy. Though Dad required round-the-clock nursing care, we wanted a family member with him as well.

In any case, I felt most myself when I was close to

Dad. I would make up for the months we'd lost; every minute by his side was precious to me.

We all held together in a silent prayer for time.

In the first few days following his release from the hospital, Dad made dazzling progress—it seemed as though he'd been shot out of a cannon. His geography was limited to his room, the adjoining den, the dining room beyond, and the garden, for a little afternoon sun, but as ill as he was, his mind seemed clearer, thanks to an improved drug regimen. I could see the sparkle in those warm blue eyes. On occasion he'd dress for dinner, a Sinatra tradition.

Some concessions were unavoidable. As Dad's peripheral vision was mostly gone (up and down, as well as to the side) and his eye-hand coordination could be affected by his medications, there were days when navigating a fork or spoon could be difficult. Our constant concern was to protect his dignity and independence. We'd give him smaller juice glasses that were easier to grip. We'd cut his food into bite-sized pieces in the kitchen, before he saw it, or serve him ziti rather than linguine. Then we'd tell him, "The steak is at the top, the corn at nine o'clock, the muffin at four o'clock."

While Dad had lost touch with the social ritual of cocktail hour, he still wanted a sip of wine for a toast at dinner before switching to Coca-Cola. He also liked a ceremonial cigarette, which we were free to give him. (The doctors told us to deny him nothing; the damage was already done, I suppose.) Foothill was a no-smoking house, so I'd bundle him up in his muffler and out to the pool we'd go. A couple of puffs and it was over—it wasn't so much a craving as a nostalgic routine for Dad. It was one of the few things he could still do with his old panache.

The evening before Thanksgiving was our first opportunity to take a breath. Rex Kennamer and his partner, Jeffrey Helfenstein, came over to give us a review of what had happened to Dad and their outlook for the future.

We learned that my father's heart attack should have killed him. What got Dad through it, according to Rex, was his iron will; most people would not have made it to the hospital.

After years of chronic cardiac disease, Rex continued, Dad was vulnerable to another heart attack, a major stroke, or an aneurysm. The key was to keep him comfortable, happy, calm, well fed, and mobile. If all went well, we might expect him to live in reasonable comfort for another two or three years.

While my father was a candidate for open-heart surgery, the doctors weren't recommending it. We all knew how much Dad despised hospitals. Rex would call him "the most difficult patient I've had in forty years" of practicing medicine. Moreover, Dad's brain scans indicated that he was suffering from dementia, an additional complication that made surgery less practical.

None of us believed that a hospital procedure would improve Dad's quality of life. We reached a quick consensus: no surgery. It just wouldn't have been fair to him.

And with that, there was a general sigh of relief. I couldn't bring back the eleven months we'd lost, but I was grateful to hear that we still had years ahead of us.

That night was the first time I'd heard "dementia" as part of the dialogue. Rex attributed Dad's condition to age, lifestyle, and the ministrokes that had shown up in his EEG. (When I asked whether the strokes might have dated back to Dad's two fainting spells onstage, Rex said it was quite possible.)

Before Dad's release from the hospital, Rex had told us exercise would be critical to get his circulation flowing and expand his lung capacity. It was easy to carry out the doctor's orders for those first few days home. But then Dad began to revert to the foggy state that preceded his heart attack.

Dad's medication remained a high-wire act. Too little and he'd get agitated; too much and he'd be groggy. I worried that Dad seemed oversedated, to the point where he was sleeping up to eighteen hours a day.

When I brought this to Rex's attention, he said that
he'd be in more direct contact with Dad's geriatric psychiatrist. But he cautioned us that there would be a lot
of trial and error before they found the right mix.

Over the next year and a half, we would learn not to
panic over Dad's ebbs and flows. He would have good
days and bad, even after his drugs were in balance.
There would be periods of real progress—and then
they'd be reversed. The sad facts were these: My father
was an eighty-year-old man with advanced pulmonary
disease. He'd survived a devastating heart attack, but he
would never be the same.

That Thanksgiving would be the most thankful of
feasts we'd ever had. We kept dinnertime loose, geared
to whenever Dad woke up. He walked to the table unas-
sisted, clean shaven and clearheaded—and obviously
moved to have his children and grandchildren around
him. It had been a long time since we'd come together
as a family.

Soon came December 12, Dad's eighty-first birthday.
After he blew out the candles on a banana shortcake,
Nancy asked him what he'd wished for.

Dad said, "Another birthday." He spoke aloud what

all of us were thinking. The sight of his somber face wrenched my heart.

It had taken me some time to come up with the right present. I didn't foresee Dad needing another tie or sweater. (Though he was still occasionally dressing, Dad's favorite uniform was the cashmere herringbone robe that I'd given him five years earlier.) I wanted to get him something meaningful, not practical; I decided on an ivory crucifix. It was immediately hung with a hat pin on the upholstered headboard of his bed.

By Christmas Eve, Dad was weaker than at Thanksgiving. He lacked motivation for his favorite holiday— it was the first time I saw him use his wheelchair. The drugs he was taking had suppressed his appetite. Midway through dinner, after a few bites for tradition, he announced that he'd go rest for a while. I wheeled him back to his room.

Less than two months away from nearly losing him, I was disturbed by Dad's regression. A few minutes after returning to the table, I excused myself and joined him in his room. He looked so small and vulnerable lying there. I crept to his bedside and laid my head on his mattress. I just wanted to be close to him.

I hadn't cried in front of Dad, and I didn't want to frighten him, but now I could not stop myself. I softly wept.

Then I felt a hand on my head, stroking my hair. I looked up—his eyes were open. He knew that someone needed comforting; it was a natural reflex for him. When he turned to gaze at me, I said, "*Please*, Poppa, you've got to try. You've *got* to be all right."

And he said, "Don't worry, Sweetheart, I'll be fine."

In these first weeks of Dad's convalescence, I'd seen glimpses of real empathy from Barbara. She'd recently told me, "I warn you, there is *nothing* like losing your father." Though she was reaffirming my worst fear, I was grateful for her compassion.

But when I emerged from Dad's room that evening, my eyes red, I could tell that Barbara was annoyed. She said, "I don't want you falling apart in front of him. If you need to do it, do it someplace else—it doesn't do him any good to see it."

I bit my tongue, as usual. While I understood she was trying to shield my dad, I thought she was wrong. I'd grown up with parents who were openly emotional in front of their children and encouraged us to be the same. (Dad would say, "If you're sad, you're sad, and that's okay.") I wasn't about to let Barbara dictate what I could feel around my father or to stigmatize something so natural. I would cry again with him, many times.

Despite our differences, however, I no longer reacted to Barbara as I once had. I'd become expert at listening to her, then moving on. What counted was for us to stay united around Dad—in public as well as in private. My sister and brother and I would be hammered repeatedly in the press, both before and after my father's heart attack, in reference to our conflicts with Barbara. Though we wondered where the leaks had originated, we were careful about what we said to reporters. We knew how much it would hurt Dad to find our family matters aired in the papers.

Despite our best efforts to follow Rex's directives, Dad could be stubborn about walking. When he felt droopy, he'd insist on using his leased wheelchair. Granted, he had the Bentley of wheelchairs, a streamlined black-and-chrome model that looked like it could go thirty miles an hour.

Then one day it was gone. In its place was an antiquated, well-used maroon chair—a hand-me-down from an uncle of Barbara's in Long Beach whom Dad had cared for financially. After the uncle died, Barbara acquired his chair and terminated the Bentley's lease.

It made me sad. Dad had a certain style even in illness; he kept a Kleenex folded like a hankie in the chest pocket of his pajamas. He deserved the best, and the sight of that secondhand chair deflated me.

Was I the only one who noticed?

In January 1997, another early-morning call from Foothill: Dad's blood pressure was erratic, and Rex wanted him back at Cedars. I beat the ambulance and waited for Dad in the receiving room. He was angry when they wheeled him in, and his mood hadn't improved hours later, when they moved him from the emergency room up to the eighth floor. They'd been able to stabilize Dad's pressure and arrhythmia almost immediately, but they wanted to keep him for another day or two, just to be safe.

This time his room overlooked Beverly Boulevard and the roof of Jerry's Delicatessen, where a big yellow smiling face had been painted on the roof, with GET WELL SOON written underneath. But Dad was not so easily mollified. He hated being in the hospital and didn't care who knew it.

The following afternoon, I arrived to find Nancy and Barbara making bets on how long it would take Dad to throw *me* out—they'd already been ejected themselves. After I took a deep breath and stepped into the room, Dad briskly said, "Hi, do you have a car?" When I told him I did, he said, "Good, I want you to get me out of here."

Though Dad seemed fine and was pacing like a cat in a cage, I knew that Rex wanted to keep him at least one more night for observation. Stalling for time, I said, "We can't go without your slippers—where are they?" As Dad started looking, I hid the slippers under my bag. We looked and we looked, and my father got louder and louder, until I said, "Pop, we have to hold it down. The patients on either side of you don't look so good."

And he said, "What do you expect? They're in the goddamn hospital!" He resumed his search, and then he said, "Well, fuck 'em, I'm going anyway."

"No, you can't."

"If you're not going to help me, get the hell out of here."

I said, "Okay, I'm going to leave."

"Okay, you leave."

I got to the door and said, "I'm really leaving."

And he said, "Fine." As I opened the door and turned my back to him, he added, "But don't be gone for too long."

⁂

After dinner, Dad and I often camped out in the den. Glass bowls of Tootsie Rolls, pistachio nuts, and cherry Life Savers were set within arm's length of Dad's "funny chair," the special recliner that pitched you up and out when you wanted to stand. (He rarely relied on it,

though; he'd prefer to have a daughter hoist him up.)
Given Dad's impaired hearing and sight, television was
less of a diversion. But he still liked *Jeopardy!*, his favorite
game show, and a familiar old movie might pique his
interest.

One evening Dad glanced back at the screen for a
moment and said, "I *know* this movie." It was a jungle
adventure with lots of pith helmets and barely clad
natives. "I remember this," Dad continued. "It was considered naughty when I was a boy, and I snuck in to see
it with some pals of mine."

The movie was *Trader Horn*. It had been released in
1930, when Dad was fifteen years old, and I thought to
myself, *Whoa!* I couldn't wait to tell the rest of the family.

My father had never been too interested in watching
his own movies, until now. The first one we happened
upon was *The Tender Trap*. (I think that he's so adorable
and sexy and funny in this film—it's one of my personal
favorites.)

Another time we laughed at *Guys and Dolls*. "He still
can't sing," Dad would say, shaking his head at his costar
Marlon Brando.

On nights like these I'd wait until he went to bed to
say good-bye. To avoid upsetting him, I'd tell him that I
was going to the den; I'd linger until he found sleep.

Good-byes were getting hard for all of us.

❈

In February, Barbara went down to the desert for her annual charity golf tournament. I was with Nancy at Foothill one evening when I looked into the guest room and noticed that the bookcases holding Dad's Oscars, Grammys, and the like were now locked behind thick sheets of Plexiglas. Nancy couldn't help but remember her recent offhand comment—that she should have taken the Oscars when Dad told us to. When I asked Barbara about it, she said there were a lot of strangers in the house and she was worried about security.

A few weeks later, when I asked Tony what was going on, he put a warning finger to his lips and motioned us out of the den. In the hallway, he said, "Be careful what you say around here."

Over time, I would learn that the additional security went beyond Plexiglas. When Tony cautioned us, my sister and I had been talking in the den, alone. What we hadn't noticed was a tiny lens hidden in the face of a clock, opposite the couch.

And that wasn't the only one. There was a second camera with a wide-angle lens in the bookcase of his room, facing his bed.

Two cameras, two VCRs—you get the picture, and so did Barbara.

I thought about the talks I'd had with Dad, the private moments between father and daughter.

Now I realized that they may not have been so private after all.

🔱

The geriatric psychiatrist was a tall, forbidding man. When he came to Foothill on his twice-weekly visits, he would loom over Dad. He'd ask my father how he was doing, and Dad would say he felt great, just to get rid of him.

We understood that this wasn't a perfect science—you couldn't just fix a medication at one level and leave it there. The psychiatrist juggled the drugs, but Dad's energy continued to wane. Nancy and I pushed for a change for months. By February Rex had found a replacement, a young doctor named Randall Espinoza.

The difference was dramatic. Dr. Espinoza was warmer and more compassionate. (He had a grandmother going through the same thing.) He also demonstrated more imagination and finesse; he suggested that we mash the pills and add them to liquids to allay Dad's concern that he was taking too many. Soon he was sleeping on a more normal schedule.

Since the day of Dad's heart attack, Barbara had been

steadfast in her attention. Aside from her golf tournament, she virtually hadn't left the house. As her seventieth birthday approached on March 10, we talked her into throwing a pajama party, so that Dad could feel comfortable without having to get dressed. A few friends joined us for an early dinner, but Dad wasn't much interested in socializing. Too much noise and activity fatigued him; he retired early.

There were a few exceptions, like Steve Lawrence and Quincy Jones, whose visits always lifted my father's spirits. I was moved by the sight of Tony Curtis cradling Dad and kissing him, as a son would his father. (I didn't realize then that Tony's own father's passing was washing over him.)

The new doctor and drug regimen were working—working so well, in fact, that Dad was too cognizant for his own peace of mind. Even in his dementia, Dad knew where he was, and *who* he was, and how little that man resembled the housebound invalid on Foothill Road.

When Barbara had retired and the house was quiet, Dad and I would have some of our closest moments. He'd talk about his grandchildren, or the good times on the road with Mom. But inevitably he'd get to his failings as a father: "I wasn't there enough, especially for you."

It was hard for me when Dad lamented the course of

his life. There were times when I'd have to leave him with Nancy and listen from the next room, wincing at each self-excoriating word.

※

As the months passed, Dad settled into a static convalescence. On his bad days he'd never make it out of his room. With the drapes closed, day flowed into night, and Dad wouldn't care.

It was a terribly gray existence—but it wasn't a crisis, and we all relaxed a little. Nancy and I spaced our visits. Barbara reverted to her busy schedule.

Dad was isolated at the opposite end of the house from his wife's upstairs suite. He had no way of getting to her, and when her intercom rang, she was not always available.

※

As Thanksgiving approached, Dad had survived a whole year without much medical ado—the fastest year of my life. We hoped against hope that there would be more years to come.

Barbara invited my mother for Thanksgiving dinner. Dad was seated in the bar area when she came in with

Frankie, and required assistance to stand. As I watched my parents embrace, I marveled at their lasting affection—how pure it was, never poised or performed.

Dad was feeling fatigued, so I wheeled him to the dining room. (As usual, he told me to slow down: "What's the hurry? You're driving too fast.") I could tell from Mom's face that she was flattened, despite Nancy's reassurances.

With everyone seated around him, Dad became emotional as he offered a toast: "To my family." It was a lot for him to take in. He couldn't make it through dinner, and excused himself before dessert: "I think I'll go rest for a while."

Could he have sensed that this would be our last meal together?

Three weeks later, we celebrated Dad's eighty-second birthday. I'd gone shopping for him but couldn't bring myself to buy anything. Perhaps I feared that this would be his *last* birthday present—I know it doesn't make sense, but the thought paralyzed me.

Still it was a good day. When we watched C-SPAN and saw the House of Representatives vote unanimously to award Dad the Congressional Gold Medal of Honor, he was overwhelmed. And he was touched to see the Empire State Building washed in blue light on the evening news. Ever humble, he said, "I don't know what all the fuss is about. I'm just a vocalist who tried to do the best he could."

My father was always flattered by honors, and these were big ones. But they were no more important than the thousands of letters and telegrams and get-well cards he'd received from well-wishers around the world. It was so important for him to know that he hadn't been forgotten.

Christmas Eve would preserve our family's open house tradition, though on a smaller scale. Mom dropped by with Sonny and Linda Golden on their way to dinner. Dad had been sitting at the table near the bar in his robe and pajamas. But when he saw my mother (looking lovely in lavender, I might add), he rose to greet her and said, "I need to go get dressed."

Mom told him to relax, as she could stay only a few minutes. After they talked and shared a laugh, she left him feeling more optimistic than on Thanksgiving. Still, she sensed that time was running out for her best and oldest friend. She knew that one of them would have to go first, and what she dreaded was apparently coming to pass: it would be him.

My mother would never see him again.

By January of 1998, Barbara had proposed a shift in Dad's nursing care, from RNs to lower-wage licensed practical nurses. "He could go on like this for years," she explained, "and the cost would become exorbitant."

I took this as great news—that the state of emergency had lifted, and that Dad might yet have many more good days ahead. If the change was all right with the doctors, it was reason to celebrate.

The transition happened so quickly that I never got to say good-bye to Rosie, Dad's night nurse.

Sadly, I would soon get to see her again.

11

With His Wife at His Side

*I*N FEBRUARY 1998, a few days before Barbara left town for her annual golf tournament, Dad went into Cedars for a follow-up physical. His urologist, Dr. Leon Bender, found a recurrence of the ureter cancer, but less than before. "This is not going to kill your father," he emphasized. He repeated the 1996 procedure and inserted another stent.

Nancy and I were a little anxious that something could go wrong while Barbara was away, especially with the recent change in nursing care. With hindsight, it would have been better to leave Dad in the hospital—we could have tended to him there. But no one could have foreseen what happened that Thursday, Barbara's first night away from home.

Nancy and Tony were on evening duty, along with the night nurse, Mario, the LPN who'd taken Rosie's place. At nine-thirty my sister called to alert me to a problem. Dad was waking up every ten to twenty minutes to pass copious amounts of clotted blood. We knew that a certain amount of bleeding was expected, but this seemed excessive—and Dad was in tremendous pain. Nancy hadn't been able to reach Barbara, who'd left strict instructions that nothing be done without her okay.

By eleven, as Dad's problem kept recurring, Nancy had grown alarmed. Dad was writhing in pain with each new episode, pleading for help; it must have felt like passing a series of kidney stones.

By midnight, Dad was visibly pale. Nancy woke up the urologist, who told her that Dad's bleeding was normal and that his pain should subside. When my sister persisted, Bender said, "Keep an eye on it, and call me in the morning."

Panicked, Nancy tried the next number on Mario's phone list: Jeffrey Helfenstein, Rex Kennamer's partner. She asked him to get Dad admitted into Cedars, so that they might avoid the chaos of the emergency room. But Helfenstein deferred to Bender, the doctor in charge.

My father was still swinging between fitful sleep and unspeakable pain, still screaming for help. Finally Nancy reached Barbara. When asked to call Bender and get Dad admitted, Barbara also deferred to the urologist, adding, "I don't want him in the hospital while I'm out of town. Give it another two hours and call me back."

My sister reluctantly followed Barbara's directive.

Dad continued to lose blood. The intervals between his episodes were getting longer, but he was still in agony, and Nancy had no help to give him.

Early Friday morning, Nancy and Tony got Dad to Bender's office. The urologist cauterized Dad again to stem the bleeding. Then we went home.

That weekend was a nightmare. We tried, without success, to entice Dad to eat, but he was too weak. He could do nothing but catch up on the sleep he'd lost.

Barbara returned to Foothill by dinnertime Sunday. Once she saw Dad's condition—thin, wan, fatigued—she asked Rex Kennamer to come out first thing the following morning. When the cardiologist gave Dad the once-over and saw that he was dehydrated and malnourished, he said, "I want him in the hospital *now*."

I left my office in Burbank and met Barbara by ten-thirty at Cedars, this time in two adjoining rooms on the eighth floor for added privacy. Dad was already on a transfusion drip, along with an IV for nutrition, and would stay that way until the following morning.

Rex was unusually stern with us. Dad was in guarded condition, our doctor said, and until he was eating and his bleeding had stopped, he was not going home. If we couldn't get Dad to eat in the next day or so, Rex would resort to a feeding tube.

Nancy was guilt-ridden about Dad's deterioration over the weekend—and she didn't feel any better when Rex told her, "You should have called me."

Toward the end of the afternoon, Bender and Helfenstein made their rounds. I was less than cordial. Then Barbara left for home, and the room became quiet.

I was delighted when Rosie resurfaced at the shift change to relieve Mario. As the two nurses exchanged notes, I could see Rosie react to what she was hearing.

When Rex Kennamer came by and saw that Dad's urine was still not clear, he ordered more blood for transfusions through the night.

As I stood at the foot of the bed, rubbing Dad's feet (he felt persistently cold and weak), another old friend of his dropped by, a prominent ENT named Ed Kantor. Ed greeted my father warmly. Then he glanced at Dad's chart and motioned Rex out to the hall.

If Rex had been unhappy with my father's state that morning, Ed was plainly upset.

When I left, after midnight, I had counted four bags of blood—and I knew that Rex had ordered at least one additional bag overnight.

I returned Tuesday afternoon, hopeful that Dad would be discharged. But they'd decided that one more night of IV nutrition was wise—and while they had my father captive, they'd run an EEG to check for further stroke activity. To move him for the scan, we wrapped Nancy's scarf high around Dad's neck. With Barbara's dark glasses, his Yankee baseball cap, and his cashmere robe, Dad was the picture of elegance—especially in comparison to how *we* all looked after that horrific weekend. With security at the wheel, we moved with the stealth of James Bond. Before Dad knew it, we had him back to his room and a meatball sandwich.

(When Rex compared the new brain scan to the old, he showed us cloudy spots in the areas of the brain that allow the mind to see. The good news was that he found no evidence of new stroke-related damage since Dad's heart attack.)

Dad was released the next day, though he'd remain on an IV at home for a day or two after that. In retrospect, we'd been fortunate. Rex would tell Nancy, "We almost lost him." The blood loss had strained Dad's heart, which was working on a thread to begin with. Dad's iron deficiency had kicked in again, and he'd lost pounds that he couldn't afford. He'd be listless and run-down for weeks.

We knew that Dad would never have let any of us suffer. Nancy and I felt that we'd let him down.

On Wednesday evening, Dr. Espinoza came to Foothill to see Dad, then stayed for dinner with Barbara and me. When the doctor asked for a quick overview, I explained that the crisis had started Thursday night—and Barbara immediately broke in and contradicted me.

When Dr. Espinoza asked me how much blood Dad had needed, I replied that I thought he'd received four units.

"Tina, that is not true!" Barbara said. "Don't be ridiculous! It was only two or three."

It was my first inkling that Barbara may have felt defensive about being away when all this began. I started to counter but thought better of it, and merely looked at Dr. Espinoza, who was staring at me.

"You're *wrong*," Barbara said. I let her have the last word.

The next time Barbara and I were alone, I proposed that we reach an understanding to alleviate Dad's problems more quickly—we couldn't just sit back if Barbara wasn't around and something went wrong.

"I don't know why you keep harping on this—everything was fine," Barbara insisted. "Your father went into the hospital as soon as he needed to. And if you girls can't

handle things while I'm away, I won't rely on you anymore."

Ever since November of 1996, Barbara had counted on
Nancy and me for relief. She'd called whenever she had a
dinner engagement, to allow us to make plans to sit in
with Dad.

But we'd never get that call again.

❋

The crisis had ravaged Dad and placed us back on vigil.
By March, however, he was getting stronger. He was
gaining weight, and the anemia was in check. But he was
still thinner than he'd been since the heart attack.

As Dad slept in his room one evening, I sat with Barbara in the den. I asked if my father had ever discussed the
option of life support. Barbara said that he hadn't, but that
he wouldn't want to be sustained artificially. That was a
great relief to me, and I said so. I didn't want to give her
any reason to shut me out at the crucial moment.

Then Barbara offered that Dad sometimes felt so
despairing and frustrated, so much of a burden, that he
had on more than one occasion wished for death. (Later
on I'd hear a similar account from Tony, who said that
Dad had gone so far as to ask for his gun. It was a subject
he never vented to his children.)

Then Barbara said, "You really don't know your father very well. You haven't been around much for the last twenty-five years."

⁂

While I knew that my father believed in a higher power, I wasn't so sure about his confidence in the afterlife—until Tony recounted a telling story. One night Dad called him into his room and whispered, "I don't know how you are going to do this, but could you get my mother out of here?"

Tony said, "I don't see her, Mr. S."

And Dad said, "She's right over there in the chair. I'm trying to get some rest, but she keeps hanging around." He'd insist that Jilly was visiting him as well.

Some would say Dad was hallucinating, but I chose to believe that two very persuasive people were beckoning him to come along.

⁂

On Saturday, May 9, after attending Amanda's graduation from Loyola Marymount University, I arrived at Foothill by two o'clock. As I walked into Dad's room, he was chatting with Ulysses, his day nurse. When Dad saw me, he went into his chivalrous ritual of standing. There was no stopping him.

He seemed especially glad to see me that day. He appeared rested and free of the aches and pains that would nag at him. His eyes twinkled and seemed unusually blue—it must have been his powder-blue pj's. I couldn't tell him enough how well he looked. The house was empty and quiet. I drew back the drapes and sunlight poured through the French doors.

When I told him about his baby granddaughter's graduation, Dad beamed with delight. But his eyes filled with tears as he said, "I'm sorry I couldn't be there. Did I get her something?"

"I'm sure you did."

"You check on it for me," he said. "This is a big day." I promised I would.

I said, "Well, Pop, you finally got your kids through college—it just took another generation." I reminded him of the opportunity he'd given me at Yale, and thanked him again for it. I wondered aloud if I'd ever get back to school.

"It's never too late," Dad said.

I'd opened the door to the patio for a spring breeze, but closed it after Dad felt a chill. He demurred when I proposed a walk to the pool. But in every other respect he seemed better than I'd seen him since before the February crisis.

The television was tuned to a golf tournament (Dad liked the vivid green on the screen), but I coaxed him to switch to a movie—I think it was *Houdini*, with Tony Curtis and Janet Leigh.

The usual finger sandwiches had been prepared, but Dad wanted something sweet, so I fed him grapes and an Oreo cookie. When some of the crumbs fell into his pajama pocket, I tried to extract them. But Dad said, "Don't worry about it—I might get hungry later."

I took out my laptop and showed him a new program I was learning. Dad remarked that it was too late for him to master computers, and I ached to hear him speak so resignedly.

We reflected on the span of his life. He'd come in when the century was but fifteen years old, and now his younger daughter was turning fifty, and the new millennium was in sight.

Dad was determined to be a part of it. "How many more months?" he asked me.

Eighteen, I told him, rounding down a bit.

"Oh, I can do that," he said. "Nothin' to it."

I was moved by my father that day—by his stamina and bravery, and his willingness to face reality.

By three, I could tell he was getting sleepy. I got up and

said that I'd be in the den for a while and that I'd see him later, my euphemism for good-bye. I hugged him gently and kissed him, and told him that I loved him.

And Dad said, "I love you, Baby, very much, *so* much."

⁂

As the next week unfolded, whenever I called for my daily update, I was told Dad was eating well, sleeping well, doing fine. I kept saying that I'd see him tomorrow, but I had an unusually rotten workweek and kept pushing my visit off one more day. I knew that I'd be with him all weekend, beginning Friday night, when Barbara was planning a spa retreat at the beach house. I was looking forward to it because our last visit had been so fulfilling. It restored my hope that there might be some good times left for us—and confirmed my sense that time was so precious.

With no clue that anything unusual was developing, I wouldn't be able to assemble the details of that fateful week until much later.

On Monday, Dad asked Tony to order in a pizza. They shared a couple of O'Doul's, a nonalcoholic beer, and had a good time.

On Tuesday, his spirits slumped. "I don't want to live like this any more," he told Tony. "This is not a life."

Dad awoke early Wednesday morning in a tempest. When Tony arrived later that day, he found my father withdrawn and nonresponsive. Dad wouldn't eat so much as an Eskimo Pie, his favorite. He perked up only when Barbara came down, on her way out to dinner. He took one look at her and said, "Oh, you still live here?"

On Thursday afternoon, feeling negligent, I rang Foothill. Vine said that Dad was tired and unsettled. She was trying to get him to calm down and rest; it wasn't a good time to visit. I meant to call back again, but I let the day get away from me. I was banking on our weekend to come. I had put off today . . .

And no one called to tell me that Barbara would be dining out for the fourth consecutive night.

I got home late from the office and rushed to put my dinner on a tray, in time to watch the *Seinfeld* finale from my bed. I switched channels midway and opened my mail.

I had one arm in my nightgown when the phone rang, at exactly 11:10 P.M. It was Rex Kennamer: "I have bad news. We lost him."

Wheeling into instantaneous defensive denial, I said, "Lost *who?*" It couldn't be Dad. My dad was still strong, my dad was doing great. Not *Dad* . . .

Rex made it explicit. "Your father," he said. "I'm sorry."

I'd always thought that Dad would pass away at home,

in his sleep. I imagined it would be in the late autumn or winter, the cold, dark time of year. This wasn't happening how or where or when I thought it would.

I was in shock, assimilating very slowly . . . but something felt wrong. I asked Rex where he was.

He said, "We're at the hospital, but we could not save him."

I asked how he'd been able to get from *his* home to the hospital before I was even notified.

Rex fumbled a little and said, "I don't know. We were too busy working on him—we worked on him for some time, but we lost him." He kept repeating that fact, as if to make sure I understood. Barbara was still at the hospital, he added, but about to go home.

"That's fine," I said, "but I want to see him."

"But they're coming to—"

"Not until I get there," I told him. For the first time in an eternity, I felt that I could make a demand and have it met. I needed to see Dad in his last setting, the way he looked at his last breath. I cannot explain how important that was to me just then.

I threw back on my clothes, flew out the door—I'd call my sister from the car. As I sped down the street, I saw the moon. It was full and bright orange, my father's favorite color—it was for Dad. I was talking to him, feeling him within me. *Oh Poppa, oh Poppa, you must still be close if you're really gone. Please wait . . .*

Transfixed, I ran a red light just north of Sunset Boulevard—and nearly got broadsided by another car, the driver honking furiously.

I kept replaying my exchange with Rex. *When did it happen? A few minutes ago. When did you get there? Too busy . . . for some time . . . lost him.*

Barbara could have called us—she could have *called!* But she did not call.

My sister was waiting outside her house and jumped in my car. We were at the Cedars emergency room in minutes.

We stopped at the admitting desk, looking for guidance. For a long suspended moment we just stood there, staring at the security guard, who stared right back. Then someone rushed over and swept us through the doors.

Adrenaline had carried me this far, but now I started to shake. I took Nancy's hand and we pulled each other down the corridor. The first person we saw was Susan Reynolds, Barbara's publicist, on the telephone at the nurses' station. In the reception area, an island with small curtained rooms surrounding it, the three doctors stood in a quiet huddle: Kennamer and Helfenstein in suits and ties, Bender in his white medical smock.

We kept walking toward them, figuring Dad had to be

close by. As we approached, Kennamer stepped toward a closed curtain and pulled it back for us.

My father lay facing us, eyes closed, hands over his chest; he lay on a lowered gurney, ready to be wheeled away. Barbara was seated in a chair to his left. We entered the cubicle without acknowledgment. I went directly to Dad and knelt beside him.

"Oh, *Poppa,*" I said. At the sight of him my tears broke their dam. I wept freely, my forehead pressed against his upper arm. I looked for fear in his face, but saw none. His strain and torment were gone—in death he looked once more to be a figure of command. When I touched him, he was still warm. For an instant, I thought I saw him move.

I silently prayed for him: *Oh God, take him and make him safe and warm, but keep him close to me.* And to him: *I am so sorry I was not here for you.* I was filled with guilt and anger, but kept those feelings contained. I just kept saying to myself that I loved him, over and over again. I believe that spirits linger with us for a time, and I dearly wanted his to hear me.

Realizing that Nancy was no longer beside me, I stood up and reached for her hand, pulled her in close to Dad at my side. I became aware of murmured noises outside our curtained doorway—there was no door, no real privacy. I moved around to Barbara. I leaned down and put my arm around her shoulder, and said very quietly, "I'm sorry." Her arms stayed tightly crossed; we would not embrace, either then or in the days to come.

I hugged Mario and told him how sorry I was that this had to happen on his watch. I thanked him for all that he'd done for my father.

Then it was time to leave. I turned to look at Dad one more time. Holding each other upright, my sister and I walked out past a small crowd of onlookers. People lowered their heads as we approached. As we reached the drive, Bob Finkelstein was getting out of his car. I told him that we were going back to Foothill, and asked him to go home and call Mom.

A few people greeted us at the house, but I went directly to Dad's room; I wanted to be alone where he had been just three hours before. The first thing I saw was Dad's bed stripped bare, and the ivory crucifix hanging over it. On the chaise longue facing the bed, I found Dad's favorite robe, the black-and-white herringbone cashmere. It smelled like Dad, along with the faint scent of lavender. I hunched over on the chaise and buried my face in the robe, rocking back and forth. Barbara entered the room, then quickly left it. I stayed there undisturbed for some time.

When I emerged to find Nancy, we traded places. I joined the people in the living room: Steve and Eydie Lawrence, George and Jolene Schlatter, Bea Korshak. I picked my place to light next to Dad's dear friend Jerry Weintraub, and nestled into him for a long time. At one point I said to him, "I'm sorry I wasn't there with Dad."

Barbara had sharp ears, and she'd heard me from over by the fireplace. "Oh, Tina!" she exclaimed. "There was no time, and what difference would it have made?"

When it was time to go, I said good night to Barbara, still clutching my father's robe.

She said, "You're going to take the robe home—oh, of course, you gave it to him."

And I thought, *What if I hadn't given it to him? Would she wrestle me for it?*

(As of this writing, more than two years later, the robe remains the only personal item of Dad's in my possession.)

By now a horde of media people had thronged around Foothill. Rather than closing in around my car in hope of a statement, they parted and let me through.

Driving home, I was thinking of how people would be waking up to Dad's death all over the world, the news moving across the globe like the dawn. It would be immediately real to them—when would it stop seeming unreal to me?

I'd had calls from friends, but it was too late to return them. I put on CNN with the idea that if I heard it announced, I'd begin to believe it.

Despite the hour, my friend Alana Stewart phoned again, concerned that she hadn't heard back from me. "I'm sorry you weren't with him," she said. "Why weren't you with him?"

When I told her that Nancy and I had gotten to the hospital as soon as we could, Alana said that all the news reports mentioned only Barbara being at his side.

As I tried to sleep, I remembered Marlo Thomas's words when her father died: *They don't belong to us.* I began to embrace that thought. It was something I'd carried dormant for many years, and now I found it a tremendous comfort.

Even as I mourned the private man, I was grateful for the public outpouring—for the millions of people who would take this loss as though Dad were one of their own.

It would take me some time to re-create the immediate events leading up to my father's death. From the time he woke up on Thursday, he was quiet and withdrawn—perhaps a carryover from his state of mind the night before. Early that afternoon, he was coaxed out into the garden for some fresh air. He requested a grilled cheese sandwich but didn't finish it. He returned to his room in a state of growing agitation.

I don't know what transpired over the next few hours, and probably never will. What I do know is that Dad was distressed, emotionally and physically.

It wasn't like Barbara to be away so much. The pity was that she didn't feel the necessity to phone Nancy or me to stay with him in her stead. Of all the nights for none of us to be there, this was the worst.

I will live with the guilt of not being there for the rest of my life.

By early evening, Dad was complaining of shortness of breath, the claustrophobe's worst nightmare. At about eight o'clock he sat up screaming. To Vine's alarm, his lips turned blue; he fell back onto the bed. Mario called the paramedics, who attended to Dad at Foothill but were unable to stabilize him. He was rushed to Cedars, where he arrived—critically ill but *alive*—at approximately nine-thirty.

In recent medical emergencies, my sister and I had been alerted—but not this time, not even by Vine, who'd been left behind at home. (Vine did call Tony, who reached the hospital in plenty of time from his home out in the Valley.) When Susan Reynolds worked the phone at the nurses' station, Nancy and I were not on her call list. But I am certain Bobby Marx was, back in New York.

Meanwhile, a medical team worked feverishly on Dad in triage. Twice Barbara became nauseated and had to leave the room. In between, she hovered over Dad, urging him on: "Fight, darling, you must *fight*." The hard reality, though, was that my father had no artillery left. As Rex Kennamer would acknowledge, they could have done an angiogram on Dad, then possibly put him through angioplasty or bypass surgery. But they'd already decided not to go that route after Dad's first heart attack, for reasons we'd all agreed upon. Those reasons stood, emergency or no.

Dad remained alive at Cedars for more than eighty minutes. There was ample time to notify his children and get them to their father's bedside.

I believe the omission was deliberate. Barbara would be the devoted wife, and then the grieving widow, *alone* at her husband's side.

❋

My father was the strongest, bravest man I'd ever known. He seemed indestructible to me; he was not one to quit. I believe that he was ready to go. He was so tired and lonely and broken. His soul had expired years before that stubborn body gave way. His future held nothing but pain. He could never be at peace, never stop running, until he *stopped*.

My father did not die. He escaped.

12

Out of the Fray

WE MET AT noon Friday to organize the funeral details. Through the night, hundreds of people had collected quietly outside Foothill; I was passing parked cars and pedestrians a quarter mile from the house. I pulled over up the street, called the house, and waited for security to open the gates before I drove down. Once again, the crowds parted respectfully. Several large flower arrangements lined the driveway and front steps.

The living room was bright and quiet. Barbara was saying good-bye to two priests from Cardinal Roger Mahony's office. After Nancy and Frankie arrived, we followed Barbara to the den. The room I'd spent so

many hours in had changed; Dad's funny chair was
gone.

Barbara ran through the agenda she'd received from
the priests for the vigil on Tuesday night and the funeral Mass on Wednesday. Though broadcasting the two
services seemed out of the question, Nancy proposed
that we mount loudspeakers outside the church for all
the people who loved Dad and could not be admitted.
But Barbara felt strongly that the proceedings should be
completely private.

We discussed other details—who would speak, hymn
selections, pallbearers, guest lists—and then it was time
for Nancy and me to go to the funeral home. To see
Dad. I couldn't wait to be with him . . . and yet I felt
strangely hesitant at the same time.

To protect our privacy, and Dad's, our trip to the mortuary was undercover. The security men put Nancy and
me on the floor of a Suburban and covered us with a
jacket. Big Harry Dice took the wheel. My sister and I
popped up after we crossed Sunset—and sure enough, a
car was following. Harry kept zigzagging through the
flats of Beverly Hills until our pursuer gave up.

After making our way through Friday afternoon traffic, we arrived at the McCormick Funeral Home near
the Forum. It seemed deserted, except for Poppa and our
own security: one man outside and one in the hall.

I'd been consumed by Dad in every way since the Kennamer phone call. I'd be brushing my teeth or driving my car, and then my grief would surge and I'd cry aloud, "Oh Poppa!" I so wanted to be near him.

Yet with each step down the mortuary's long hallway, I felt more and more ambivalent. I'd found comfort in Dad's human form in the hospital. But when I saw my father in the viewing room—lying in his blue blazer, surrounded by candles—I knew he was *gone*.

Nonetheless, I wanted to be near him. To touch him. I placed my right hand over his heart, which couldn't hurt him anymore. His hands were so cold—they reminded me of the times that he would warm my cold hands with his gentle rubs and warm breath, and I would do the same for his.

But now I could not warm him, ever again.

When I returned to Foothill late that afternoon, I peeled away to be in Dad's space again. At the doorway to his room, I stopped dead in my tracks. There was Bobby Marx relaxing in Dad's bed, reading a magazine. I could see his fiancée, Hillary, at the sink in my father's bathroom. She was brushing her hair; her face reflected in his mirror.

My first thought was, *These strangers are in my father's room.* And then I realized that this was *their* house now, not his. Jarred and disoriented, I mumbled my apologies

and made a quick retreat. (I shouldn't have been so surprised. Dad's clothes had been in storage for months.)

Eliot had arrived from Florida; he and Harvey Silbert
had been visiting Barbara while Nancy and I were at the
mortuary. They were on their way to a meeting with
Bob to review Dad's will, which had already been distributed. (There was little suspense over the will, since
the bulk of Dad's estate had already been assigned
through joint tenancy or other agreements.)

As I passed him in the living room, Eliot murmured,
Free at last—free at last! Over the next few days, it became
a running gag—that Barbara was nearly out of my life.

The next day, Saturday, I faxed my invitation list to
Foothill via Dorothy. Within minutes, Barbara called.
Everything seemed fine, she said, with one exception: "I
don't think that we need to include Mrs. Reagan."

I wasn't going to wait to hear her reason—this was
my personal list, and I held firm. Not only did Mrs. Reagan represent a former president, I said, but she was one
of Dad's oldest friends, and a close friend of mine and
Nancy's and Mom's as well.

Barbara weighed my response a moment before
relenting. "And by the way," she added, "I think you're
right about Sonny." I'd had to lobby for Sonny's inclu-
sion as a pallbearer the day before—I'd told Barbara that

it would be a terrible omission, and that Dad would have expected Sonny to be part of his funeral.

On Sunday I opened my home to twenty or so close friends. They needed a place to express their grief; I needed their comfort, too. Dad's music pervaded the sunny afternoon. There were paintings and photographs of him everywhere, even in my garden. Every guest wore a powder blue ribbon, provided by my housekeeper, Lucy.

The songs and pictures were healing and uplifting. Everyone relaxed—we cried and laughed together, hugged and kissed one another. I assumed that people would stay a couple of hours, and they stayed for four. I would finally slip out, to return to McCormick's.

I had to see Dad while I still could. I felt oddly reunited with him in death, where no one stood between us. Nancy, A.J., and Mia had already been there, leaving many of his favorite things—we'd wanted to give him a big send-off. There were cherry Life Savers and a few Tootsie Rolls from Nancy, a small bottle of Jack Daniel's from our cousin Shell, a pack of Camels and a Zippo lighter from Bobby Marx. A.J. and Amanda had left a few stuffed animals to keep him company on his long journey. My contribution was a small dog biscuit, for Dad's love of little critters. (When I was a child and asked him where heaven was, my father—who was named for St. Francis of Assisi—would reply, "Heaven is where all the animals go.")

∭

By Monday the strain was telling. Normally this would have been the end of it, but the funeral had been delayed two days to accommodate Cardinal Mahony.

I put my nervous energy to work by taking care of a few things at my office at Warner Bros. that morning. I was touched to see the studio's flags at half-mast.

Bob Finkelstein reached me there on his way to a most unexpected meeting at Harvey's office: "It seems that there's a second will."

Later that day, on my way from the mortuary to Foothill with Bob and Eliot, Bob filled me in. Harvey, blaming his secretary for the blunder, had produced a will dated September 3, 1991—just four days after the one we'd already received. The two documents were virtually identical, except for one curious paragraph. In the second will, Dad gave Barbara an additional $3.5 million from his share of community funds.

I found the development fascinating, since Dad's will was supposed to be confidential, its contents known only to Harvey and his client. But now it seemed fair to conclude that Barbara had been privy to what she would get.

The mistake was a revealing one. After signing his will on a Friday (in the presence of a psychiatrist, captured on videotape), Dad was somehow persuaded to return to Harvey's office on the following Tuesday and execute a second will.

This sequence of events was just a little suspect. It didn't take much to imagine what might have transpired in his home in the period between the two wills. (I'd later learn, from what was overheard that weekend, that it was a time of havoc and bitter argument between Dad and Barbara.)

I turned to Eliot and said, "This is something we weren't ever supposed to know about, right?"

"It was something that had to be done," Eliot told me. "It was miserable for him."

I found it sad to be reminded how Dad's life had played out amid such tawdry maneuvering—even his will was a negotiation. The truth of the matter was this: Barbara probably ended up with exactly what Dad would have given her anyway. My father was going to make sure that both his wife and his children were well taken care of.

But I didn't care about Harvey Silbert's gaffe, or who would benefit from the fallout. I was mourning my father; I had no energy or interest for anything else.

When we got to Foothill, I broke from Bob and Eliot

to say hello to Barbara. She was behind the marble-topped bar, facing Arthur Crowley. They had drinks in hand, and I could tell that it wasn't their first round.

Seeking a point of common interest, I asked if they'd heard anything about Dad's military burial. My sister, the driving force behind Dad's Medal of Freedom and his Congressional Gold Medal of Honor, was on another mission. Over the weekend her inquiry had been routed to President Clinton, who quickly authorized a full military honor guard and an American flag draped over Dad's coffin.

I found the prospect exciting, because I knew how much my father would have been pleased. What I didn't know was that Barbara and her divorce lawyer (a World War II veteran, as he'd be quick to tell you) were adamantly opposed to the idea—and that Barbara had rejected the president's offer.

"There's been a misunderstanding," Arthur said. "Your father didn't serve in the armed forces—they don't just hand these things out."

. "I won't have it," Barbara said. "It would be a dreadful embarrassment to your father. It just isn't appropriate."

I was confused. How could a military burial be inappropriate if it was approved by the President of the United States?

But Arthur said, "Forget about it—really."

I was livid, and too close to tears to stay in their company. I went into the den, sat down on the ottoman, and cried. Bobby Marx came over and asked what had happened. I explained what I could and said, "Does it still have to be this way, even now? Because I hate it."

Then Barbara was in the doorway, telling Bobby she needed to speak with him—leaving me with Arthur, who placed a consoling hand on my shoulder. By that point I was sobbing. I wanted to scream; the flag was just the tip of it.

"It's going to be all right," Arthur said. When I looked up but didn't respond, he added, "Do you remember the day in Sonny's office when you insulted my hairpiece?"

"I do remember," I said.

"I didn't forget that," Arthur said. "That really hurt my feelings."

Arthur left. Bob and Eliot and Bobby Marx came in and gathered around me. "I've had enough," Eliot said angrily. "I'm going to get to the bottom of this."

And Bobby said, "My mother is nuts. We're going to work this out."

When I left Foothill that afternoon, it would be for the last time.

On Tuesday I kept my own company at home with my assistant Lisa Tan. I was marking time to the vigil service that evening.

As I sat in my upstairs office, I glanced up through the large skylight and saw someone skywriting a heart. Then came the initials: *F . . . S.*

It seemed that Dad was everywhere.

Upon arriving at the Church of the Good Shepherd in Beverly Hills, I walked in the side entrance and was directed into a small anteroom. I'd counted on meeting Nancy, Frankie, and A.J. and Amanda. I was very pleased and a little surprised to see Mom there. I was *really* surprised to see Mia, accompanied by her son Seamus. My sister had invited the people closest to us and to Dad, and I got a giggle out of it. If Ava had been alive, she would have been there too.

As we waited, we could hear Bill Miller and Al Viola playing "In the Wee Small Hours" from inside the chapel, a song so strongly reminiscent of my father's wistful core. When Barbara came into the anteroom to join us, I could see that she was startled, but she kept her poise.

When it was time, we were led around the church to a side door, and took our places behind the pallbearers. The musicians were concluding their set with "Moonlight in Vermont"; I could almost hear my father's voice filling the cavernous space. After a moment's pause, the resounding chords of the organ marked the start of our procession. The congregation's murmuring hushed as we followed behind my father. The surreal was becoming real to me—this was the beginning of the very end.

We took our seats in the two front pews, just a few feet from Dad. The Paul Clemens portrait sat on an easel to the right of the altar. It was strange to see Dad before us with that lonely, faraway look.

My sister spoke that evening, as did her two extraordinary, eloquent daughters. My nieces had lost their father, Hugh Lambert, when they were small, and now they were losing their grandfather. Amanda chose to read a poem by e. e. cummings, while A.J. selected an essay Dad had written years before about intolerance. As I listened to her speak about Frank Sinatra the patriot, the child of immigrant parents who was so devoted to his country, I wondered how anyone could want to deny him his flag.

As the guests filed out, the last to say good-bye was Harvey Silbert, who stood before us hat in hand. He apologized profusely about "the confusion" over the wills. We made light of it—what was there to say?

Before departing, I needed to leave one last gift for Dad. It was a small white envelope containing a card and ten dimes—the change he'd carried for his faithful phone calls. I left it with Kevin, the mortician, who promised he would place it in Dad's jacket pocket. I kissed the casket good night.

The next morning—the sixth interminable day since Dad's death—was bright and clear. When Barbara led us out of the anteroom and into the chapel, it was standing room only. Sunlight played through the stained glass behind the altar. The church was awash in thousands of white roses, lilies, and gardenias, Dad's favorite flower.

The splendor, the fragrance, the music, the affection that filled that room—it would be a funeral worthy of my father.

Barbara took her seat in the front pew, along with Bobby, Hillary, Vine, Frankie, and Cynthia, his girlfriend. I sat directly behind Barbara in the second pew, between Nancy and Bob, with Mom to Bob's left.

Before the service began, a priest assisting the cardinal spoke to us from the aisle. Near the end of the Mass, he informed us, the cardinal would distribute a dozen or so blessed metal crucifixes, identical to the one on Dad's casket. The priest said they were for family and anyone else we wanted to have one. More would be made available if needed.

The religious service lasted more than two hours, and I thought it was glorious—Dad deserved every second of it. For the most part it represented him well, with the possible exception of Cardinal Mahony's homily. The cardinal didn't know my father and hadn't had the time to speak to his children. I thought his talk was impersonal. But when words failed, the music took over. Dad would have liked that.

The mass concluded with "Ave Maria." As we sat in silence, the cardinal approached the front pews to present the crucifixes, with the assisting priest directing him. When I saw that there were several crosses left over, I caught the assistant's eye as instructed.

The cardinal moved to his right and reached through to me, between Barbara and Bobby. As I took the cross over Barbara's right shoulder, she grabbed it and my hand—hard. Without turning to address me directly, she said, in a voice easily heard around us, "Who is that for?"

Then I made my big mistake: I told her the truth. "I want to give it to Bob," I said.

Barbara paused a beat. Looking straight ahead, just inches from my mother, less than a yard from my father's casket, she said, *"No!"* with a tone of pure disdain.

And she tore the cross from my hand.

Bob gasped. I felt Mia's hand at my back. My mother squeezed Frankie's arm. My sister was steaming—I was worried that she might smack Barbara upside the head.

By then the choir was finishing its hymn. The befuddled cardinal handed the remaining crucifixes to Barbara. I didn't know whether to laugh or cry. Then I realized that my hand was bleeding—the metal had sliced across my palm.

I could only hope that Dad was watching.

As the last echoes of "Ave Maria" faded, the church was filled with an unmistakable swell of strings. It seemed that everyone softly expelled a breath in unison—a sort of celestial sigh. At Friday's family meeting, it was the one thing we'd all agreed upon: that the secular portion of the service should begin with "Put Your Dreams Away," Dad's old signature song, my long-ago lullaby.

Put your dreams away for another day, and I will take their place in your heart . . .

I felt his gentle strength and comfort in every word as his voice filled the pillared church. There was heavenly splendor in that moment, absolute perfection. As the music worked its cathartic magic over the assembly, we released our sadness. Everyone broke down, but no one more than Bob.

A number of Dad's closest friends would remember Dad from the altar that day, and many funny and familiar anecdotes were shared. But the warmest response went to Frankie, who spoke without notes—and with the ease and command of his father's son.

At the end, the guests filed past the closed casket, then returned to their seats and stood for the recessional: the priests and attendants, the pallbearers and Poppa, then the first pew and the rest in order. As Barbara reached the top of the church steps, overlooking Santa Monica Boulevard, she was stopped for several minutes while they brought the hearse around to the front. It was quite a photo opportunity, and Barbara would share it only with Bobby and his fiancée. (In the photographs taken at this time, you can see Barbara clutching several crosses to her breast.)

The burial was restricted to the immediate family; two limousines were lined up behind the hearse to take us to the airport for a private plane to the desert. (Our benefactor was Kirk Kerkorian, who'd also provided the plane that took us home after Grandpa's burial in New Jersey.) Barbara took the first limo, with Bobby and Vine. As everybody milled about, Nancy put Mom in the second one, with Bob and Lisa Tan.

The three cars pulled off. It took six or seven minutes to get another car around front for my sister and brother and me—and then we realized that none of us knew where we were going, including the driver. Was the plane leaving from Van Nuys, or from Burbank? Our problem was compounded by a massive satellite breakdown that intermittently jammed our cell phones.

We couldn't help but start laughing; Dad must have been howling somewhere. Nancy eventually convinced a receptionist at Van Nuys Airport that we were who we were—and that we'd lost our father. No one could make this up.

Our security people were frantic. When we boarded the plane, we found Barbara looking concerned: "My God, what happened to you?"

And I said, "You've heard the expression 'Fuck up a two-car funeral'?"

It was time to take Dad home. Tired and numb, we passed most of the twenty-minute trip in silence. As we approached, the air traffic controller said: "You're clear for landing—and welcome home, Mr. Sinatra."

We stood at attention as the ground crew placed Dad's casket on the conveyor belt, which gently rolled him down to us. From a distance I noticed a dozen airport workers scattered about the tarmac, caps in hands. En route to the burial, we'd see other men in the same posture. I flashed back to the motorcade for Grandpa, nearly thirty years before.

We arrived around four at the cemetery, where an area had been cordoned off for us. They'd laid artificial turf atop the real grass that led to Dad's plot, but I knew that we were walking over Grandma, Grandpa, Uncle Vincent, Jilly. The burial site was tented for privacy, to shield us from the photographers just beyond the cemetery walls. The space was dark and dreary; I would have preferred the desert sky and warm breezes.

The service was brief. Father Jack Barker, from St. Francis of Assisi Church in nearby La Quinta, spoke about Dad with a familiarity that pleased me.

We'd learned of how the flag issue had been resolved only moments before the funeral. After two days of negotiations with Barbara (represented by Susan Reynolds) and the White House, Bob had arrived at a compromise: Dad would have a scaled-down honor guard, and a folded flag would be presented to his widow, rather than draped over the coffin.

I'd suggested to Barbara that if she was still uncomfortable about the flag, she wouldn't have to keep it—she could give it to Dad's son.

The end result was very moving. A marine major general, spanking clean in his white pants and blue jacket, touched the flag to Dad's casket, pivoted smartly, and extended the flag to Barbara "on behalf of a grateful nation."

Barbara thanked him, turned to my brother, and said, "Frankie, I would like you to have this."

I thanked her.

We stayed until Dad was at rest in the desert earth.

He was home and safe beside the parents he'd been missing all these years.

We flew back into the setting sun even quieter than when we'd come—we were without Dad, without words. Nancy and I sat holding hands. We watched Frankie sitting alone, staring out the window, clutching the flag on his lap.

After twenty-two years, I said good-bye to my father's wife. There was nothing to hold us together any longer.

I was glad to get home that night. Tired and aching, I soaked in a hot bath, then fell into bed. Feeling lonely for Dad, I turned on the television, where I knew I would find him. A local newscast was signing off with a montage of our day's events, ending with our plane taking off from Van Nuys. It was overscored with Dad singing "Come Fly with Me."

I curled up under my father's robe, smelled his scent, and smiled at the sound of his voice. And I thought of my last note to him, enclosed with the ten dimes: *Sleep warm, Poppa—look for me.*

Epilogue

THE MOURNING WAS worse than I'd imagined. I had been given the time I'd prayed for, and did not fear the inevitable. But I learned that you cannot prepare for the death of a parent—for its awful finality, for what it takes from you.

When my father died, I truly lost a piece of myself.

For several months, each day began with a small reprieve, a blank moment. Then the void tugged at my gut, and harsh reality returned. The lingering aftershock played tricks on me. Whenever my phone sounded at dusk, I'd think—for a fleeting instant—it was *him*. I'd call my mother and tell her to stay well, but the resonance of that instant remained with me into sleep.

And then I'd wake up, and start the cycle again.

More recently I have moved into the dull numbness of acceptance, a lifeless gray zone. My heart no longer leaps at that early evening ring. And yet before I answer, I will pause and think, *This is the time he would have called.*

At the beginning I cried, conscious of my sadness. Now I cry for no apparent reason; my tears come to me unbeckoned.

My friend Bob Finkelstein, who lost his father when he was eighteen, told me that grief never goes away—it just changes. As usual, he was right.

Any number of things will evoke my dear Poppa. The play of light and clouds after a storm. A dinner with simple food, nice wine, and the people I love. And his music, of course. Most often I play the lonely, plaintive songs, the ones where he transformed his anguish into art.

To me, the tragedy of Dad's life was that he never found respite. He was so full of worry, so *tormented*, right up until the end. If you dream of the dead only after they are settled in the next life, I'm afraid that I dream little of Dad. I fear that he has yet to find the peace that eluded him on earth.

In undertaking this book, it was never my intention to place my father on some cold marble pedestal. I wanted to remember him as he was. I had the best times of my life with him, and felt privileged to be his child. He taught me so much: conviction, loyalty, the dangers of deception and prejudgment—and a capacity to live life to its fullest.

He was far from a perfect father. (And I was far from a perfect daughter, as we have seen.) But whatever his flaws or weaknesses, I never loved him any less. I believe that we choose our parents; I could not have made a better choice.

And if our family had more than its share of adversity, it made us try all the harder to hold ourselves intact.

Nancy will tell you that Dad is best recalled by "Something Wonderful," from *The King and I*:

> *This is a man who thinks with his heart,*
> *His heart is not always wise.*
> *This is a man who stumbles and falls,*
> *But this is a man who tries.*
> *This is a man you'll forgive and forgive,*
> *And help and protect, as long as you live.*

Incredibly, more than two years have passed since Dad's death. After all that we went through together, everything has washed away but our love.

In that love I am my father's daughter, and always will be.

Tina Sinatra
August 8, 2000

Index

Photo Credits

(8) Pictorial Press, London
(14) Ted Allan/MPTV
(19) Private collection
(23) Neal Peters Collection
(26) Ben Polin
(27) Ben Polin
(29) ABC Photo Archives
(31) ABC Photo Archives
(35) AP/World Wide Photos
(36) Dan Dorman
(37) © 2000 Archives of Milton Greene, LLC/www.archivesmhg.com
(38) Ted Allan/MPTV
(40) Neal Peters Collection
(41) AP/Wide World Photos
(46) David Sutton
(47) Peter Borsari
(53) Bill Mark
(55) CBS Photo Archive

(56) Bernie Abramson/MPTV
(57) Alan Berliner
(59) "It Happened in Brooklyn" © 1947 Turner Entertainment Co., a Time Warner Company. All Rights Reserved
(61) CBS Photo Archive
(62) Quincy Jones Productions
(65) Nancy Sinatra Lambert
(66) White House Photo
(70) Private collection
(72) Warner Bros./CBS
(73) Warner Bros.
(74) Nancy Sinatra Lambert
(78) Amanda Lambert
(79) AP Wide World Photos
(81) George Kalinsky

Tina Sinatra was the executive producer of *Sinatra*, an award-winning five-hour mini-series based on her father's life that aired in 1992 on CBS. She lives in Los Angeles.